THIS BOOK IS FOR YOU

- Are a conscious business owner or team member who recognises that the current ways of leading and operating a business is unsustainable? Most likely, you:

    - run your own business and are seeking a way to become more productive and make more profits so you can leave a legacy in the world;
    - work as part of a larger organisation and are frustrated by the lack of co-operation and collaboration that exists;
    - and you are looking for a new way of doing business, one that aligns with your values and enables sustainable change.

- Are frustrated that you and your team members are not delivering to their full potential.
- Are seeking ways to motivate and engage your team members.
- Want a framework to help you develop your leadership skills and expand as leader.
- Are passionate about finding another way to run a business, one based on co-operation and collaboration.
- Are frustrated by all the resources – time, energy and money – that are wasted every day in business.
- Want to understand how to leverage all the benefits of Big Data.
- Are seeking a simple model to follow that helps align your people, processes and playground (environment) to help energise a collaborative and effective culture for maximum results.

If you're still reading, you clearly resonate with the content of this book and have taken the first step to helping change the shape of how we lead and run businesses in the future.

As you read on, you'll find loads of strategies, tactics and worksheets to help you create what I refer to as a *Joined Up* business, where no resources are wasted. The impact will be greater productivity and profitability, as well as a more engaging place to work.

I can't wait to share this amazing content with you.

> *"Progress is impossible without change, and those who cannot change their minds cannot change anything."*
>
> **George Bernard Shaw**

PRAISE FOR THE ALCHEMY OF CHANGE...

"Julia is brilliant in the way she has integrated nature in business. In this insightful book, Julia Felton shares with you the three cornerstones every business needs to create a high-performance business culture, and it all starts with the leader. If you're looking for a new perspective on how to leverage your current resources in an authentic and collaborative way, then I urge you to dive in; you won't be disappointed!"

"In this brilliant book, Julia Felton provides a new blueprint for running a business, one based on co-operation and collaboration, where Shared Leadership is the norm. If you are frustrated and struggling with the constant day-to-day demands placed on you, then this book provides a step-by-step guide of how to create a *Joined Up* Business where no resources are wasted."

"In this insightful book, Julia Felton shares with you the three cornerstones every business needs to create a high-performance business culture, and it all starts with the leader. If you're looking for a new perspective on how to leverage your current resources in an authentic and collaborative way, then I urge you to dive in; you won't be disappointed!"

"Julia Felton clearly understands that frustration that comes from operating in a dysfunctional team. In *The Alchemy Of Change*, she provides a blueprint of how to lead and inspire teams to create lasting transformation by getting all team members into flow. And the result is a high-performance business where no resources are wasted. This book is long overdue and should be read by every business executive."

PRAISE FOR THE ALCHEMY OF CHANGE...

"In *The Alchemy Of Change*, Julia Felton teaches us that when team members are aligned to a powerful purpose, extraordinary things are possible, as team members' hidden potential is unlocked. For business, the rewards are immense – increased productivity, profitability and team engagement result. If you only read one business development book this year, let this be the one."

"Finally, a book to acknowledge that the current leadership paradigm is no longer working and that a different approach is needed. One based on collaboration and connection where all aspects of the business (including the people) are aligned and *Joined Up*. Through *The Alchemy Of Change*, Julia Felton cleverly shows us that there really is a different way to operate and run business which makes it more fun and engaging."

"I LOVE this book! It's packed full of practical tools, tips and techniques to help you transform the way you lead your business so that no resources, in terms of time, money and effort, are wasted. What a gift!"

At the heart of *The Alchemy Of Change* is a simple message: if you're feeling frustrated that the current ways of leading and operating business are unsustainable and you are looking for a new blueprint, you will find it in this amazing book!"

"It's reassuring to know that a simple model exists that helps align your people, processes and playground (the environment) to help energise a collaborative culture for maximum results. All that is required is a shift in perspective and when this happens, you can create a *Joined Up* Business where no time, money or energy is wasted. And who wouldn't want that?"

ABOUT JULIA FELTON

Julia Felton is passionate about inspiring business owners to unlock the hidden potential in their people, processes and playground (environment) to create high-performance *Joined Up* businesses. By unleashing their own powerful potential, "grabbing the reins" of their business and becoming proactive leaders, individuals and teams can get into flow and work together with a singular purpose.

By each individual focusing on their unique natural strengths, individuals, teams and organisations are able to become more engaged and motivated. Collaboration reigns and competition is banished. The result is increased productivity and profitability as twice as much is achieved with significantly less effort.

Her innovative coaching and development programmes, for individuals, teams and organisations, are inspired by nature and her herd of horses. She is committed to creating positive transformation and getting outstanding results through streamlining and systemising businesses so that all the aspects of the business are aligned and no resources are wasted.

Julia's extensive corporate experience includes building businesses and teams from the ground up. During her 12 year career at Andersen and Deloitte, she was responsible for developing a business from an idea on a piece of paper to creating and then building a million-pound business unit that became firmly established as the global market leader, providing business intelligence solutions to the hospitality industry. Her unique ability to work at both a strategic and tactical level means that she is sought after as a high-performance consultant, mentor and coach.

Julia holds a degree in Hospitality Management and is a member of the Chartered Institute of Marketing and the Institute of Leadership Management. She is also a Fellow of the British Association of Hospitality Accountants. As a Master Coach and qualified NLP practitioner and trainer, she enjoys mentoring young entrepreneurs and recently became a Young Enterprise Coach. She is also a Talent Dynamics Performance Consultant, a Trusted Sales Dynamics Coach and a Certified Money and Marketing Business Coach.

Julia's passion is horses, and, as a natural horsemanship coach and a Licensed HorseDream Partner, she often incorporates sessions working with the horses into her Business HorsePower leadership and team working programmes and Unbridled Success Retreats.

Julia is an accomplished international speaker and in addition to *The Alchemy of Change: Ancient Wisdom Re-invented To Unleash*

The Potential of Leaders and Teams, she is the author of *Unbridled Success – How the Secret Lives of Horses Can Impact Your Leadership, Teamwork and Communication Skills.* Her keynote speech *Straight From The Horses Mouth: Leadership Lessons From The Barn To The Boardroom* is provocative and thought-provoking, making her a sought after speaker.

Connect with Julia at Julia@juliafelton.com or via her websites

- Speaker: www.juliafelton.com
- Workshops: www.businesshorsepower.com
- Author: www.on-the-hoof.com

Follow Julia on the following social media sites:

- LinkedIn: www.linkedin.com/in/juliafelton
- Twitter: www.twitter.com/julia_felton
- Facebook: www.facebook.com/businesshorsepower
- YouTube: www.youtube.com/juliafelton

> Change is the law of life.
> And those who look only to the
> past or present are certain
> to miss the future.
>
> John F. Kennedy

THE ALCHEMY OF CHANGE

THE KEY TO THE FUTURE
LIES IN THE PAST

ANCIENT WISDOM RE-INVENTED
TO UNLEASH THE POTENTIAL OF
LEADERS AND TEAMS

JULIA FELTON

PART OF THE BUSINESS ON-THE-HOOF SERIES

Filament Publishing

Published by
Filament Publishing Ltd
16 Croydon Road, Waddon, Croydon,
Surrey, CR0 4PA, United Kingdom
Telephone +44(0)20 8688 2598
www.filamentpublishing.com

© Julia Felton 2015

ISBN 978-1-910819-14-2

The right of Julia Felton to be identified as the
author of this work has been asserted by her
in accordance with the Designs and Copyright Act 1988.

No portion of this book may be copied by any means without
the prior written permission of the publisher.

Printed by IngramSpark

DEDICATION

To my horses – Toby, Charlie, Bracken,
Thistle, Bunny and Red –
and all the others that have
passed through my life.

Thank you for teaching me
the best leadership lessons ever
and for modelling the way to show
humanity a better way of being,
one based on collaboration
and connection,
rather than command
and control.

TABLE OF CONTENTS

This Book Is For You If You...   1
Praise For *The Alchemy Of Change*   3
About Julia Felton   5
Foreword   17
Introduction   19
How This Book Is Structured   23
Glossary   26

SECTION ONE   29

CHAPTER ONE: THE QUEST   31
    Business Is Changing   35
    Why Is This Critical Right Now?   36
    Shared Leadership   40

CHAPTER TWO: WHAT'S NATURE GOT TO DO WITH BUSINESS?   49
    Collaboration Continuum   53
    The Five Elements Found in Nature   57
    How The Five Elements Impact Business   60
    The Natural Rhythm To Business   66

CHAPTER THREE *THE JOINED UP BUSINESS BLUEPRINT™*   69
    The Joined Up Business Blueprint™   70
    Positions of Perspective   75

CHAPTER FOUR: SETTING THE GPS FOR YOUR BUSINESS   79
    Business Intelligence Dashboards   81
    Types of Business Intelligence Dashboards   82
    Making Sense of Decisions   84

CHAPTER FIVE: TRUST THE *JOINED UP* BUSINESS GLUE   87
    Trust: The Hidden Business Lubricant   88
    What is Trust?   89
    The Consequences of Lack of Trust   89
    Measuring Trust: Value and Leverage   90
    The Joined Up Team Equation   93

CHAPTER SIX: APPLYING TRUST IN A *JOINED UP* BUSINESS   97
    Building Self-Trust   98
    Honest Intentions Create Trust   104
    Breaking the Rules   104
    The Trust Mirror   105
    Virtual Trust   107
    Trust Your Instincts   108

SECTION TWO   111

CORNERSTONE ONE: Expand The Leader   113

CHAPTER SEVEN: PURPOSE AND VALUES   117
    The Power of Why   120
    Why Having A Why Is Important For Business   122
    The Leader's Values   127
    Values Based Leadership   130
    Shared Purpose Can Create Massive Change   133
    Importance of Hiring People With Aligned Values   135
    A Purpose-Driven Culture Drives Profits   137
    Conditions of Success   140

CHAPTER EIGHT: LEADING WITH COURAGEOUS IMPACT   143
    Collaborative Leadership   145
    Attributes of Successful Leaders   147

Leadership is a Relationship	156
Inspiring Others To Access Their Hidden Potential	159
Women, Leadership and Relationships	160

CHAPTER NINE: EMPOWER RATHER THAN DELEGATE	**163**
Empowerment versus Delegation: The Difference	164
Delegate or Stagnate	166
Positions of Leadership	168
Lessons from the Horses: Wild Herd Leadership	170
Which Leadership Position Is Optimal?	171
The Empowerment Matrix	174

CORNERSTONE TWO: Empower Others To Act	**181**

CHAPTER TEN: KNOW YOUR ROLE IN THE HERD	**185**
Why Teams?	190
Benefits of Being in a Team	192
The Talent Dynamics Framework	193
The Eight Talent Profiles	200
Common Team Roles For Each Of The Five Energies	202
Team Dynamics: Know Your Role in the Herd	203
Optimal Team Size	209
Visible Results	210
Shared Leadership and Teamwork	211

CHAPTER ELEVEN: THE POWER OF COURAGEOUS CONVERSATIONS	**215**
Accessing the Other 90%	219
Positions of Perception	221
How To Prepare for a Courageous Conversation	223

CHAPTER TWELVE: PURPOSE-DRIVEN DECISION-MAKING 231
    Data Deluge 233
    Inattention Blindness 235
    The Dopamine Rush 236
    Give Authority To Those Closest To The Information 237
    The Joined Up Business Decision Making Framework™ 238
    In The Data Jungle Which Metrics Should You Focus On? 241
    Intuition v Logic 244

CORNERSTONE THREE: Engage The Environment **249**

CHAPTER THIRTEEN: IS THE BUSINESS ENVIRONMENT KILLING YOU? 255
    The Hidden Dangers in Business Today 256
    Your Boss Can Seriously Harm Your Health 259
    Our Human Make-Up 261
    The Ripple Effect of The Business Environment 268
    Herd Dynamics 269

CHAPTER FOURTEEN: HARNESSING NATURE'S NATURAL RHYTHM 273
    The Seasons of Business 275
    Balanced Business Systems 279
    The Integrated Performance Model 281
    Productive Work Spaces 282
    Teams Unplugged 287

CHAPTER FIFTEEN: CREATING A WIN-WIN SITUATION 293
    Balancing Entrepreneurship with Bureaucracy 296
    Putting The Cart Before The Horse 298
    Systems Failure 299

SECTION THREE — 303

CHAPTER SIXTEEN: ENERGISING A HIGH-PERFORMANCE CULTURE — 305
    Cultural Erosion — 307
    Beyond The Call Of Duty — 310
    Improved Culture: Improved Results — 312
    Cultural Mismatch — 318

CHAPTER SEVENTEEN: ALL *JOINED UP* — 323
    Common Barriers To Success — 325

CHAPTER EIGHTEEN: FINAL THOUGHTS — 333

Acknowledgements — 337
Appendix — 339
Endnotes — 343
Bibliography — 350

FOREWORD

I'd love to say that this book was many years in the planning and a lifelong dream to write, but that simply isn't true. This book just evolved and took on a life of its own whilst I was in the process of updating my first book, *Unbridled Success: How The Secret Lives Of Horses Can Impact Your Leadership, Teamwork and Communication Skills*.

During my 20+ years in the corporate world, something always really used to irk me. It was the fact that time and time again, I witnessed colleagues re-inventing the wheel and, in doing so, wasting valuable resources. Maybe it was because I was so curious, but my role as a Global Knowledge Manager led me to have a central role liaising with all the different hospitality disciplines within my firm. I also had a specific expertise in business intelligence and gathering data for benchmarking purposes, and so was often called on by other business divisions to help them in this regard.

From this elevated position, I was well placed to observe the silo business practices that occurred around me and how knowledge was held onto rather than shared. One of my biggest joys was seeing the sheer relief on people's faces when they came to me and I was able to direct them to resources that would significantly make their job easier, as we had already completed something similar to that project in the past.

Now, over the past decade, my horses have become my best coaches teaching me business and life lessons. Unfortunately, it was not until I left the corporate world that I really appreciated what they had been teaching me. And, as I reflected on this fact, I realised that my herd of horses live in a state of harmony. They act as a single unit and there is collaboration and shared leadership. A wild horse simply cannot afford to live alone; it is simply too dangerous and so the herd band together with a shared purpose of survival. To act in silo groups would be detrimental to the overall success of the herd, and yet that is what I witness in business day in, day out.

This got me to thinking about what we can learn from nature and specifically my herd of horses that can help us create more effective organisations that ultimately deliver more productivity and profitability. Organisations where everyone is operating as a team and working at their full potential, and where no resources are wasted.

The result was the *Joined Up Business Blueprint*™, a model for creating a purposeful, empowered, aligned business that serves the needs of all its stakeholders at multiple levels. I do hope that you enjoy this book and it stimulates you to think and act differently. How you show up and lead impacts business and contributes to creating a high-performance business culture that inspires team members and delivers results. Not because they have to, but because that is the outcome of having a purpose-driven culture where all the resources are aligned.

INTRODUCTION

We are at a pivotal point in the development of our society. The world economy is in dis-ease. There is tension everywhere, challenges abound, there's financial crisis and a lack of trust permeates. The bonds that have long held society together – family bonds – have all but evaporated. People have become isolated, spending more time on computer technology than with each other. We delude ourselves that, with all our Facebook and other social media friends, we are connected, when in reality we are more disconnected than ever. Isolation is a way to keep ourselves safe but it creates challenges in communicating and engaging with others.

Change has become the norm; in fact, change is happening so fast that we can no longer keep up with it. We are inundated with a tsunami of data and information, resulting in this becoming known as *The Big Data Era*.

The insights this data can potentially yield to help improve business performance is astounding and yet we are less prepared than ever to deal with it and make good use of it. We are in a place of shift and that shift is happening at lightning speed. This is why we need to learn how to ignite, energise and lead change *On-The-Hoof*, with dexterity and agility.

The old paradigm of command and control leadership won't serve us in *The Big Data Era*, where collaboration is a necessity. There is simply too much going on for one leader to be able to manage it all. This in itself creates blind spots for businesses. We need a new paradigm of leadership – one that is flatter, more collaborative and more responsive. We should consider adopting *Shared Leadership*, where everyone looks out for the needs of the business, not in a self-serving ego way, but from a place of contribution to the community.

The problem is that our society has become selfish. It is all about "me" and this formula is not viable long term. The "me" culture has created many of the challenges we face today, and if business is to navigate the current winds of change, we ought to adopt a new approach. We need to move from the "me" to the "we" economy, entering an arena of collaboration and caring for others. Remaining successful requires a new way of doing things, and business leaders will need to master a different skill set from that they are using today.

Visionary, forward-thinking leaders know that if we are to survive and thrive, something has to change. If we do what we've always done, we'll get what we've always got. What we've always got simply won't serve us going forward.

As leaders, we need to become compelling and create collaborative, supportive workplaces. By engaging team members, we unleash high-performance teams who can operate at their full potential, who give the best of themselves day in, day out – not because they have to, but because they want to. And why would they want to do this? Quite simply because the business they are working for has an inspiring reason for existence that motivates them to want to be part of it.

Through my extensive experience of working at companies like Andersen and Deloitte and of running my own business, I'm sick and tired of observing all the wasted time, energy, money and effort that is expended every day, simply because activities are not aligned, not *Joined Up*. In the corporate world, this manifests itself in a silo, non-cooperative mentality, where there are power struggles and everyone is trying to protect their own turf. There is little camaraderie; instead team members spend their time trying to outperform each other. People are focused on themselves and "What's in it for me?" rather than appreciating and recognising that the business's success comes from everyone working collectively together. Success, in life and business, is a team sport.

We've created the current, dysfunctional, attitude and approach; and we are responsible for changing it.

I can't count how many times I've observed different teams (or even team members within the same team) actively sabotaging each other's success by not sharing valuable resources. Just think about it. How much more could be accomplished if everyone worked together in any and every business? If we all shared the same goals and contributed to them?

The exponential impact on performance would be incredible. Productivity and profitability would increase. People would be more engaged, and there would be an energised buzz in the workplace.

This is what happens when you create a *Joined Up* business: a business that is aligned across all areas and where no resources – time, energy or money – are wasted; where everyone collaborates and connects. Where everyone feels valued and has a contribution to make.

Luckily, creating a *Joined Up* business is simple. Maybe not easy, but simple nevertheless. It is nothing new, as we have before us a blueprint for running a *Joined Up* business that has existed for hundreds of centuries. There is an ancient wisdom that prevails that we can use to guide us.

That model is found in nature – specifically in a herd of horses. In nature, there are no wasted resources; everything happens for a reason. There is an ebb and flow to the rhythm of life and this is what keeps it in balance.

If we could mirror the rhythm of nature and align all our resources, we would eliminate the current self-serving, short-term approach of business and make decisions that collectively benefit us all.

The purpose of this book is to share with you how you can create a sustainable *Joined Up* business by aligning your resources; a business where hidden human potential is unleashed and productivity and profitability increase. I will share with you how this is possible through referencing the natural world and the behaviour of my herd of horses.

HOW THIS BOOK IS STRUCTURED

This book is structured in three sections to enable you to dip in and out as you wish.

Section One – *Out Of The Starting Gate* – sets the scene and provides the background to why you would want to create a *Joined Up* business. In Chapter One, we look at why now is the right time to start questioning the way that we operate and lead businesses. In Chapter Two, we review the five natural elements and how this directly correlates with business. In Chapter Three, we introduce the *Joined Up Business Blueprint™*, before sharing in Chapter Four how Big Data can be used to help keep your business on track. Then, in Chapters Five and Six, we discuss the importance of trust in business and how it is the glue that keeps everything operating in harmony.

Section Two – *The Journey* – describes the three cornerstones of the *Joined Up Business Blueprint™* in detail. In Chapters Seven, Eight and Nine, we examine **Cornerstone One: Expand The Leader**. Firstly, we examine why purpose is so critical for giving your business a GPS and raison d'être for being. Then, in Chapter Eight, we look at the role of the leader and the key attributes they need to successful embody to be a *Joined Up Leader* that is impactful, courageous and compelling to follow. In Chapter Nine, we discuss the difference between delegation and empowerment, and how empowered team members are more motivated and engaged.

In Chapters Ten, Eleven and Twelve, **Cornerstone Two: Empower Others To Act**, we examine how to create high-performance teams by leveraging all the resources at our disposal. Specifically, Chapter Ten looks at how we can get team members into flow so they can access their hidden potential.

In Chapter Eleven, we discuss the power of having Courageous Conversations before looking at Purpose-Driven Decision-Making in Chapter Twelve.

Cornerstone Three: Engage The Environment is covered in Chapters Thirteen, Fourteen and Fifteen. In this section, we examine the role that the environment plays in developing and sustaining a high-performance culture within business. Specifically in Chapter Thirteen, we look at how many business environments are literally killing their team members – both physically and also through stifling creativity. In Chapter Fourteen, we share how harnessing nature's natural rhythm can help increase productivity in the workplace whilst in Chapter Fifteen, we look at how to create a Win-Win situation and so avoid the systemic failure that so often occurs in organisations.

Section Three – *Over the Finish Line* **–** brings everything together in Chapters Sixteen and Seventeen by examining how to evolve a *Joined Up* business that energise a high-performance culture.

In my final thoughts, I share a pioneering and innovative way of developing all the skills required to become a *Joined Up Leader* and so create an aligned, purpose-driven, productive and profitable *Joined Up* business.

On the next pages, you will find a glossary and, at the end of each chapter, you will find list of key takeaways and also links to checklists, assessments and resources that you can download. I would strongly urge you go and get all these great resources, as they will help you create your *Joined Up* business with less effort. After all, the quest that all *Joined Up Leaders* are on is to find innovative ways to leverage their resources through sharing and collaboration.

Finally, in the true spirit of collaboration and to fuel my business purpose, a percentage of the sale of this book is being contributed to two organisations that I resonate with. The first is B1G1 (www.b1g1.com) who connect businesses with high impact projects across the world, so that business can truly be seen as a force for good. The second is Friends Of A Legacy (FOAL) which is a horse advocacy group with a mission to preserve and protect the wild horses of the McCullough Peaks Wild Horse Management area (www.friendsofalegacy.org).

GLOSSARY

Big Data Paradox: a term to describe the ironic situation that businesses find themselves in today. On one hand, there is an avalanche of data that should enable better business decisions to be made, and yet team members are either afraid, or fail to understand how to use the data in a constructive manner, so instead the data is ignored.

Business Intelligence Dashboards: a way to display a multitude of different data variables in an easy to understand way to enable better monitoring and evaluation of performance.

Circle of Safety: a term coined by Simon Sinek referring to an environment that is free of danger and gives team members a sense of belonging, the power to make decisions, and where the leader offers trust and empathy.

Five Element Business Focus Model: a way of looking at the five main business activities of mission, merchandise, magnetise, monetise and mechanise in a way that leverages the laws of nature.

Five Element Energy System: The unique interaction of the five elements – water, wood, fire, earth and metal – which forms a system of creation and destruction.

Joined Up **Business:** a sustainable business where no resources – time, energy or money – are wasted because everything is aligned and working in harmony.

Joined Up Leaders: the leaders of *Joined Up* Businesses who are self-aware and conscious of the impact that they have on those around them.

Joined Up Business Culture: the business environment that results when all aspects of the business are aligned and working synchronistically.

Joined Up Business Blueprint™: a business framework that helps organisations become more efficient and effective by aligning their people, processes and playground (environment).

***Joined Up* Data:** the process of ensuring that all the data and business intelligence within the organisation is complementary and interfaced to enable better decision-making and to provide clarity on how the business is performing.

Joined Up Decision Making Framework™: a way to make decisions using the five natural elements that exist in nature.

On-The-Hoof: a term to describe the agile way that leaders need to be in order to effectively respond to the sea of change that surrounds them.

Secret Energy of Business™: based on the premise that everything in the universe is comprised of energy and that like energy attracts like energy. So, in business, your personal energy field impacts the type of customers, suppliers, stakeholders and team members that are magnetised to you. Everyone emits an energy field unconsciously, and if this is negative, it can repel business opportunities.

Shared Leadership: the concept that, given the rapidity of change, there is no way one person can know about everything in the business. For a business to be successful, leadership and decision-making needs to be shared.

> It is better to lead from behind and to put others in front, especially when you celebrate victory when nice things occur. You take the front line when there is danger. Then people will appreciate your leadership.
>
> Nelson Mandela

SECTION ONE:

OUT OF THE STARTING GATE

"For the first time ever, everyone in the organisation – not just the boss – is expected to lead."

Seth Godin

The quality of a leader is reflected in the standards they set for themselves.

Ray Kroc

CHAPTER ONE: THE QUEST

"THE GREAT QUEST OF
LIFE HAS ALWAYS
BEEN TO
DISCOVER TRUTH."

JOYCE MEYER

He was number 0786 and he stood looking forlornly at me from his pen. In the hot Wyoming sun, his head hung low and he looked dejected with life, really fed up. Yet despite his outer appearance, there was curiosity and inquisitiveness in him. Number 0786, the horse with no name, was a year old and he had been rounded up from the Salt Lakes reservation. He had been part of the Bureau of Land Management (BLM) mustang roundup, designed to control America's wild horse herd population. In a second, his life of freedom on the range, living as a wild horse with no worries and fears, had been traded for a life in captivity. He was separated from his family herd and was alone. I'd love to say he was one of just a few unlucky ones, but every year around 9,500 wild horses are removed from the lands in an effort to control the population.

Number 0786 was a stunning roan mustang with a dark brown face and speckled brown and white coat. He stood about a metre high at his shoulders. He was just a little guy who was now forced to face the world on his own. As he stood trembling before me, I reflected on the fact that he had been given no choice in the matter. His whole world had been changed in a heartbeat. Standing there, what hope did he have in his future?

Number 0786, whom I named Cody, was to become my responsibility for the next seven days as I sought to get him accustomed to domesticated life, so that he could be safely adopted. That was his only ticket to a future of some degree of normality and freedom. It was his ticket to avoiding becoming like 46,000 other mustangs that live in confined holding pens across the USA.

As I looked at him, I reflected that his situation was not very different from what I continuously witness in the business world. People stuck in jobs they don't love, doing things they don't want to do, just because they feel they have no choice. And yet each of us does have choices in how we approach the situations we find ourselves in.

How I could help Cody reach his full potential became my focus for the next seven days. I knew that if I could help him find his strengths and find the courage to trust and connect, then all kinds of opportunities could open up for him. And, with luck, we could find him a home on a nice ranch where he would be loved and cared for. I began thinking about what I could do to enable him become his very best and bring out his hidden potential. What transitions could I help him make? What kind of environment could I create to enable this transformation to occur?

It is the same in business. We need to ask what we can do to create high-performing individuals and teams operating at their full potential? What types of environments and situations can we evolve to bring out the best in our team members? What kind of leader do we need to become to inspire change? There are literally millions of people in business not living up to their full potential just because they have not been given the chance to shine; and it's the same with the 9,500 mustangs that are rounded up each year. Some of the mustangs make it, fulfilling their full potential and become solid citizens, contributing and fitting in to society, whilst others fall by the wayside and are destined to a life of less than mediocrity. What factors can we put in place for them to not only to survive but thrive in this very different environment? How can we help them cope with all this uncertainty and change and still embrace life, not from a place of fear but from a place of courage and empowerment.

As I ruminated on this, a hawk swooped down, and, with an effortlessly flap of his gigantic wings, soared upwards again towards the thermals. There he flew majestically in circles, riding the thermal currents whilst searching out his next meal. From that high perspective, and with his laser-like vision, he could see everything that was happening on the ground below him. I couldn't help but wonder at the great view he had of Cody and me, and how different life must look from up there.

As I sat in the corner of Cody's pen and watched the hawk high above, I got to thinking about what makes some people, teams and businesses soar and achieve amazing success whilst others flatline.

What secrets would we be able to see if we stepped out of the busyness of life and took a new perspective on things, just like the hawk?

What would happen if we really grabbed the reins and became leaders of our lives, rather than fall victim to circumstances?

What more could we achieve? What impact could we make?

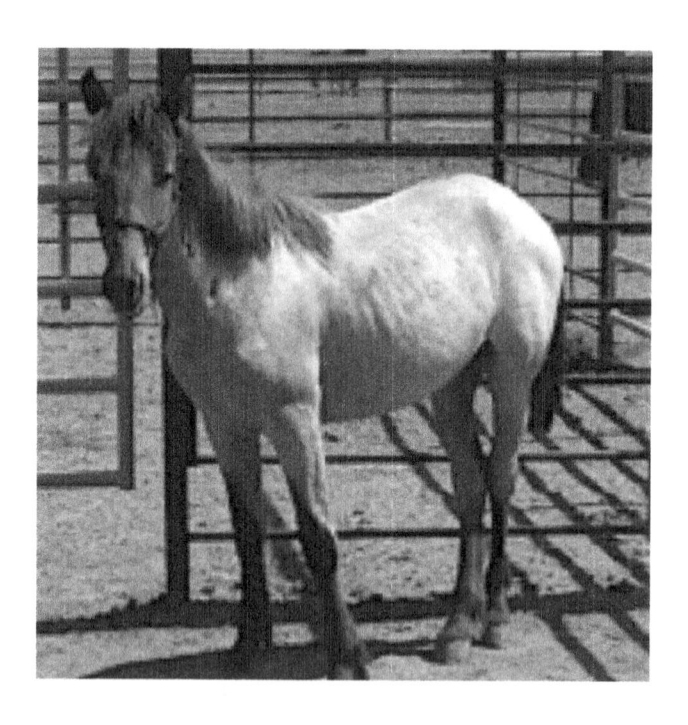

Cody – Number 0786 – the inspiration for this book.

BUSINESS IS CHANGING

We live in challenging times. Uncertainty is everywhere. The only certainty is the level of uncertainty that surrounds us. The pace of change is relentless and we are expected to achieve more with less. Periodic economic downturns make businesses leaner and yet ironically not always more effective. Businesses need to become more efficient and squeeze every ounce of productivity out of their teams if they are to remain profitable; more than that, though – they must engage team members and align all their resources, people and processes, if they are to deliver long-term sustainable results.

At the same time, life is busier than ever. We are drowning in information. On average, 122 business emails are sent every day.[1] We are bombarded with information, which, rather than bolstering performance, is now hampering productivity. Technology has become a curse as well as a blessing; but this deluge of information can also provide us with a way to navigate the storm of relentless change as it can show us what is working and what is not working.

Business intelligence, or what is now being dubbed "Big Data", has been available for years and when used well can provide great insights on how a business is performing. We can see what areas are performing well, and where we should place our focus. What has happened in recent years is that technology has enabled us to collect and analyse more data than ever before.

> ## The Data Tsunami
>
> **On average, every minute on the Internet:[2]**
>
> - Facebook users share nearly 2.5 million pieces of content.
> - Twitter users tweet nearly 300,000 times.
> - Instagram users post nearly 220,000 new photos.
> - YouTube users upload 300 hours of new video content.
> - Apple users download nearly 50,000 apps.
> - Email users send over 200 million messages.
> - Amazon generates over $80,000 in online sales

In our interconnected society, we can now measure virtually any business metric – in finance, marketing, social media campaigns, customer satisfaction, etc. – with more accuracy than ever before. BUT, this deluge of data also hinders performance, as most people simply don't know what to do with it. The question that needs to be asked is, how can all this date be used effectively to manage business through ongoing rapid change?

WHY IS THIS CRITICAL RIGHT NOW?

There is a massive shift happening in business right now and *Joined Up Leaders* are waking up to the fact that the old ways of leading teams and business are no longer working. Although many people believe businesses have become global, the stark reality is that we have barely scratched the surface of this transition.

It is anticipated that globalisation will continue at lightening pace and will bring more new challenges for business leaders trying to manage across borders.

The need for team working will increase, but there will also be a need for *Shared Leadership* due to the sea of information out there. There is simply too much data for one leader to manage and assimilate alone.

We're on a seismic shift where a number of megatrends will converge to change the way we live and work. You might say we are in the void before the perfect storm. How we navigate this change is fundamental to our success and sustainability as a species.

So what are these megatrends? According to the Hay Group, the six major trends that will impact leadership competencies as we move towards 2030 are:[3]

1.   ACCELERATING GLOBALISATION

The global balance of power is shifting towards Asia and the rising global middle class. This means that international companies will need to adapt global strategies for local markets. Leaders will need to be culturally sensitive and master the art of collaboration; they will need excellent conceptual and contextual thinking ability.

2.   CLIMATE CHANGE

A growing scarcity of strategic resources such as water, minerals, metals and fossil fuels could cause price hikes and trigger regional and global conflicts. Leaders will need to balance the competing demands of financial success, social responsibility and environmental custodianship.

3. DEMOGRAPHIC CHANGE

The war for talent rages on and, whilst, the world population is growing, there are demographic imbalances. In the industrial countries of the West and China, life expectancy is rising but populations are stagnating or declining, whereas populations in developing countries are booming. Leaders will need to understand, lead, integrate and motivate increasingly diverse teams.

4. INDIVIDUALISATION AND VALUES PLURALISM

With greater convergence between private and working lives, there is a need to redesign work processes to suit the team members rather than the organisation. Leaders will need to work harder at generating personal loyalty, through accommodating team member's requirements, enabling self-directed working, and individualised leadership.

5. INCREASINGLY DIGITAL LIFESTYLE

Online media continues to blur the boundaries between private and working lives. There is a real need for leaders to bridge the information gap between team members whilst ensuring that over-reliance on technology does not hamper the development of key social skills, such as communication.

6. TECHNOLOGY CONVERGENCE

Miniaturisation and virtualisation will drive the convergence of nano-, bio- and information technologies and cognitive sciences, spurring innovation and accelerating research and development in many fields. The result will be more collaboration and cross sector partnerships, which leaders will need to learn how to influence.

In other words, organisations will have to radically adapt their cultures, structures, systems and processes in order to survive in the new world order. Managing in matrix structures – where information flows around the globe in a way that renders traditional hierarchies and reporting lines redundant – is one of the biggest challenges that leaders will face. Leaders will need to learn to lead through influence rather than authority, and this will have an impact on them at a cognitive, emotional and behavioural level.

According to the Hay Group, *"Leaders will have to be multilingual, flexible, internationally mobile and adaptable. But most crucial of all, they must be highly collaborative and have strong conceptual and strategic thinking skills."* [4]

Clearly then, our existing ways of working and leading will no longer serve us. Change is in the air and, quite frankly, if we don't change, then nature will do it for us. That's the challenge and the beauty of where we are now. In a dysfunctional society, which for so long has been self-centred, with an ego-based economy, nature is stirring things up to restore harmony. In nature, harmony reigns. There is a natural ebb and flow to life, a rhythm and predictability, and when things get out of flow and balance, nature naturally steps in to realign things.

The move from the "me" to the "we" economy, where we collaborate, connect and care for others is needed for a number of reasons:

- Business is set to become even more global, with the pace of globalisation increasing.
- The fast pace of change of technology will continue.
- Leadership is no longer a one-man job but rather a shared responsibility.
- The level of team members engagement and commitment needs to rise.
- The true potential of each team member needs to be fully leveraged.

SHARED LEADERSHIP

Leadership is no longer a title for those at the top; rather there is a need for each and every person to become a leader. There is a need for individuals to evolve their own personal leadership, to expand themselves and take responsibility for their impact on the world. Without each of us stepping up, our world and business environment is unlikely to thrive (yet alone survive) in the future.

In today's complex workplace, a leader's success is directly related to the effectiveness of their teams. These teams contribute to the culture of the organisation, and their health is a reflection of that culture's health. To realise the high-performance results we are after, we have to understand the power of these essential and healthy collaborations.

To deal with this complexity, we need teams of leaders working towards a common purpose with a *Joined Up* approach. We no longer live in a world where individual stars can carry the day on their own.

So how can we collaboratively steer our business to reach its highest potential and, in doing so, become the best version of ourselves? The new phenomenon of Big Data provides us with the means to do this. It enables us to create checks and measures to ensure we are all pulling in the same direction. It can help eradicate the "I" in organisations because the data never lies. To do this, we must learn how to interpret the data correctly, create Business Intelligence Dashboards aligned with the values of the business, and then manage the outputs.

To achieve this, collaboration and co-operation is key. Just like a leader can no longer lead in isolation, team leaders and business units can no longer work in isolation. A business – just like everything else in nature – is an ecosystem made up of parts; one can't exist without the other. Business units and team members need to communicate and find collective solutions to problems because changes in one area of business will impact other areas.

In the Global Human Capital Trends 2015 Survey by Deloitte, 78% of global companies cited building global leadership capability as being the biggest challenge facing them right now[5]. This need for leadership is across all levels, geographies and functional areas. In a world where knowledge doubles every year, and skills have a shelf life of two and a half to five years, leaders need constant development.

And yet it is not just leaders who need constant development; it is also team members. Hiring team members based solely on their skill set (their competency) is no longer a sustainable solution; the skills you hire for today won't be the skills you need in 2.5 years' time. It is better to hire team members based on their character, people of integrity with sound judgement who are adaptable, flexible and able to problem solve. People with these types of characteristics can then adapt and learn the competency skills needed for their role as and when required.

This effective model of leading *On-The-Hoof* already exists in nature. Specifically, horses operate as an efficient herd with a collective responsibility for keeping each other safe. Each herd member knows his or her role in the team. Although a hierarchy does exist, it is flexible, with herd members losing their rank and authority if they fail to perform. There is accountability and there are rules of engagement. There is also collective decision-making, particularly in times of danger, when the horse closest to the danger signals to the others to take action by fleeing.

In nature, life exists in perfect harmony. There is a system and ebb and flow to life. Everything knows its role: the plants know when to flower, the animals know when to hibernate, and the farmer knows when to harvest. There is a rhythm to everything. No resources are wasted – everything happens for a reason. Yet this is rarely the case in life and business where resources – time, energy and money – are thrown away on a daily basis. Against this backdrop, how do we achieve more with less?

The answer is to help our team members become more effective and productive – to operate as high-performance teams – by tapping into the unused 90% of their potential. As Robert Cooper in his book *The Other 90%* notes: *"The dinosaurs of the future will be those who keep trying to live and work from their heads alone".* [6]

We need to become heart-centred; to access the brilliance of the second and third "brains" – the heart and gut – as the highest reasoning and creativity involve all three brains working together. This is something that occurs naturally in nature but that human logic has dulled down over the years. We have become a reasoning society and have forgotten how to access our intuition (gut instinct).

Joined Up Leaders energise a culture where accessing the Other 90% is possible; the net result is more engaged and productive team members. In fact, employee engagement and culture issues were cited as the number one challenge companies face around the world right now, according to Deloitte's 2015 Global Human Capital Trends Survey[7].

Culture drives many outcomes in organisations, perhaps most prominently employee engagement and retention, and with more than half of respondents in the Deloitte Human Capital Survey admitting to having either a poor program or no program to measure and improve engagement, this does not bode well for businesses. Particularly when the research also reveals that when team members are engaged and motivated and in a state of Flow, productivity increases by 22%.[8]

Flow is an optimal state of consciousness, when you feel and perform your best. It's the moment of total absorption when time speeds up or slows down like a freeze-frame effect. Mental and physical ability go through roof, and the brain takes in significantly more information per second, processing it more deeply. Productivity rises and business results improve; team members have more fun and are more engaged in the business.

Sometimes called "being in the zone," Flow isn't just an experience for record-breaking athletes. Anybody anywhere can apply the triggers for any task. The amount of time someone spends in Flow has a massive and powerful correlation to life satisfaction, as when someone is in Flow they are automatically accessing their hidden potential. Unfortunately, according to Steven Kotler, author of *The Rise of Superman: Decoding the Science of Ultimate Human Performance*, "the average business person spends less than 5% of their day in flow".

The great news is that the behaviours required for creating a *Joined Up Business Culture* are the same that people need to create a fulfilling life. As *Joined Up Leaders*, we need to create a culture that empowers team members to get into Flow. A *Joined Up Business Culture* means collaboration, personal responsibility, learning and growing, respect, and trust to name just a few. These are behaviours that show up automatically when we are at our best, in Flow, accessing the hidden 90% of our potential.

If prompted, many people would realise that collaboration and communication skills are necessary for success and that success is not solely the responsibility of the leader of the business. Everyone needs to take personal responsibility for their own actions and the impact they have on others.

Leaders of today need to become emotionally self-aware and understand how they impact others on a physical and energetic level. I call this the *Secret Energy of Business*™. We can't see it, but we know that energy is everywhere. Humans emit an energy vibration and like attracts like. When everything and everyone is aligned within a business venture, things are magnetically attracted – like a cosmic force is at work. This creates harmony. Team members are excited by the vision and want to be a part of the success; this in turn attracts more opportunities.

Leaders of today really need to understand that leadership is an *Inside Out Job*. And it is not just the ones with the title of Leader – in fact, everyone in society needs to recognise that they are part of this ecosystem and everything they do impacts the system, as it has a ripple effect. Abdication, blame and lack of responsibility will continue to harm the system. Only co-operation and collaboration will ensure that everyone and everything survives in a sustainable way.

This might seem daunting – few people like change; and yet it is the only answer. Change has been fast in the past, and as the speed of technology is set to increase ever more rapidly; it will only become faster. This is why the blueprint of a collaborative society with shared leadership where everyone feels part of the community is so useful, and so important. This model has been working for tens of thousands of years, has been right in front of us, and we have never seen it. Welcome to the power of the herd.

Horse herds provide a model of the way we can live and work in collaboration. The herd is always about the "we", never the "me", and the reason is simple: at the mercy of the elements and natural predators such as mountain lions, the "me" option is simply not viable. Alone in the wild, they surely wouldn't survive. This is why there are no egos in the herd – they live in a perfect herd system with basic rules that ensure harmony and ease. Self-serving actions are quickly dealt with and the overriding need for community to fulfil the powerful basic requirements of safety, security and survival prevails.

How different business and life would be if we all operated from a place of collaboration rather than a place of isolation and me-ness. This is the quest that all *Joined Up Leaders* are on: to find a way to get more commitment from themselves and others, and, in doing so, create a sustainable workplace, one that meets the needs of all its stakeholders and adds value to the community within which it operates. For business to succeed in the future, it can no longer be based on exploitation and coercion, but rather co-operation and voluntary exchange. Trust must be fostered, both individually and collectively, so that a win-win situation exists for everyone and harmony rules.

John Mackey, CEO of Whole Foods, calls this "Conscious Capitalism", where we are *"fully awake and mindful, to see reality more clearly, and to more fully understand all the consequences – short term and long term – of our actions"*.[9]

The only way to make sense

out of change is

to plunge into it,

move with it,

and join the dance.

Alan Watts

Chapter One:

The Quest

Takeaways:

- Current command and control leadership models will not serve us in the future.
- Six megatrends will fundamentally alter how we lead and run businesses.
- Successful businesses of the future will need to be *Joined Up* to maximise the use of resources.
- Finding ways to help team members tap into their hidden 90% of potential will provide untold results, both for the individual and the organisation.
- Nature and herds of horses provide a blueprint of the way that we can live and work in collaboration and harmony.
- Business needs to move from a "me" model to a "we" model to foster co-operation and collaboration.
- When team members get into Flow, the results are a 22% increase in productivity which translates to increased profitability, fun and engagement.
- Team members typically spend less than 5% of their day in Flow.

Nature is an inherently complex system built on interdependence and it is this interdependence that keeps it working so efficiently.

Julia Felton

CHAPTER TWO: WHAT'S NATURE GOT TO DO WITH BUSINESS?

"Dependent people need others to get what they want. Independent people get what they want through their own effort. Interdependent people combine their own effort with the effort of others to achieve success."

Stephen M. R. Covey

What's nature got to do with business? Quite a lot, it seems. My herd of horses have taught me some of the best business lessons I have ever learnt, although admittedly at the time I did not fully understand them. As soon as I recognised this, I started partnering with my horses to help other business leaders develop their leadership skills. You can read all about the business lessons I learnt from horses in my book, *Unbridled Success: How The Secret Lives Of Horses Can Impact Your Leadership, Teamwork and Communication Skills.*

It doesn't matter what way you look at it, business is a system made up of a number of interrelated parts. However, many of the clients I work with regard business as a combination of separate business units. Unfortunately, this sets up a situation where these "independent" units tend to operate with a silo mindset, and that means the individuals and teams do not share information with others in the company.

Rather than creating an interdependence on one another, as exists in nature, organisations tend to build walls around their internal departments. Business leaders create their own chiefdoms, led by ego and desire to succeed at any price. This can lead to the demise of company culture, kill communication, waste people skills and resources, and get in the way of the communal, aligned focus required to move the business forward.

Instead of building walls, companies need to collaborate across departments and towards common aligned vision and goals in order to maximise effectiveness and make a positive contribution.

Nature, too, is an inherently complex system built on interdependence and it is this interdependence that keeps it working so efficiently. There is a symbiotic relationship between the animals and the environment where everything impacts everything else. Within this ecosystem exist harmony and balance – imbalances occur only when some aspect does not have enough influence. Nature moves forward with stable improvements rather than the boom and bust cycle that we experience in business ecosystems.

I witnessed a great example of the symbiotic relationships that exist in nature whilst I was living in the African bush. Parasites are a problem for the water buffalo that graze on the African plains. They get into their hair and, if not removed, get under their skin. So what do the water buffalo do? They allow the cattle egrets to sit on their backs. The cattle egrets pick off the parasites, a source of nourishment for them; they also provide a warning system of upcoming danger.

Nature always seeks to stay in harmony; it is only when the natural rhythm is disturbed that some cataclysmic event needs to happen to restore order; sustainability is the norm. Short-term gains never serve the longer-term game for any element of nature, which is why when things get out of balance, harmony must immediately be restored.

In nature, animals understand that if conflict arises, it needs to be dealt with swiftly. Conflict can be viewed as a disruption to the harmonious state. If everyone is not aligned, then normal operating procedures cannot be maintained. Within a herd of wild horses, we clearly see this happening: on a regular basis, the lead stallion of a band of mares will have his leadership position challenged by a younger bachelor male, a disruption to the status quo. What then happens is that the lead stallion and bachelor stallion get into a flight. It is quick and fierce, and at the end of the ruckus, harmony is restored. Either the lead stallion retains his herd of mares, or he loses them and is forced out of the herd.

Unfortunately, this desire to maintain balance and harmony is not something that I often experience in organisations. In fact, many businesses I work with could be viewed as actively sabotaging their success, so focused on short-term gains that they fail to recognise their actions are not sustainable. This is the challenge we have of living in a society where we reward short-term gain and immediate gratification over longer-term sustainability.

For many companies, the "boom-bust" cycle is their winning formula. Each individual leader is rewarded based on their results right now rather than the impact their actions will have in the future. I'm sure you can think of many examples of this in your own experience. This very thing drove the recent financial crisis: banks eager for short-term profits loaned money to individuals who did not have the capacity to repay their loans.

What these organisations have failed to appreciate is that business is a living organism – a system of interdependent and interrelated parts that need to co-operate together in order to achieve success. For many, this represents a paradigm shift in how we look at a business: not as a linear structure, made up of independent units, but rather there is an energy and flow to how it operates.

Businesses exist as an integrated system on many levels – at the individual level, at the team level, and at the organisational level. On the individual level, each team member is made up of a complex series of cells that interact with each other. Human health is only maintained when everything is in balance (homeostasis). Dis-ease is the result of some element falling out of alignment. And so it is in organisations: they thrive when everyone is aligned behind a shared purpose and vision, where everyone has shared values and where a culture exists that supports each part of the business.

When conflict arises, the business as an entity starts to fall ill, witnessed by poor performance, inefficiencies and lack of productivity.

Contrast this with a *Joined Up* business, which has a unified focus and encourages collaboration and teamwork, ultimately resulting in the accomplishment of the goal, despite the difficulties that present themselves.

Unlike the human body, which fights dis-ease by creating antibodies to attack the invading virus, organisational leaders are often less aggressive in pursuit of removing the toxic influence from the office. When internal conflict occurs, silo mentality and a negative culture often emerge, serving to harm and, in the worst cases, such as that of the accountancy firm Andersen, kill the organisation.

Joined Up Leaders understand the power of having honest, courageous conversations (something we will explore further in Chapter Eleven). Honest conversations are a powerful tool to prevent disharmony, resentment and misunderstanding developing within a business and killing it.

COLLABORATION CONTINUUM

Nature provides a blueprint on how to collaborate, yet few people truly understand what collaboration really means. Many think that collaboration means giving up something to accommodate someone, whereas it actually means creating a win-win situation where all parties benefit. One person contributes something that is built on and leveraged by someone else.

The Joined Up Business Blueprint™ (described in the next chapter) is a great example of what can result from collaboration. I came up with the concept, which was then amended, and developed through a series of conversations and brainstorming with my team. The end result is something much better than any of us individually could achieve. That is the power of true collaboration, where the outcome is more than the sum of the parts.

Collaboration is a powerful competitive force as the benefits escalate through the organisation. Nature is full of examples of the power of collaboration: bees and ants work in collaborative and collective ways to establish their hives and colonies. Bees and ants understand the benefits of co-operation over conflict and operate on the basis that collectively the group is more powerful than any one individual.

Control, co-operation and collaboration exist on a continuum based on the level of trust. At one end of the continuum is control, where there is competition and no sharing of resources (silo mentality).

There is little or no trust and turf wars abound as everyone is looking after themselves. At the other end of the spectrum is collaboration, where high levels of trust pervade and team members work together to achieve shared goals. Co-operation is somewhere between. A collaborative business is *Joined Up* with no resources unnecessarily wasted.

Key Attributes of Control, Co-operate and Collaborate Environments		
Control Environment	**Co-operate Environment**	**Collaborate Environment**
Characterised by: • Competition for clients, resources, partners and public attention. • Silo mentality. • No sharing of resources. • No systematic connection between parties.	Characterised by: • Sharing of information happens as needed. • Often informal in nature and occurs for discrete activities or projects.	Characterised by: • Longer-term interaction based on shared purpose and mission and goals. • Shared decision-making and resources. • At its highest level results in a fully integrated business which is *Joined Up*.
Increasing levels of trust →		

There are many different ways to create a collaborative workplace. To achieve this outcome, leaders must be agile and adopt the best leadership style in the moment. They need to engage team members and groups outside of their formal control and inspire them to work towards common goals – despite differences in convictions, cultural values and operating norms.

Most people understand intuitively that collaborative leadership is the opposite of the old "command and control" model. Key differentiators between these two leadership styles are summarised below.

Organisational Structure	Command and Control	Collaborative
Who Has the Relevant Info?	Hierarchy	Dispersed, cross organisational network
Who Has Authority to Make Final Decisions?	Senior Management	Team members at all levels and locations, and a variety of external stakeholders
What is the Basis for Accountability and Control?	People at top of organisation have clear authority

Financial results against plan | The people leading collaborations have clear authority

Performance on achieving shared goals |
| **Where Does it Work Best?** | Works well within a defined hierarchy; works poorly for complex organisations and when innovation is important | Works well for diverse groups and cross unit and cross company work, and when innovation and creativity are critical |

Collaborative efforts are highly fluid and not confined to company silos. In many cases, they are project based and the leaders are adept at creating and disbanding teams as opportunities arise. And to avoid the trap of endless pointless meetings, where no decision is made, clear rights and responsibilities are assigned so that there are clear next steps.

In this way, *Joined Up Leaders* can harness ideas, people and resources from across boundaries of all kinds.

The challenge comes in getting all these disparate players to work together effectively so they need to know when to wield influence rather than authority to get things moving forward and when to halt unproductive discussions and activities.

Clearly there are times when the command and control model of leadership is appropriate (such as in a crisis) but in today's dynamic business environment, more sustainable long-term results are achieved when a collaborative style of leadership is adopted, as team members feel more empowered and engaged. The challenge for *Joined Up Leaders* is to know when to apply each style of leadership for maximum results. (This is something we will explore further in Chapter Nine: Empower Not Delegate.)

THE FIVE ELEMENTS FOUND IN NATURE

There are five natural elements found in nature and they each represent a different season of the year. These elements and their seasonality can help provide us with a blueprint of how to run our businesses by keeping our people, teams and processes in flow.

Element	Season
Water	Winter
Wood	Spring
Fire	Summer
Earth	Late Summer
Metal	Autumn

The interdependence of these elements is clearly seen in the *Five Element Energy System* below derived from Chinese medicine philosophy. Each element supports and destroys each other in order to maintain balance and harmony.

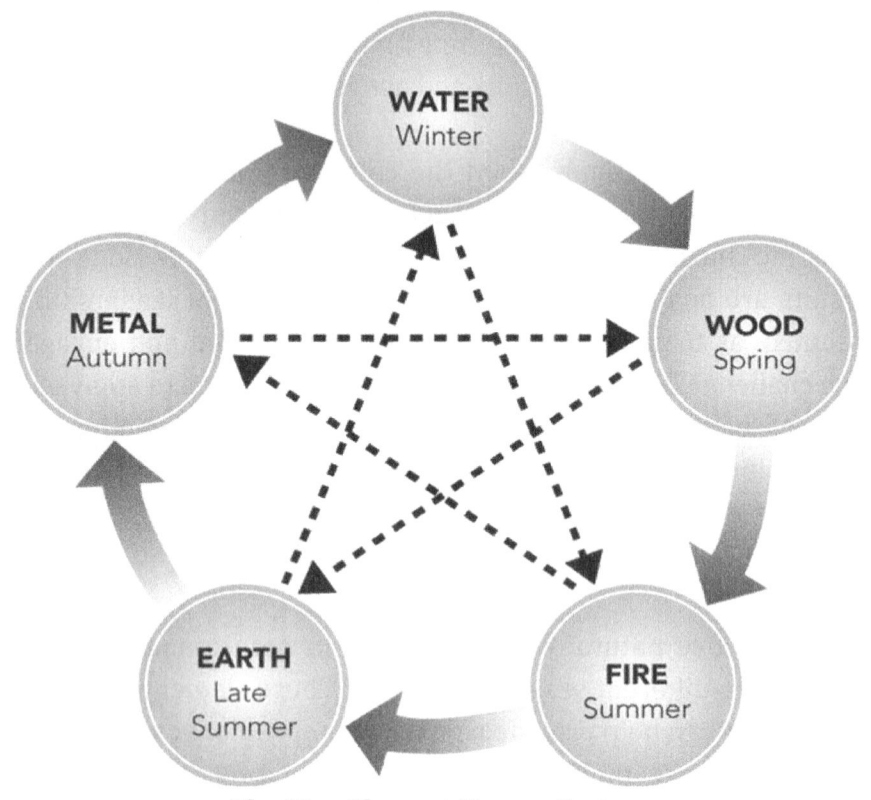

The Five Element Energy System

In this diagram, the large black arrows show the relationship between each element, as one leads into the next. This is the cycle of construction or creation. The other dynamic is the cycle indicated by the thin dotted black arrows. This is a cycle of control or of destruction, one of consequences and effect.

This Five Element system sat at the heart of one of the most complex and successful dynasties in ancient China, a dynasty that lasted nearly a thousand years.

Cycle of Construction (Positive Effect)	Cycle of Destruction (Negative Effect)
Wood feeds Fire	Wood leeches Earth (of minerals)
Fire creates Earth (ash)	Fire melts Metal
Earth bears Metal	Earth absorbs Water
Metal enriches Water	Metal destroys Wood
Water nourishes Wood	Water extinguishes Fire

From historical texts, we know this ancient wisdom influenced governments, commerce, business, medicine and education; the wisdom has remained hidden for over 2,000 years within the classical medical texts, waiting to be decoded and reawakened for integrating into modern-day business and life.

In its simplest form, this *Five Element Energy System* is a set of patterns or groups of characteristics that repeatedly occur; it helps us make sense of the world, our businesses and ourselves.

The ancient Chinese observed what was happening in their world, saw these elements as energies in action and classified them. Since then, people throughout history have commented on them or observed their effect in the wider world, notably Carl Jung, Albert Einstein and Richard Buckminster Fuller, to name a few.

The *Five Element Energy System* is a way to understand what is happening in the world and the influence it has upon us. It's like a map, and, when understood, shows us the quickest path to operating at our full potential and to leading a business towards collaboration, harmony and success.

HOW THE FIVE ELEMENTS IMPACT BUSINESS

The same five elements that provide the foundations for the natural world also exist in business – they are fundamental in helping us understand how business is shaped.

Each of these different elements corresponds with a different energy that is found in any business. For example, we need to understand each team member based on their energy frequencies and then recognise how this impacts the team and the business.

The combined frequencies of individuals create the frequency of the team, which in turn drives the energy of the business. It all starts with the smallest unit and ripples out to the rest of the organisation.

In Chapter Ten: Know Your Role In The Herd, we will be deep diving into how team members can understand their value to the business and where they are most trusted; for now, we will look at the five elements and the five energies they bring to the business overall.

Water Energy has a duality; it can be fast moving and powerful, or still and peaceful, allowing reflection. It is the Energy that teaches us about rest, action and sustainability. It allows us to reflect, learn and move on to a higher level of success. It is the Energy that drives our willpower and purpose. Water Energy is associated with winter. In an economic winter or recession, we live with the consequences of our previous actions, as we would if we were growing crops. This can be a time of plenty, with lots of future opportunities, or hardship and constant struggle. Water Energy and winter are points of transition, consequence, reflection, and future potential.

Element	Energy	Focus	Business Activities
Water	Contemplative	Why	Mission: Reason Why. Purpose of Business
Wood	Creative	What	Merchandise: Innovation, Strategy, Creation and Planning
Fire	Connective	Who	Magnetise: Customers and stakeholders. Marketing and Sales
Earth	Consultative	When/Where	Monetise: Service and follow through. Customer service
Metal	Calculative	How	Mechanise: Systems and Process

Wood Energy is associated with spring, the first of the five seasons, which epitomises the qualities of this powerful and forceful Energy. Spring is a chaotic time of new beginnings and growth; everything is fresh and alive. As a new seed grows, it pushes through the earth consistently and steadily, pushing everything out of its path. In business, this is associated with ideas, innovation and determination. Each plant has a very clear and focused plan for what needs to be done to achieve its aim or destiny. In business and life, this Energy is about planning, drive and clear aims.

Fire Energy is associated with summer, when there is lots of heat and energy and an outward expansive movement. This will show up in people as being more extrovert or expansive in nature and personality, connecting and communicating with others. In business, fire energy is associated with sales and marketing activities, and with energising team members and inspiring them to new heights.

With so much energy associated with fire, there can be issues around balancing activity with rest. A common concern is that of team members being too busy to be conscious of the consequences of their actions.

The ideal balance is where they are active and enthusiastic but mindful of their actions and outcomes; being passionate but selective.

Earth Energy is associated with late summer, a lazy, hazy time when much of the work has been done. In fact, this "season" was created especially to enable the link of the four seasons with the five Energies.

Late autumn is a slower time with less growth, a time to look after each other, a time where the frenetic nature of spring and the heat of summer had passed. This grounded stillness and caring are some of the key characteristics of Earth Energy types. In business, earth energy is associated with customer service and nurturing relationships. It is a time for developing joint ventures and collaborations.

Metal Energy is associated with autumn, the culmination of all the previous seasons. In order to capture what has been produced, one must harvest the crop. This is a process of detachment and efficiency. There can be no waste, with only a short time to complete the task at hand.

Team members with Metal Energy hate waste and are super-efficient; they will make sure that you don't waste a penny of your hard-earned cash. They are also trustworthy and would be devastated if they let someone down or failed to deliver on a promise.

When we look at the business attributes of each of the elements, we notice that they map directly across to the five main areas of focus in business as illustrated below: I call this the *Five Element Business Focus Model™* and it is represented by:

MISSION
Water
WHY

MECHANISE
Metal
HOW

MERCHANDISE
Wood
WHAT

MONETISE
Earth
WHEN/WHERE

MAGNETISE
Fire
WHO

Five Element Business Focus Model™

- Mission (water energy) – the business purpose
- Merchandise (wood energy) – what products/services are we offering?
- Magnetise (fire energy) – who are our customers?
- Monetise (earth energy) – where and when should we distribute our products?
- Mechanise (metal energy) – how should we organise things? What systems and metrics do we need to monitor performance?

Every organisation needs a combination of these energies to prosper and succeed. Just like in nature, the energies must be aligned to keep the entity in harmony. When the organisation falls out of balance (harmony), that is when poor performance arises and trouble occurs.

In the worst case scenario, everything implodes, reflected in the boom-bust cycle that we so often experience in business today. Fuelled by short-term gain and the pursuit of instant gratification, team members (the leaders included) focus on self-serving aims and desires. These make them look good in the short term but often involve them sabotaging the success of others by not sharing information.

Silo mentalities emerge which threaten the survival of the business. Just like in the natural world, we experience cataclysmic events, the equivalent of the hurricanes, tsunamis and floods that address the imbalances in nature, causing the bust side of the boom-bust cycle.

The famous balance
of nature is the most
extraordinary of all
cybernetic systems.
Left to itself, it is always
self-regulated.

Joseph Wood Krutch
(1893-1970)
Saturday Review
June 8, 1963.

These "busts" allow business to consolidate and harness its resources, to look at things differently and then, when trading improves, step up activity again. Unfortunately, many companies believe they have to live by this rhythm. The more socially conscious businesses, however, have realised that this approach is not a long-term sustainable solution. Instead, by focusing on the long-term outlook and having developed a culture that rewards contribution to the longevity of the organisation, they don't suffer as severely as others through the downturns.

THE NATURAL RHYTHM TO BUSINESS

The chart shows the natural rhythm that exists in business and how every business evolves through these different stages. Every business begins with the water energy giving the business its purpose. It then moves into the innovation and creation stage as represented by the wood energy. This is when products and services are birthed.

These then need to be communicated to the marketplace and this is when fire energy comes into play. Then the products/services get delivered and the customers nurtured; this happens through the application of earth energy. Once all these phases have been completed, metal energy enables us to harvest the fruits of our labours, and processes and procedures are put in place. Finally, we complete the circle by reflecting on what worked and what didn't and making adjustments so that we can move effortlessly around the circle again.

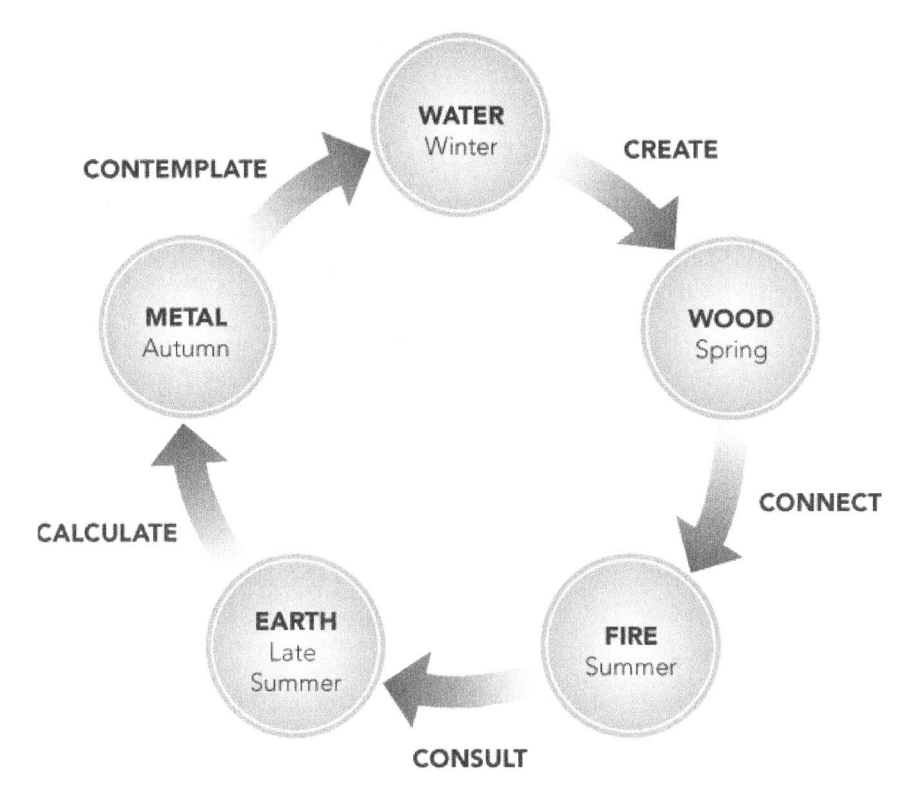

The Natural Cycle of Business Creation

Just like the *Five Element Energy System*, every business has a natural cycle of creation that it follows. Challenge occurs when, rather than following the creation cycle of business, leaders become self-serving and move into a cycle of control and destruction. They seek to miss out stages.

This can have dire consequences, particularly in the longer term when the system seeks to rebalance itself in order to re-establish its rhythm. The boom and bust cycles, both at individual business and wider economy levels, are direct results of business leaders trying to alter the course of nature and not allowing businesses to follow the natural flow.

Chapter Two:

What's Nature Got To Do With Business?

Takeaways:
- Business is a system made up of a number of interrelated parts. All need to work in harmony for the organisation to prosper.
- The same five elements that provide the foundations for the natural world also exist in business entities – water, wood, fire, earth, metal.
- All businesses can be built around these five different elements – which have both a constructive and destructive cycle.
- The business energies need to be aligned and in balance to ensure harmony in the workplace.
- Focusing on short-term gains is not sustainable.

Action:
Look at the activities you have in your business plan. Do you have a range of projects reflecting the five different energies planned, or are you dominate in one type of energy? Reflect on this and explore if there is anything you are overlooking or not focused on because it is not part of your natural energy flow.

CHAPTER THREE: THE JOINED UP BUSINESS BLUEPRINT

This is Wilkins, he believes in joined up thinking and aligning facets so no resources are wasted!

"WHEN A BUSINESS IS JOINED UP SO THAT ALL FACETS ARE ALIGNED, THERE ARE NO WASTED RESOURCES IN TERMS OF TIME, ENERGY AND MONEY."

JULIA FELTON

In the previous chapters, we have looked at why business needs to adapt and change to survive and that a blueprint exists within nature of how we can do this by working with the five different elements. This chapter examines the cornerstones that every business must have in place to allow a *Joined Up* business to evolve. And why would you want a *Joined Up* business?

Well, simply, a *Joined Up* business will result in increased productivity and profitability as resources are utilised to their maximum potential; and, more importantly, the business model is sustainable.

THE JOINED UP BUSINESS BLUEPRINT™

I coined the term *Joined Up* Business from a mentor of mine, Monty Roberts, who is the original Horse Whisperer. In the equestrian world, the term Join Up® is synonymous with a set of principles and training method that Monty uses for creating a willing partnership with a horse based on mutual trust and respect. A methodology that advocates collaboration and connection, rather than violence and force. So it seemed appropriate that the term *Joined Up* business should reflect the new paradigm that we are seeking to implement when leading business in this new era.

So what is the formula for creating a *Joined Up* business?

$$JUB = T(EL+EO+EE)$$

Where:
- JUB = *Joined Up* Business
- T = Trust
- EL = Expand The Leader
- EO = Empower Others To Act
- EE = Engage The Environment

The Joined Up Business Blueprint™

The three cornerstones that must be aligned in order for a *Joined Up* business to emerge are:

- Expand The Leader (EL)
- Empower Others To Act (EO)
- Engage The Environment (EE)

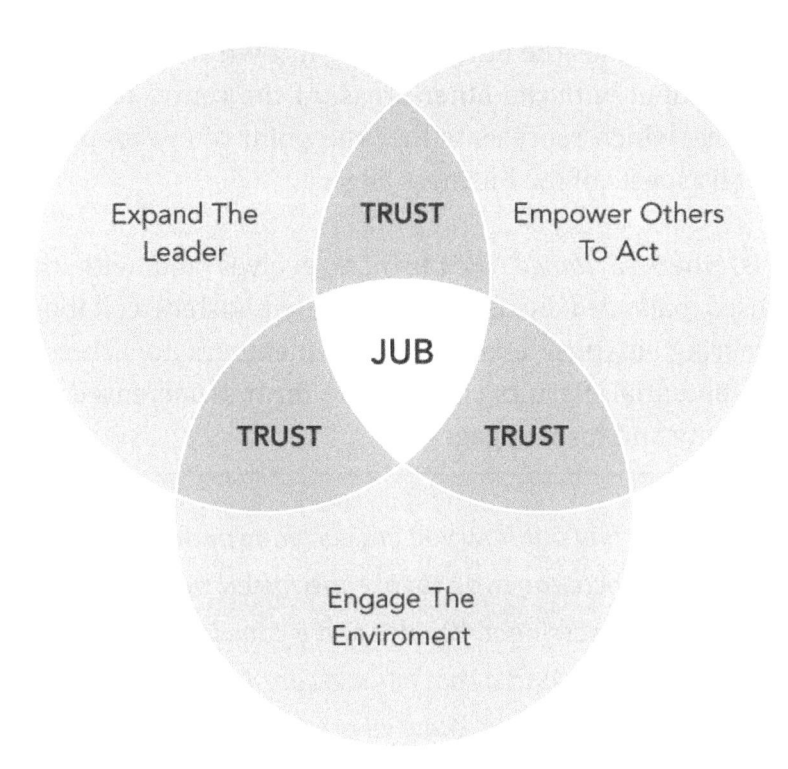

Trust (T) is the glue that holds these three cornerstones together. When all these items operate synchronistically together, then the outcome of this is an energised *Joined Up Business Culture* where collaboration and contribution are the norm, and high-performing teams work together across the business.

The three cornerstones of the multidimensional system, which I call the *Joined Up Business Blueprint™*, are illustrated by the circles.

Each circle overlaps the others, having its own attributes, but also interdependent with the other areas. At the centre of the model is the area, which represents the true point of interdependence, where all aspects of the business align.

This is where a *Joined Up* business evolves and with this an energised balanced business culture that fosters collaboration and sharing, in turn enabling team members to access their hidden potential. Results come in the form of increased profits, productivity and team engagement.

> **ACTION:** *To find out how you are currently performing in business, I encourage you to take the Joined Up Business Blueprint™ assessment. You will find a copy in the Appendix, or you can download a copy at www.on-the-hoof.com/resources. You will then know where to focus your efforts first to begin creating a Joined Up business.*

Expand The Leader (EL)

This cornerstone is all about the individual and their personal leadership style. Everything starts with the leader because unless they are *Joined Up* and aligned, it is challenging for the rest of the business to grow. Within this cornerstone, we'll examine how to instil purpose into a business and look at the attributes of courageous leaders and the difference between empowerment and delegation.

Empower Others To Act (EO)

This cornerstone is all about developing the team and the stakeholders. We'll review how to create a high-performing team by getting the right people in the right roles, how to make effective decisions and how to have courageous conversations.

Engage The Environment (EE)
This cornerstone is all about creating a business environment that supports business growth in terms of people and process. We'll look at how current business environments sabotage business performance; we'll learn how to create win-win situations, and how to work with the rhythms of nature to support the engagement of the environment.

Trust (T)
Trust holds these three cornerstones together enabling everything to occur interdependently. Without trust, there is no collaboration, and, without collaboration, there is no sharing of resources, so productivity and profitability diminish as team members are not operating at their peak performance state.

Traditional v *Joined Up* Business

The best way to understand the massive benefits that evolving a business that is *Joined Up* brings is to contrast it with what is perceived as a traditional business structure – one that operates from place of command, control and compartmentalisation, rather than a place of collaboration and connection.

Traditional	Joined Up Business
Leadership • Command and control • Hierarchical organisation structure • Low level of trust • It's a job – forced to follow • Tell people what to do • Inauthentic leaders hide behind the mask of the role • High level of control	• Collaboration and connection • Flat organisation structure typically incorporating matrix-style management • High level of trust • Has a clearly defined purpose • Empower team members • Leaders are authentic and bring whole self/real self to work • Balance creativity with controlled risk
Teams • Limited teamwork – silo mentality • Individuals strengths not utilised and wrong people in wrong roles • Centralised decision-making • Avoid difficult conversations • Sabotaging of others for own personal success • Slow to respond	• Build high-performance teams quickly • Align best people to best roles • Decentralised decision-making • Engage in honest conversations • Work in collaboration and harmony to avoid silos • Execute with speed across functionality i.e they operate On-The-Hoof
Environment • Create a win-lose environment • It's all about 'me', not 'we' • Low levels of happiness and productivity as teams not engaged • Lack of clarity on role and how it fits into the bigger picture	• Create a win-win environment • It's all about 'we', not 'me' • Balance between productivity and playfulness • Clear metrics and accountability – we're in this together
Culture • Low performance culture based on blame and self-preservation	• High-performance culture that inspires and results in greater productivity, profitability and passion

There are many advantages to creating a collaborative business that is *Joined Up* including the following:

- Creates a win-win for both the business and the team members.
- Team members are fully engaged and willing to take on new projects and challenges.
- Team members innovate at a faster rate; "two heads are better than one", giving the ability to develop and bring products faster to the market.
- There is improved organisational flexibility and agility which enables the business to keep up with the fast, global pace.
- Working in a team allows team members to showcase their diverse skill sets and play to their specific strengths.
- There is improved employee health, wellness and performance.
- Retention rates are extremely high.
- There is a competitive advantage when attracting top talent.
- There is increased revenue and profitability.

POSITIONS OF PERSPECTIVE

Each of the cornerstones is influenced by the five elements and five energies discussed earlier. Everything is interdependent and aligned. These three cornerstones also work well as they examine the concept of creating a *Joined Up* Business from three different perspectives: self, other and observer. In NLP, these are referred to as the three Positions of Perspective[10].

In every interaction, there are at least three viewpoints, and, in my experience looking at every situation through these three lenses gives a much more balanced view of what is happening.

                    OBSERVER

    SELF   OTHER

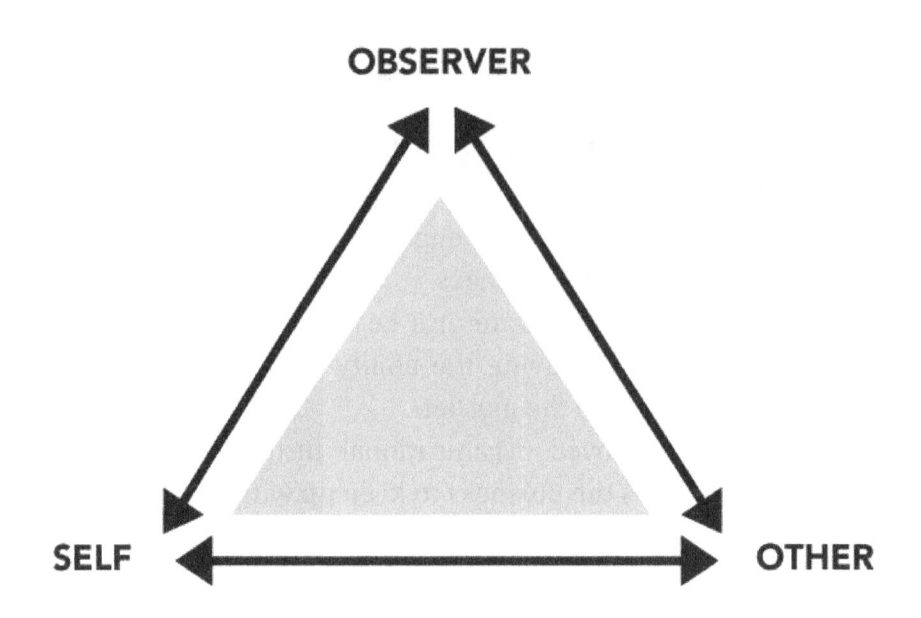

Cornerstone One looks through the lens of Self; Cornerstone Two looks through the lens of Other, and Cornerstone Three looks through the lens of the Observer.

Before we move on to review each of these cornerstones in depth and explore the key activities that define each cornerstone, let's see how we can measure the effectiveness of a *Joined Up* business by using Big Data, and how we can benefit from the glue that holds everything together: Trust.

Chapter Three:

The Joined Up Business Blueprint

Takeaways:
- *The Joined Up Business Blueprint™* is a multidimensional system which outlines the three cornerstones which must be aligned and in harmony before an organisation can energise its culture.
- The three cornerstones are: Expand the Leader, Empower Others To Act, Engage The Environment. These cornerstones are interdependent and, where they all converge, a Joined Up business emerges, fostering an energised culture.
- Traditional business structures operate from place of command, control and compartmentalisation whilst a Joined Up business operates from a place of collaboration and connection.
- Trust is the glue that holds the three cornerstones together; without trust, there is no collaboration, and, without collaboration, there is no sharing of resources.
- The cornerstones can be viewed from three positions of perspective, giving a holistic view of what is happening.

Action:
To find out how you are currently performing in business, I encourage you to take the *Joined Up Business Blueprint™* assessment. You can find this in the Appendix, or you can download this at *www.on-the-hoof.com/resources*. You will then know where to focus your efforts first.

The two words 'information' and 'communication' are often used interchangeably, but they signify quite different things. Information is giving out; communication is getting through.

Sydney J. Harris

Chapter Four: Setting the GPS for Your Business

"If you can't measure it, you can't improve it."

Peter Drucker

In today's society, there is no shortage of information. Collectively this information is being referred to as Big Data, due to the large volumes of high velocity, complex and variable data that requires advanced techniques and technologies to capture, store, distribute, manage and analyse.

Big Data pervades our life. The term relates to all the data that is available from a myriad of sources, including email, social media, social demographics and financial information. Never have we had access to so much information and, ironically, never have we had so little insight into what is really happening. This is the *Big Data Paradox*.

Big Data is both a blessing and a curse. When converted into insights, it enables us to monitor and measure the success we have at creating a *Joined Up* business. The curse or the challenge is that the data comes from disparate sources and so it relies on technology to join it all up. Thankfully, recent developments in technology make aggregating and aligning the data easier than before, so obtaining *Joined Up Data* metrics on your business is becoming easier.

We all realise that we are drowning in data. What we need is a way to interpret the data so that we can have direction. Direction is different from information. Information represents the entire gambit of knowledge whereas direction shows us how to get from point A to point B. Just like your GPS in your car, Big Data can – when organised into an effective business intelligence data dashboard – show you the best route to take to reach your destination. It helps you take the blinkers off your business to see where you are going; data helps us measure the success in evolving a *Joined Up* business.

Like all GPS systems, you need to know where you are now and where you want to get to. You must have a vision for your business and be realistic about the challenges that face the business today; then using a Business Intelligence Dashboard can help you stay appraised of roadblocks and traffic congestion on your journey to success. It can highlight for you when to speed up and slow down, when to course correct, and when to just pause and wait. As with all technology, it is foolhardy to blindly follow the GPS without any appreciation of external influences. We've all had an experience of plugging a destination into the car GPS, only to end up somewhere else, as outdated software did not reflect changes to the road system.

Business Intelligence Dashboards provide us with a road map of the upcoming dangers and how we can manage business to achieve more growth and success. They can pinpoint for us a myriad of business variables including: underperforming product lines, less profitable services, effectiveness of marketing campaigns, etc. Never have we had so much data available to enable us to make better decisions. However, none of this makes any difference if the data is not being used in context or if team members are manipulating it for their own personal ends. In other words, the data outputs are only as good as our ability to read the data in an objective way.

BUSINESS INTELLIGENCE DASHBOARDS

A Business Intelligence Dashboard is a visual way of displaying data in a *Joined Up* way. *Joined Up Data* is the collection of disparate bits of data that are filtered and used to create insights enabling tangible, aligned actions to allow the business to grow sustainably. It shows you exactly what is going on in your business in real time so that you can make effective decisions.

It can:

1. Show what is working (so you can do more of this)
2. Show what is not working (so you can fix this)
3. Measure individual performance
4. Enable effective decision-making

Armed with this information, you can clearly steer the direction of the business and navigate the relentless change that is occurring. The Aberdeen Group's research has shown that companies using Business Intelligence Dashboards generally have[11]:

- Three times higher revenue growth than those who do not
- Two times higher profit growth than those who did not

This makes sense, as companies using Business Intelligence Dashboards as their business GPS have total insight into their business performance, whilst their competitors don't.

TYPES OF BUSINESS INTELLIGENCE DASHBOARDS

As with a vehicle, a myriad of different gauges are needed to monitor what is happening in a business. These are the most common gauges found on Business Intelligence Dashboards today:

1. Financial Performance: profit margins, cash balances, accounts receivable and payable
2. Revenue: revenue per day, by product/service, monthly revenue trends, turnover
3. Website: traffic, top keywords referring traffic, top referring websites
4. Sales: number of leads/proposals by salesperson, closing rates, sales by lead source, conversions

5. Advertising: number of leads generated, cost per lead, advertising expense as percentage of sales
6. Customer Service: monthly refunds, call handling time, number of calls/emails processed
7. Email Marketing: open rates and click through rates, unsubscribe rates, revenue generated per email or per click
8. Social Media: Facebook fan engagement, number of Twitter followers, leads and sales generated from social media, traffic to website from social media
9. Product/Service Fulfilment: number of products/services delivered, change in inventory levels, on-time completion percentage
10. Team: employee attrition, engagement, acquisition costs, satisfaction

These different gauges also relate to the different elements discussed in Chapter Two. For example, financial metrics relate to the metal element, marketing metrics to the fire element, customer service metrics to the earth element and product innovation ideas to the wood element. It is important to ensure a balanced mix of gauges on the Business Intelligence Dashboard to enable the creation of a sustainable *Joined Up* business.

> **BONUS:** *You can download a checklist of some of the data variables that you might want to include in your Business Intelligence Dashboard, categorised by element type at www.on-the-hoof.com/resources*

The number of gauges your business selects will depend on the type of information your specific business needs to monitor and the complexity of the data required.

The one thing to remember is that no single metric can be meaningfully interpreted when viewed in isolation. The context of the information is important.

For Business Intelligence Dashboards to have maximum impact on the business, team members need to be educated and encouraged to interpret the data. If team members have any fear about the data, there is a danger they might manipulate the results; and since all aspects of the business are interrelated, this could have far-reaching consequences for other areas of the business.

In the 2013 EMA/9sight Big Data research report, the authors discovered that some of the biggest obstacles to leveraging the power of Big Data related directly to corporate culture[12]. Issues of stakeholder communication and buy-in as well as co-ordinating implementation strategies were cited as common challenges. This is why evolving a business that is *Joined Up* and energising the business culture is so important to successfully enable the use of Big Data to monitor *Joined Up* business performance.

MAKING SENSE OF DECISIONS

If team members are in information overwhelm, it is challenging to use the data to create meaningful insights; too much data results in avoidance, and, since it can't easily be converted into insights, it gets put in the top drawer of the filing cabinet. The data may signal trouble on the horizon, but put away in a drawer, no one sees it. Decision-making becomes impaired when team members become frightened of the data; they ignore, avoid, sandbag or manipulate the data for their own purposes. This is a real problem for business. The very thing that could help a business to reach new levels and achieve its full potential for all the stakeholders – team members, investors, suppliers, local community – is not being utilised, resulting in *The Big Data Paradox*.

It is natural to be overwhelmed by so much data; it is easy to get caught firefighting the current problems and never looking up to see what is on the horizon; being caught below deck stoking the fire to propel growth forward with no idea of where you are going. The signs – the data – are all there that you are heading for the perfect storm, but, stuck below deck, you don't see this. Business blunders on regardless until a big wave consumes it, and, in the worst-case scenario, this literally sinks the ship.

What needs to shift? The answer is to energise a culture where team members and leaders are empowered to look at the Business Intelligence Dashboard and make pro-active decisions based on the results; where there is no fear of reprimand; where collaboration and *Shared Leadership* is rewarded and there is an engaged environment where harmony reigns. In this case, there is no need to manipulate the data for personal gain.

In terms of the *Joined Up Business Blueprint™*, Big Data can be used as the metric to help us measure our success in creating a business that is *Joined Up*. As such, it plays an essential role in the creation of Business Intelligence Dashboards. Big Data is a metal element – used for analysing performance – and so helping us navigate through the blind spots to our destination.

Chapter Four:

Setting The GPS For Your Business

Takeaways:
- Big Data can help us navigate change but we need to know where we are heading first.
- Big Data cannot just be viewed as a technology solution to giving business insights, as it still relies on people to interpret the data.
- Businesses using Business Intelligence Dashboards generally have:
  - Three times higher revenue growth than those who do not.
  - Two times higher profit growth than those who did not.
- There are different *Joined Up* Business Data Metrics which relate to the five different elements.
- The *Big Data Paradox*: Never have we had access to so much information, and, ironically, never have we had so little insight into what is really happening – creating a Business Intelligence Dashboard can help us overcome this challenge.

Action:
Download the Business Intelligence Dashboard checklist at *www.on-the-hoof.com/resources*

CHAPTER FIVE: TRUST THE JOINED UP BUSINESS GLUE

"Trust is the biggest business commodity of the decade. Without trust relationships and businesses falter."

Stephen M. R. Covey

In today's networked and interconnected world, trust has become the new currency – the critical competency for individuals, teams, organisations, and even countries. Trust impacts every situation and relationship, whether personal or professional.

In fact, trust is a bit like water, which is the vital substance that sustains all life on this planet. When it's there, everything flourishes and grows. When it's not there, everything withers and dies. The same is true for trust. Without trust, projects slowly die, employees lose interest, and strategies fail. Trust has a lasting impact on your team, and in your organisation.

Here again, horses have something to teach us. Horses have such a sensitive radar that they are masters in giving feedback to help us learn. Many of my clients come and spend 1-2 days with my herd of horses at my *Unbridled Success* Retreats. Unlike with people, you can't use your authority to get a horse to do something. They respond only to influence. If you can learn how to inspire and influence a 600 kg horse to follow you, this readily translates into becoming a compelling, trusted leader that your team members want to follow.

TRUST: THE HIDDEN BUSINESS LUBRICANT

Trust acts like a lubricant. It reduces friction and creates conditions for evolving a *Joined Up* business. How well the team works together is the true indicator of future success and ability to lead through change.

Robert A. McDonald, Chairman, President and CEO of Procter & Gamble, when referring to Stephen M. R. Covey's book *Smart Trust*, states: *"It is both a mindset and a toolbox for 21st-century leadership"*. Trust is an important commodity that cannot be overlooked when building business. Trust is the glue that holds relationships and is the common denominator that integrates the three cornerstones: expand the leader, empower others to act, and engage the environment. Without trust, there is no harmony in the team or in business, and dis-ease prevails. Interestingly, if there is no trust in a herd of horses, they fight and live in fear for their lives, because there is no safety – lack of trust brings chaos.

WHAT IS TRUST?

A great analogy to understand trust is to compare it to money. Each time you make a good leadership decision, you build trust (earn more money). Conversely, each time you make poor leadership decisions, trust is eroded (money lost).

All leaders start with a certain amount of money in their pockets or piggy bank; how they act determines whether that sum of money grows or becomes depleted. If a leader keeps making bad decisions, then eventually the pile of money disappears – they have run out of trust with those they influence. It doesn't matter whether the last blunder is big or small, it will be the straw that breaks the camel's back.

THE CONSEQUENCES OF LACK OF TRUST

Trust needs to be reciprocal and shared. We don't trust rules, we trust people. Courage comes from leaders whose responsibility it is to protect the people working below them. People have confidence to do the right thing when they feel trusted by their leaders. It is leaders who energise the business culture to enable team members to reach their full potential, resulting in superior business performance.

Leaders cannot break trust with people and continue to influence them; it simply does not happen. This is much the same with horses. Horses thrive on a trusting relationship with their handler/owner. If that trust is breached, it takes a long time to repair, and, in some instances, is never repairable.

Lack of trust is prevalent in business today. Team members no longer trust employers to look after them. Long gone are the days when people had a job for life. Today businesses quickly downsize when economic conditions get tough. There is little loyalty from team members to employers or vice versa. The financial crisis of 2008/9 has made more and more people distrustful of banking institutions, as well as the government's ability to handle these situations.

To earn the trust of their team members, leaders must first care for their well-being and connect with them. To earn trust, trust must be extended. The best way to do this is to create a caring environment that enables people to fully engage their heads and hearts.

MEASURING TRUST: VALUE AND LEVERAGE

Team members deliver the most value to the business when they are undertaking a task that they are trusted to complete. Often then they are in the state called Flow since they find doing the task enjoyable and effortless.

Value is determined by the level to which a team member's talents are of value to those around them and a team member's effectiveness in business is measured by the amount of value they deliver to the business.

Value results in attraction whereby people are drawn to your goods and services. Wherever you see people getting attracted – whether to a product, person or company – you will find value. Value creates market attraction. This is the *Secret Energy of Business*™. When value is created, it acts like a magnet, attracting resources to it.

Products and services are vehicles for delivering value and are perceived as valuable when they meet a need, satisfy a desire, or appreciate over time. Value is created when someone is willing to pay for that product or service.

Businesses that add value build trust in the marketplace. The more value is created, the more trust is built and the bigger the market the business can command. However, if the value provided decreases, trust will diminish and so will market share. Therefore, how trusted a business is can be measured by the amount of revenue it generates.

> **BONUS:** *To discover where you are most trusted in business, take the Trust Test at http://bit.ly/trusttest*

Leverage allows the value to be delivered effectively and sustainably. If a business delivers value and leverages its resources effectively, it will be profitable. Increasing leverage results in growth and reveals the level at which each team member is having an impact.

Leverage is about doing more with less and this is where profit is produced. Value in itself does not ensure a healthy business. Leveraged value ensures that you not only have attraction but the attraction results in profitable results for everyone involved.

Leverage creates conditions for increased flow of resources – information, opportunities, ideas and money. Consequently, if a business does not leverage effectively, then flow is obstructed or limited, and resources are not used effectively.

In some cases, the business can consume more resources than it provides. When this happens, profitability levels decline and losses result, jeopardising the business's survival.

Effective leverage comes from having the right people and resources in the right place at the right time doing the right things for the right reason. In other words, having everything and everyone *Joined Up*. Everything that blocks and prevents flow of resources prevents leverage occurring and so makes an organisation less profitable, as it is not achieving its full potential.

Clearly an organisation needs to add value before it can leverage. Then once it has established leverage, it can then add more value and leverage this. It is just like walking. The first step is value and the second step is leverage. It is about balanced movement.

If not balanced adequately, there is potential for overvalue and overleverage, for example, investing in adding features to a product or service that the consumer does not use, or which make producing the item cost-prohibitive. It is a fine balance to add value without over-delivering.

	Measure	Outcome
Value	**Trust**	**Revenue**
Leverage	**Flow**	**Profit**

THE JOINED UP TEAM EQUATION

The impact that team members can have on the business is also a function of value and leverage. When team members are in flow and operating at their full potential, they are naturally adding value by operating at their best, and when they align this with other resources in the organisation, they can leverage for optimum impact. This is what happens when we create high-performing teams. One team member adds value and this is leveraged by someone else. This is the magic of a *Joined Up Team*.

The *Joined Up Team Equation* can be summarised as follows:

Joined Up Team Performance = Value x Leverage

The talent of an individual is their personal, sustainable value to the team. The talent of a team is the team's sustainable value to the company. The talent of a company is the company's sustainable value to their market. In this way, we can see how interconnected an individual's performance is to the success of the team, which in turn impacts the success of the company.

CASE STUDY:

CREATING VALUE AND LEVERAGE IN A TEAM

Holistic Enterprise Realising Opportunities (HERO) was a project funded by Blackpool City Council to deliver Enterprise Education across Blackpool. It was tasked with providing young people with access to skills training and knowledge they would otherwise have never received. The HERO team inspired many young people into a career in business and entrepreneurship. Its work had been incredibly well received by young people, Blackpool schools and parents alike.

The team knew approximately 18 months in advance that their LEGI funding (Local Enterprise Growth Initiative) was due to end and that they would lose their entire £300,000 a year funding for activities. This meant an end to Enterprise Education, as Blackpool knew it. If the team wanted to continue, it had to find a sustainable and scalable solution that didn't require public sector funding, and fast!

After completing a one-day Value and Leverage Workshop, the team members began to understand the best way to create value within their group and how to leverage that value with each other.

They started to have some real 'aha' moments about why the ideas they previously had were not coming to fruition in the way they had set out in the new HERO vision.

They experienced a unique process of creating Flow and learnt how to immediately apply that to the ideas created that day. The programme created situations that allowed participants – both as individuals and as a team – to experience Flow for the first time together. It was highly empowering.

The change in the mindset within the team was dramatic and instantaneous. Team members were open to change, much more flexible in their approach, more committed and, most importantly, were having more fun!

HERO has now become a Community Interest Company and is no longer funded by the government, but through its commercial activities. Forward orders have already been placed for programmes by schools that will be run by this "new company" in Blackpool. It is estimated that revenue of £50,000 will be achieved as a minimum in the next 12 months. As a community interest company, it can now apply for funding streams that were not open to it previously. This is likely to generate a further £30,000.

Productivity has increased because each person is working to roles and accountabilities that keep the team in Flow. The team was awarded a Prime Minister's Big Society Award (one of only a handful presented across the country!)

Chapter Five:

Trust: The Joined Up Business Glue

Takeaways:
- Trust has become the new currency – the critical competency for individuals, teams, organisations, and even countries.
- Trust impacts every situation and relationship, whether personal or professional.
- Trust is an important commodity that cannot be overlooked when building a culture that supports high-performance teams.
- Trust acts like a lubricant. It reduces friction and creates conditions for evolving a business that is *Joined Up*.
- Any team member's effectiveness in business is measured by the amount of value they deliver to the organisation.
- Value is measured by trust. The result is revenue.
- Leverage is measured by Flow. The result is profit.
- The *Joined Up Team Equation* is: *Joined Up Team Performance* = Value x Leverage.

Action:
Take the Trust Test at *http://bit.ly/trusttest*

CHAPTER SIX: APPLYING TRUST IN A JOINED UP BUSINESS

"Trust is like a mirror ... once its **BROKEN** you can never look at it the same again..."

Unknown

BUILDING SELF-TRUST

So how does a leader build trust in those that follow them, and also in themself, since good leadership involves leading from the inside out? The answer lies in consistently exemplifying:

- Competence
- Connection
- Character

Ralph Waldo Emerson states that *"Self trust is the first secret to success"*, because just as you can't lead others until you can lead yourself, you can't trust others until you can trust yourself.

In his book *The Speed of Trust*, Stephen M. R. Covey describes the first wave of trust as self-trust. It is all about being credible and developing integrity, intent, capabilities and results that make you believable, both to yourself and others.

Building trust with yourself starts with the small things in life: doing what you say will do. For example, being on time to meet friends, not finding excuses for cancelling just because you don't feel up to it, putting personal appointments in your diary and then making sure you keep them (e.g. going to the gym).

I know from my own experience how difficult it can sometimes be to keep those appointments with myself. It is so easy when the alarm goes off in the morning to find an excuse for not exercising today, or not getting up and writing my book. Over these last few months, it has taken courage and determination for me to set aside time to write. Sure, there is always something else pressing to do, but I know that every time I fail to keep these commitments to myself, I feel my self-esteem and self-confidence slipping away and I fail to inspire others to believe in me. They lose trust in me and the net result is that my business suffers.

We all know it intuitively, and research also confirms that a person's self-confidence affects their performance. This is why Jack Welch of GE always felt so strongly that *"Building self confidence in others is a huge part of leadership."* Furthermore, a lack of self-trust also limits our ability to trust others. In the words of Cardinal de Retz, "A man who doesn't trust himself can never really trust anyone else."

It is the small things we do that ultimately impact how people trust us. We might not realise it, but telling a white lie here and failing to keep an appointment there all impact our credibility. And if we are not credible, then we are not trustworthy; people simply don't believe that we will follow through on our actions. We lack integrity when we fail to keep our own standards, and when we fail to live up to our own standards, our colleagues see no reason to meet them either.

> ## CASE STUDY:
>
> ## BUILDING TRUST WITH SMALL ACTIONS
>
> *Beaver Trees and Landscaping, a small company based in Christchurch, New Zealand provides a perfect example of a company that has fully embraced the power of building trust by small actions. Given the nature of its business, the company has many client appointments to quote for work. So after hearing about the Power of Small from Paul Dunn of B1G1, the owner Bryce Robb implemented a policy of making all the appointments for quotations at unusual times, such as 10:25am.*

> *This was such a small change to the business, but it had massive impact. Firstly, a customer's surprise at the times of the appointments prompted them to be on time; they were then delighted when the Beaver Trees representative turned up on time.*
>
> *In fact, people are so surprised that they are often found waiting on their driveway for the representative. Now, of course, the Beaver Trees representative is always on time and just this simple act has built massive trust with prospective clients. The net result is that the company's sales conversion rate has jumped to a massive 80% and they are not the cheapest game in town. This proves the power of making a commitment and sticking to it. Furthermore, the company was recently judged to be the Best Company To Work For In the World with under 50 team members.*
>
> *That's the power of building trust by doing what you say you will do.*

My recent personal experience with Bracken, a young horse in my herd, demonstrates perfectly the impact that failing to be consistent and credible in your actions can have. Bracken came to me having been found abandoned. She was weak and frail, and quite afraid of humans. Over the following few months, I cared for her, and we developed a great bond and friendship. She trusted me implicitly to keep her safe, as I never did anything to harm her.

However, as sometimes happens in great relationships, she gradually began to lose respect for me. Why was this? Well, it crept up on me so slowly I barely noticed, but on reflection I realised I was making requests to her, like moving out of my space, and if she failed to move I didn't ask again, making allowances for the fact that she was young and had just started her training. However, when I did this, from Bracken's perspective I lost credibility. If I made a request and she did not oblige, it wouldn't matter, as I would just quit. Quickly, Bracken lost trust in my abilities and therefore my leadership as well. Regaining her trust has taken many months of hard work and has reinforced for me the need for consistency in my behaviour.

I wonder how many leaders in business quit before they get the outcome they desire. The ramifications are huge as not only do they then fail to complete the task they are undertaking, they lose credibility with their peers and ultimately, therefore, their trust and respect. In my experience, leaders often quit before they get the outcome they desire because they lack trust in their own decisions and defer to the influence of others.

In *The Speed of Trust*, Stephen M. R. Covey identifies that there are Four Cores of Credibility which make a person believable to both themselves and others[13]. All are necessary for self-trust:

Core One: Integrity
- Walking the talk and being congruent both inside and out
- Having courage to act in accordance with our beliefs and values
- The biggest violations of trust are violations of integrity

Core Two: Intent

- Our motives, agendas and resulting behaviour
- Trust grows when we genuinely care for the people we interact with, lead or serve

Core Three: Capabilities

- Our talents, attitudes, skills, knowledges and style. These are what inspire confidence – they are the means by which we produce results
- Our ability to establish, grow, extend and restore talent

Core Four: Results

- Track record, performance and ability to get the right things done
- Credibility increases when we accomplish what we say we will do and diminishes when we fail

The first two cores deal with character, and the second two with competence. If we visualise these four cores of credibility as a tree, then character forms the roots of the tree – only once that is established can trust and leadership follow. Importantly, our character determines our success at leadership and whether people will trust us. No one likes to spend time with, or follow, people they don't trust.

A person's character communicates many things to other people:

Character Communicates Consistency

- A leader needs to act consistently, day in day out; they can't decide just to quit because they are having a bad day

Character Communicates Potential

- When a leader's character is strong, people trust them and trust in their ability to release their potential. This gives people hope for the future and boosts their personal self-esteem

Character Communicates Respect

- If you don't have character within, you cannot earn respect from others; respect is essential for lasting leadership

How ironic it is that we spend millions of pounds annually developing competency skills in our team members when really our focus should be on developing character skills in the areas of integrity, authenticity and discipline. To develop integrity requires being scrupulously honest, telling the truth even when it hurts. To be authentic requires being ourselves with everyone and not playing politics or pretending to be anything we are not.

> *"95% of all leadership failures in the last century have been failures of character."*
>
> **Norman Schwarzkopf, United States Army General**

Finally, to strengthen discipline, we need to do the right thing regardless of how we feel. (Horses are masters at teaching discipline. Regardless of the weather, I have a commitment to go and check them, feed them and water the horses twice a day. It is amazing how disciplined we can become when we know that someone or something is relying on us.)

HONEST INTENTIONS CREATE TRUST

A high-performance culture can only occur when team members know that the leader's intentions are honest. Being open is perhaps the most powerful way that a leader can create trust. When a leader opens up and has honest conversations, people tend to be more open in return and a genuine interest and respect can develop. Conversely, if the leader is a "closed book", people find it difficult to connect with them; there is no commonality of purpose. This is the reason why open-plan offices have become more popular in recent years. The lack of closed doors makes managers and team leaders more accessible and some of the physical barriers to communication are broken down.

Leaders are also more likely to instil trust in their team members if they demonstrate fairness, especially when making contentious decisions, and if they can admit to their own Achilles' heel and seek to address this. Ultimately though, trust is developed through serving others (and/or a higher cause), as opposed to serving self. Building trust in your abilities is achieved through exuding appropriate optimism and confidence and ensuring that your accomplishments are recognised appropriately.

BREAKING THE RULES

Trust is the biological reaction to the belief that someone has our well-being at heart – that they care about us. Great leaders are trusted by others to obey the rules. They are also trusted because they are flexible and know when to break them. The rules are there for normal operation. When a situation dictates it, we want team members to break the rules and go the extra mile for customers. This is how great customer service results.

In *Entrepreneur Magazine*, Richard Branson shares the story of when one of his team members did exactly this[14]. They broke the rules to provide exemplary customer service. The essence of the story was that a passenger was flying from New York to London in Virgin's Upper Class and, as a result, was entitled to a complimentary limo pick-up to take them to the airport. For whatever reason, the limo didn't arrive and the passenger was forced to make their own way to the airport.

When the passenger arrived at the airport, they informed the check-in attendant of their experience, and, from her own pocket, the check-in attendant refunded the passenger the cost of his taxi fare to the airport. When the check-in attendant sought to reclaim the money from her superior, her request was declined because she did not have a receipt.

Eventually this story reached the Virgin head office and the check-in attendant was immediately refunded the money and praised for her initiative, which had created great customer loyalty. Conversely, the check-in attendant's supervisor was reprimanded for blindly following the rules without recognising that this was a case where breaking the rules was acceptable because of the customer loyalty that resulted.

THE TRUST MIRROR

Working with animals, and horses in particular, can provide us with a perfect mirror of how trustworthy we are as a leader. When two horses meet for the first time, or indeed when a person meets a horse, the horse is asking three questions:

1. Who are you?
2. What do you want?
3. How do you operate?

Effectively the horse is seeking to assess how trustworthy you are in your intentions. Are you greeting the horse in order to make him do something for you, or are your intentions simply that you want to say 'hello'? How the horse answers these questions will influence the response that you get.

During the summer of 2004, when I was having an ongoing issue catching my horse, Toby, I suspect his answers to these questions would have been something like:

1. That is my miserable owner who only turns up at weekends
2. She wants to throw a saddle and bridle on me and expects me to take her for a ride.
3. She is again being really self-serving. It is all about her, she cares nothing for my feelings or what I want from this relationship.

Against that background, it is hardly surprising that he opted to vote with his hooves and did not allow me to catch him for the entire summer.

Reflecting on this situation made me think about similar questions that team members might unconsciously pose when they meet another person in the organisation. Some of the questions that might run through their head are:

1. Do you care about me?
2. Do you have the knowledge to help me?
3. Can I trust you to make unbiased recommendations that meet my needs and not your own agenda?

The last question is particularly relevant when creating a culture that supports effective decision-making and promotes high-performance teams; if there is any doubt of the intentions of the other individual, then there will be no connection or trust.

VIRTUAL TRUST

In our interconnected virtual society, it is easy to think that we can build trust online. However, there is also no such thing as virtual trust. Whilst we might initially get to know our team and our customers by the Internet and emails, nothing can substitute for face-to-face interaction and the power of proximity. All great leaders and business owners recognise that they can't build trust without direct connection and communication. This is why in person business meetings continue to abound and have not significantly declined with the advent of video conferencing.

Our societal need for connection makes us want to be with others; you can only truly get to know someone when you are face-to-face and you get to experience their energy and how they show up. So much is revealed in a face-to-face meeting that can't be gleaned on the phone or via Skype. And it is the same for your customers and other stakeholders too. They want to be able to connect with you and make an assessment as to whether they trust you. This is why video has become the largest medium for sharing data. Over 300 hours of video are uploaded to YouTube every minute and over six billion hours of video are watched each month on YouTube – that's almost an hour for every person on Earth. While not as good as an actual meeting, at least when our potential clients can see us and hear us they are more likely to make a positive assessment that they want to do business with us.

TRUST YOUR INSTINCTS

At the beginning of this chapter, we discussed the fact that no one will trust you unless you trust yourself. Listening to the gut instinct deep inside your body is perhaps one of the greatest gifts you can give yourself. It is there for your self-preservation; but time and time again I find myself and my clients ignoring this inner voice, preferring to listen to the rational, intellectual left-brain.

Being around horses teaches us never to ignore our instincts, but rather to rely on them as credible, unquestionable sources of information and communication. Put simply, if we don't listen to our instincts then we can get ourselves (and our equine friends) into danger. Once we begin to trust our instincts then a whole new world of opportunities and possibilities opens up for us as we tune into things that we never saw before.

As prey animals, horses have to listen to and trust their instincts in order to survive. This makes them great teachers and role models for us. By contrast, over the years we humans have forgotten to listen to our natural instincts. Many of us never listen to that inner voice, or if we hear it we ignore it and then we wonder why things turn out badly.

I recall when I was working in the corporate world that I consistently failed to listen to that inner voice. I made decisions that I regretted and kept taking on new projects even though I barely had time to complete the work I already had on my desk. Quite frankly, I didn't trust the gut instinct that was telling me to slow down and stop taking on more work. The net result was that I burned out, experiencing extreme fatigue. This was the ultimate way of my body telling me to stop. I couldn't help but hear the message loud and clear when I was drained of energy.

Why was it that I never listened to what was going on and blindly carried on regardless? I guess it was because I rarely trusted myself, so I could not listen to that inner voice with all its wisdom. I did not listen to my heart and gut. The funny thing is that despite this being our instinctive response and deep survival mechanism, society conspires to numb this feeling and discount its wisdom from the list of rational solutions that are available. And yet, listening to our instincts isn't a sign of weakness; it is a sign of strength.

Another word for our natural instincts is our intuition. I remember a number of coaches suggesting that I listen to my intuition but quite frankly I was never really sure what they meant. What was this illusive quality called intuition? I'm ever-indebted to Liz Mitten-Ryan of Equinisity who shared with me that "intuition" is made up of two words: "inner" and "tuition" – so to her intuition is about listening to our inner teachings, the things that we just know about the world, our gut feeling. There is nothing to learn; we just know when something is right or wrong.

Listening to the ancient teachings that have been handed down from generation to generation can help us live a more fulfilling, authentic life. I know at times in the past that I have believed I don't have any intuition but then I remember that my intuition is always working; it is just that I'm not tuned to the right "radio station" to hear it. If I focus and make myself open to tune in and listen to my intuition, then I can hear it loud and clear – just like the radio station playing in the background in my kitchen.

Chapter Six:

Applying Trust in a Joined Up Business

Takeaways:
- Build Trust in those who follow you, and also yourself, by consistently exemplifying: Competence, Connection, Character.
- It is the small things we do that ultimately impact how people trust us.
- There are Four Cores of Credibility, which make you believable to both yourself and others: Integrity, Intent, Capability, and Results. All are necessary for self-trust.
- Building sustainable trust allows the organisation to Flow.
- There is no such thing as virtual trust.
- Listen to your intuition (inner teaching) as it always knows what to do.

Action:
- Go to *www.on-the-hoof.com/resources* and download the Trust Worksheet and then;
- List all the areas where you are trusted in business.
- List what actions have done that have caused an erosion of trust.
- Consider how can you build self-trust so that you can build trust with others.

SECTION TWO:

THE JOURNEY

"Sometimes it's the journey

that teaches

you a lot about

your destination."

Drake

In this section of the book, we will focus on the three cornerstones that enable a *Joined Up* Business to evolve. To recap, these cornerstones are:

- Expand The Leader (EL)
- Empower Others To Act (EO)
- Engage The Environment (EE)

By aligning these three cornerstones, we allow a *Joined Up* business to emerge; the outcome of this is an energised *Joined Up Business Culture*, where collaboration and contribution are the norm, and high-performing teams work together across the business.

Each of the three cornerstones is sub-divided into three chapters, which reflect the activities that must be undertaken to create a business that is *Joined Up*. Many of the activities are interdependent and so rely on alignment elsewhere. For example, courageous conversations are challenging unless the business leader is fully in integrity and leading from a place of courageous impact.

Each of the cornerstones is examined using the three Positions of Perspective framework. This helps us to see business from three different viewpoints: Self, Other and Observer.

> **Cornerstone One:** Expand The Leader – most closely corresponds with the perspective of Self.
> **Cornerstone Two:** Empower Others To Act – examines things through the lens of Other.
> **Cornerstone Three:** Engage The Environment – relates to the perspective of Observer.

CORNERSTONE ONE: EXPAND THE LEADER (EL)

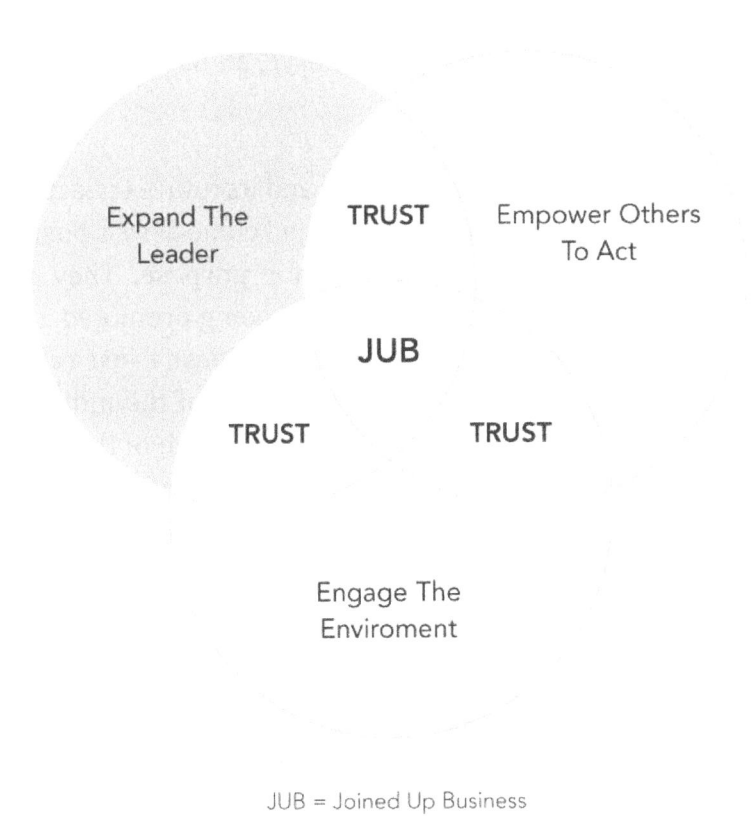

Expand The Leader   **TRUST**   Empower Others To Act

JUB

TRUST   TRUST

Engage The Enviroment

JUB = Joined Up Business

"Before you are a leader, success is all about growing yourself. When you become a leader, success if all about growing others."

Jack Welch

Expand The Leader is the first cornerstone that we will examine in creating a *Joined Up* business where everyone is contributing at their full potential. This is the logical place to start as everything stems from you, the leader, and then permeates out into the team and the environment. Just like the creation of a tiny baby starts with the first cell in the embryo, all businesses a start with the leader.

The impact a leader has on the business and its future trajectory is of paramount importance, and yet so often I come across business leaders who quite frankly are not fit for purpose. They have succumbed to the classic *Peter Principle* of being promoted above their level of competence. And competence doesn't just refer to skills but rather to the emotional development of the individual. Many leaders simply are just not self-aware enough of the impact they have on others. They simply don't have the emotional agility and intelligence to manage their emotions and recognise the impact they are having on others.

Given that this cornerstone is all about *Expanding The Leader*, it makes sense that in this section we are looking at the business through the lens of self – in other words, how the leader sees things, and how the leader feels and responds to the many events that occur.

Joined Up Leaders recognise how essential it is to integrate their hearts with their heads by developing self-awareness and emotional intelligence whilst empowering others to do the same.

As the saying, purportedly attributed to Lao Tzu goes, *"the longest journey that people must take is the eighteen inches between their head and their heart".* *Joined Up Leaders* work on expanding themselves by learning to master their emotions and trust their intuition and judgement.

They work to build up the emotional resilience to deal with the myriad of situations that present themselves every day without getting out of balance. As a result, they are able to stay focused and not get diverted off course.

Before we delve into this cornerstone, I want to address the concept of personal leadership. I truly believe that everyone in society can be a leader in one or more specific aspects of their life. Let's face it; we are all leaders of own lives, making choices on a daily basis of what to do next. These choices influence the direction of our lives.

Parents are leaders of their children and many people are leaders of local entities such as churches. Whilst in this book we are looking at leadership from the perspective of how you show up in business as the business leader, leadership is not a rank exclusive to those at the top of the organisation. Leadership becomes a choice to serve others with or without any formal rank. As we move forward, more and more of us will need to adopt leadership roles if we are to create the collaborative and connected businesses and society required to respond positively to the various megatrends.

Focus on the journey,
not the destination.
Joy is found not
in finishing an activity
but in doing it.

Greg Anderson

CHAPTER SEVEN: PURPOSE AND VALUES

"IF YOU HAVE A PURPOSE AND CAN ARTICULATE IT WITH CLARITY AND PASSION, THEN EVERYTHING MAKES SENSE AND EVERYTHING FLOWS."

ROY SPENCE JR.

Society is changing at relentless speed and so is our team members' motivation to work. A recent study by Deloitte of the millennial generation showed that 77% considered it their duty to improve the world for everyone through their lifestyle and careers[15]. Gen Y are no longer interested in just a job, they are seeking an experience, a rationale to contribute something. The monthly pay cheque is not the motivation to work for much of the younger generation. They want more.

Increasingly, leaders are waking up to the fact that they need to have a bigger social purpose than just making money. A philosophy that resonates with team members and so allows them to access the hidden 90% of their own human potential. Business leaders need to create an environment that inspires and motivates team members. The business needs to stand for something bigger and have ambitions to make a real difference in the world. It needs to have a big purpose for its existence, something that is often referred to as the Business Promise. This states clearly why the organisation is in business.

Interestingly, the 3rd annual Deloitte Core Beliefs & Culture Survey noted that organisations with a strong sense of purpose – defined as a focus on making a positive impact on customers, employees and society in general – are more confident in growth prospects, more likely to invest in initiatives that lead to long-term growth and enjoy higher levels of confidence amongst the key stakeholders[16]. Organisations that are stronger attract better talent and retain motivated team members, creating a virtuous circle.

The Business Promise or Why is represented within the five elements by water. A business's Why is the lifeblood of the organisation. It is what sustains "life" when the business faces challenges and tough times arrive – and there will always be tough times. Without a great Why, it is easy to lose the heart and motivation to continue. The big Why of the organisation's existence is what gets its leaders and team members out of bed in the morning on those tough days.

At a macro level, the Business Promise should be to add value to the community it serves, profitably. This may sound obvious but too often I see businesses that are no longer adding sufficient value. As customers and employees move elsewhere, they fall into a spiral of despair, as trust is broken. Often I see businesses continue to deliver value but no longer profitably. The business starts incurring losses or making cuts that take it down a similar death spiral.

Even though all businesses are different, in essence they have the same shared purpose. When they fail in this purpose, they cease to exist. When they achieve this purpose each day, they thrive. There is a parallel in the natural world. When we look at the natural world, we see that all living things, despite their diversity, have the same primary purpose: to preserve and propagate life.

Since the nineteenth century, when rise of corporations as we know them today began, companies have been treated as living individuals, with tax liabilities, legal and ethical responsibilities and clear guidelines for when they can be said to be "alive" and when they are declared "dead". When we think of a company as a living thing to be grown instead of built, we become interested in its life cycle.

As we saw in Chapter Two, every business has a natural life cycle that it passes through which corresponds to the cycle of seasons. The duration of these seasons are not fixed, however, and great *Joined Up Leaders* can shorten or extend any of these seasons, with the one certainty that the rhythm will ultimately prevail.

The success of the company is not to be measured by how long it lasts but by how full a life it led, the example it set and the legacy it leaves behind.

When we focus everyone on the two performance measures in this Business Promise:

1. "How well are we adding value?"
2. "How profitably are we achieving this?"

we align everyone to the two most important drivers that ensure the success of the business.

THE POWER OF WHY

The importance of Why in business was proposed by Simon Sinek in his book *Start With Why: How Great Leaders Inspire Everyone To Take Action*. He conjectured that businesses usually look at the what, how and then the why they are in business, and suggested they do the converse.

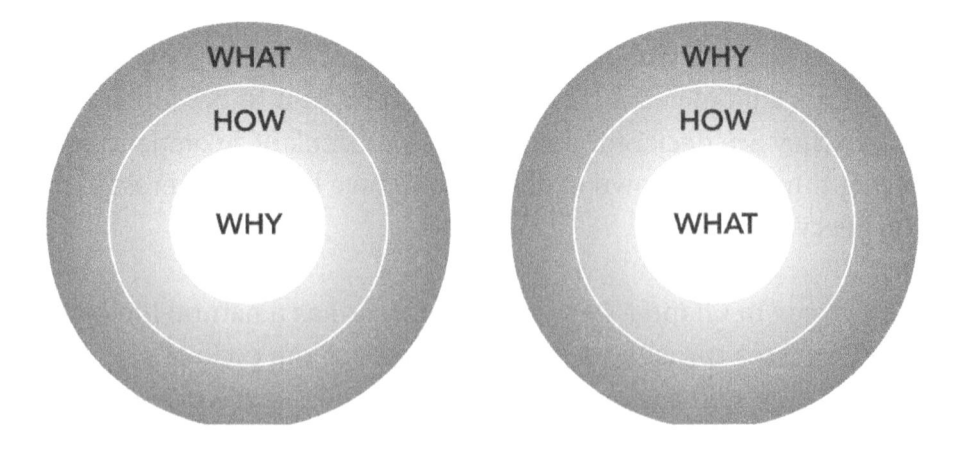

Focus on the Why you are in business, and the What and the How will follow. This relates back to the *Five Element Energy System* we looked at in Chapter Two, with the Why at the top of the system, as it drives everything else.

Let's take Apple as an example. Their Why is to "challenge the status quo and create innovative products that are personal and people just love". They have a holistic view for being in business, which is not product-driven or channel-specific. This is why they have been able to launch multiple products under the Apple brand – iPhones, iPads, iPods, iTunes, iMacs – and, more recently, Apple Watch.

Their Why provides an umbrella for what they do. Contrast this with a company like Dell who tend to focus on what they do, which is make great computers. Do you see how limiting this purpose is? It only allows Dell to make computers and in fact, if they supply anything other than computers, as consumers we doubt their ability to do this.

The power of having a Why in business was one of three factors that a recent Deloitte Review showcased as being important conditions of success when a large number of people collaborate effectively[17]. The three factors were:

1. Belong: people collaborate on behalf of an organisation they feel connected to. In other words, they have a reason why.
2. Believe: people collaborate when they commit to carry out a specific action. They have a common what.
3. Behave: people collaborate when they share a common understanding of how things are done. They know how to do things.

WHY HAVING A WHY IS IMPORTANT FOR BUSINESS

A company's purpose is the reason that company exists. *Joined Up Leaders* are motivated by service to the company's highest purpose whilst creating value for all the stakeholders. Leaders understand the interplay of all the elements and see the business as a whole rather than the sum of many parts.

For companies, purpose matters. It energises the system and allows the business to transcend the narrow concerns of individual stakeholders. It creates the vision, which everyone lives by. When all the stakeholders are aligned around a common higher purpose, they are less likely to care only about their immediate, narrowly defined self-interest. Having a higher purpose is the first step in being a *Joined Up* business – one where everyone involved understands the value it can bring to the larger community. Core values create the guiding principles within the business to realise its purpose.

The business purpose holds the organisation together and nourishes and encourages the team members and other stakeholders to excel. It can galvanise an organisation to achieve greatness. Jeff Bezos, founder and CEO of Amazon.com, suggests that we: *"Choose a mission that is bigger than the company".*

Like a magnet, a business's purpose attracts the right resources – team members, customers, suppliers and investors – to the business and aligns them. A compelling purpose reduces friction within the business ecosystem as everyone is aligned and pointed in the same direction and is moving in harmony – just like a herd of horses.

Examples of company purpose are:

- Disney: to use imagination to bring happiness to millions
- Zappos: to make customers happy
- Southwest Airlines: to give people a reason to fly
- RSPCA: to prevent cruelty, promote kindness to and alleviate suffering of all animals.
- Sainsbury's: to provide a quality shopping experience for their customers with great products at fair prices
- Whole Foods: to bring whole foods and greater health to the world

If a business has a purpose and it can be articulated with clarity and passion, everything makes sense and everything flows. Purpose always comes before strategy, so what is the difference between purpose, mission and vision? In *Conscious Capitalism*, John MacKay describes the difference as being:

- Purpose: the difference you want to make in the world
- Mission: the core strategy that must be undertaken to fulfil the purpose
- Vision: the imaginative view of how the world will look once the purpose has been largely realised

> *"Individual action and commitment to a common goal. That is what makes a team work, a company succeed, a society flourish and a nation triumph."*
>
> **Deloitte, from the book**
> *As One: individual action collective power*

Well-run, values-centred businesses can contribute to humankind in more tangible ways than any other type of organisation in society. Bill Gates did not start Microsoft with the goal of becoming the richest man in the world. What he saw was the potential of computers to transform our lives and he strived to create software so that there could be a computer in every home. In the process, he got rich. He delivered value to consumers, and, in turn, he got paid. Money is purely a vehicle for exchanging value.

FOR TEAM MEMBERS

Having a business Why is also important as it engages team members to become part of a movement – something bigger than themselves – and everyone likes to be part of a movement. It appeals to our basic human need to belong; we are a social species. People naturally love connecting with others, and having a shared purpose and vision is one way that disparate groups of individuals can connect and interrelate.

For team members, happiness results from living a life of meaning and purpose, although this is best achieved when not directly aiming for it – just like profits.

An absence of purpose results in work that is devoid of meaning and that does not tap into our higher human capacities, resulting in a negative effect on the productivity and profitability of any business.

Purpose-driven motivation is intrinsic motivation and far more effective and powerful than extrinsic financial incentives. When emotionally invested in work, team members can overcome almost any challenge with ease.

The importance for team members of connecting the company to a purpose beyond profits and growth was summed up by Unilever CEO Paul Poleman when he said: *"Having a deeper purpose to what we do as people makes our lives more complete, which is a tremendous force and motivator. What people want in life is to be recognised, to grow and to have made a difference. That difference can come in many forms; by touching someone, by helping others, by creating something that was not there before. To work for an organisation where you can leverage this and be seen to be making a difference is rewarding."*[18]

> **ACTION:** Think about your own business; do you have a clear purpose, mission and vision? If not, take a few minutes to consider what each of these elements looks like. Then consider the values required to help you achieve these goals.

When companies lose their connection to purpose, the business falters. This is in part what happened at Tesco and what prompted the new CEO Dave Lewis to say: *"I do think it's pretty clear we have to get back to the core of our business in price, availability, and service. What it is that customers need from us so that they reward us with their loyalty."*[19]

FOR CONSUMERS

Evidence shows that we are experiencing something of a "values revolution", where consumers are increasingly aware and concerned with the social responsibility of the companies they do business with. According to a study by Edelman, ethics as a purchase trigger has risen 26% globally since 2008.[20] Now more than ever, consumers resonate with a business having a Why. This is because the primary purpose of any business is to add value. If you don't add value to your consumer's life, you won't stay in business long. Consumers only exchange money for value. They part with their hard-earned cash when the corresponding benefit they receive back is worth it to them.

As an analogy, imagine you have a burst water pipe in your home that is spewing water into your kitchen. The longer the water runs, the more damage is being done. At this point in time you have a real need for a plumber and you will pay over the odds to get someone to fix it. The value of the plumber's service in fixing the broken pipe exceeds the amount of money you are willing to pay. If, however, you just have a dripping tap, while the constant drip is annoying, it might not be worth paying the same amount as getting the broken water pipe fixed. Simply stated, the value exchange at that point in time is not a match.

Consumers feel motivated and emotionally connected to a company with a big Why. Contrary to popular belief, we buy with our emotions and these are governed by the limbic part of the brain rather than the logical neocortex. There is a saying:

EMOTIONS SELL – LOGIC JUSTIFIES

This is also the reason for Apple's success. They appeal to people's emotions. This is why people queue up overnight on street corners to purchase the latest device.

Having just seen the latest commercial for the new Apple Watch, I experienced exactly this phenomenon. I don't need a new watch, but the commercial appealed to my emotions – the sleek design, the gadgetry, the functionality – it created a desire to have one. Now logically, I really don't need one, but as I sit here my emotions are finding all kinds of ways to convince my logical brain why it would be a great idea to invest in one; and given time, I'm sure they will convince my neocortex of the logic of having this watch.

THE LEADER'S VALUES

The founder of a business typically sets out the Business Promise, and if it becomes ingrained in the culture, it permeates throughout the entire organisation. The Why is typically a reflection of the founder's values, and for team members to be highly effective in the business, they need to resonate with the company Why.

Arthur Andersen, the now defunct accountancy firm, is one company that had a great Why. Based on the philosophy of the founder, Arthur E. Andersen, its founding premise was One Firm, One Voice, and the business was structured to reflect this. It also had the following ten values that were prominently displayed around the organisation.

1. Client Service: delivering value without compromise
2. Hard Work: being responsive and timely
3. One Firm Concept: many independent nationals with common objectives
4. Recruiting Quality People: the first major firm to do campus recruiting
5. Training and Development: leadership in professional development
6. Meritocracy: people rewarded based on their own merits
7. Integrity: objectivity in all that we do, without fear or favour
8. Esprit de Corps: pride in the organisation and belonging to it
9. Professional Leadership: acknowledged leader throughout our history
10. Stewardship: making long-term decisions to benefit the Firm

Underpinning of these values was the idea that the firm should always be truly independent, putting the needs of its stakeholders before that of the clients. Many reports exist of the founder Arthur E. Andersen refusing to cede to client demands to "tamper" with their accounts if that would in any way jeopardise the reputation of the firm.

In the book *Inside Arthur Andersen: Shifting Values, Unexpected Consequences,* the authors provide a detailed account of why and how the once largest accountancy firm in the world failed. In essence, the main driver was that the culture and the values of the firm shifted significantly away from the principles that Arthur E. Andersen imbued when he established the firm in 1913. As audit services became more commoditised in the 1970s, the firm sought to venture into consulting engagements to supplement its revenues. However, the drivers of the consulting business meant that it had very different values and culture to that of the original firm. Although the audit and consultancy arms tried to align their values on paper, the underlying differences continued and ultimately resulted in the acrimonious splitting away of Andersen Consulting in 2000 to form what is now known as Accenture.

Andersen still appreciated the value of being able to offer its clients a one-stop shop for professional services, however, and so developed its own business consulting division within the accountancy firm. The dynamics within the consultancy division led to pressure to sell at any cost. The independence, credibility and integrity of the firm were lost in return for short-term gains.

The crushing blow to the firm came when the audit partners, even those who had some reservations, acquiesced to Enron's request to restate their accounts, wiping out some 20% of Enron's earnings for the previous five years. It was a case of undermining its core value and putting the client before the firm. The pressure was great, with the fear of losing the company's biggest account, reportedly worth over $100 million at the time.

Even though, in May 2005, Andersen was finally acquitted of any wrong doing, the damage to its reputation had already been done – the firm had imploded as its clients left in droves. Its credibility in tatters, and having been forced to surrender its CPA licenses and its right to practice before the SEC, there was no option but to shut up shop. On August 31st 2002, the firm ceased trading, with many of its divisions being acquired by other accounting and consultancy practices across the world.

I share this story from a personal perspective as I was leading a division with Andersen's London office during this time. The experience certainly helped me hone my own personal skills in leading teams through adversity, but it serves to illustrate how a business's viability is dependent on the value it brings to its customers. When customers can no longer see and/or understand the value offered and trust and credibility is lost, they leave. They no longer have an emotional connection to the company and so seek this elsewhere.

The story also illustrates how a business culture that once sustained great growth can morph in a way that, rather than helping business grow, contributes to its downfall. One of Andersen's challenges was that, with business becoming more global (in 2000, it had 300 offices in 84 countries), team members became disconnected from the founding principles and value of the company. With business today becoming more global than ever, this is a real challenge for leaders – to ensure that everyone is aligned and operating to the same values.

VALUES BASED LEADERSHIP

Values are defined as the core beliefs by which individuals guide and conduct their lives in a way that is meaningful and satisfying to them. Values are the things against which people measure their choices, whether consciously or not. They are used to rationalise behaviour to themselves and others. They determine the level of satisfaction with choices, even if decisions are not freely made but constrained by other factors. As such, business values are at the core of a business culture.

Values come from the heart and not from the head (even though we often try to rationalise our behaviour) and therefore they are not attributes that we can teach people, they need to be experienced. Most people have a sense of their own values, although they may have stopped listening to them. Helping team members and business leaders connect to their own values and those of the organisation is one of the activities that we engage in during my *Unbridled Success* Retreats. Through partnering with horses, team members come to acknowledge their own personal values and what makes them tick.

Armed with this clarity, they can then see how their values align with those of the organisation and if there is not a match, they can decide how to move forward.

> **CASE STUDY:**
>
> **CLARITY OF PURPOSE BOOSTS BUSINESS PERFORMANCE**
>
> *Last summer, I was working with a business owner who wanted to grow her business to the next level. Her existing business was successful but she was struggling to move it up. She had no motivation and was starting to fall out of love with her business. During her private Unbridled Success Retreat, we started to examine why she was in business. What was the purpose of her business and what impact did she want to make in the world?*
>
> *She gave me all types of logical reasons for being in business and what she wanted to achieve, but as I sat there in the round pen with my horse Charlie, I instinctively knew, as he did, that her answers lacked any conviction. There was no passion in her voice and, energetically, she was flat. I continued to ask her questions to help her get to the root of her purpose for being in business and she kept giving me "lame" answers. Throughout this, Charlie stood next to me, unwavering.*

> *I then asked the business owner to take a deep breath and to really imagine what she wanted to achieve in the world. Then, out of nowhere, she said: "I want to save the elephants".*
>
> *This was so far removed from what she had been saying that I was initially taken aback; in that moment, Charlie walked up to her and put his head on her chest. From a heartfelt state, she had connected to the real reason why she was in business and Charlie now sensed she was congruent and aligned.*
>
> *The transformation in her business over the following months was incredible. Connected to her passion and purpose, her business had real meaning and she found many ways that she could support the elephants, including volunteering at an elephant sanctuary twice a year. Her desire to save the elephants gave her momentum to get out of bed in the morning and find innovative ways that her business could grow, so that she could contribute more financially to elephant rescue projects.*

The performance of a company is closely tied to the personality and values of the person at the top, since these define the culture of the enterprise. Not many people will have heard of James Sinegal but he was the co-founder of Costco and ran the company from 1983 until his retirement in January 2012. Sinegal believed in creating a balanced culture, one where looking after the team members was a priority. He believed that if the company treated team members like family, then the team members would reciprocate with trust and loyalty. He rejected the notion that in the retail, and in the warehouse sector, you had to keep wages and employee benefits to a minimum.

His people-first attitude was the foundation for a culture that allowed trust and co-operation to develop. Workers are praised for finding solutions and better ways of doing things. They look out for each other rather than competing against each other. The net result is that the share price of Costco has exceeded industry averages since 1986 and the company has enjoyed consistent growth, rather than the roller coaster ride that many of its peers have experienced. Today, Costco is the second largest retailer in the USA and the world. It is focused on a long-term game rather than the short-term results required by Wall Street. As Sinegal once noted:

"Wall Street is in the business of making money between now and next Tuesday. We're in the business of building an organisation, an institution, that we hope will be here 50 years from now."

SHARED PURPOSE CAN CREATE MASSIVE CHANGE

Business is a vehicle for creating massive change in the world and when all team members align behind a shared vision, the business is capable of achieving amazing results. And not just financial results. Of course, all businesses need to create financial success as cash is the lifeblood of society, but for business to be sustainable and successful, its purpose needs to be more philanthropic.

It needs to contribute something to society in order to be perceived to be of value.

Contribution is one of the six human needs identified by Tony Robbins and ultimately, once our basic human needs of safety, security and companionship are met, our natural desire is to be of service to others and make a contribution. Successful businesses are those that play a long-term game and whose focus is on serving others. The US retailer Whole Foods is a great example. Their company purpose as stated by Walter Robb, their co-CEO, is: *"We are not so much retailers with a mission as missionaries who retail. The stores are our canvas upon which we can paint our deeper purpose of bringing whole foods and greater health to the world".*

There is immense pressure in business today to focus on short-term gains. We have become a results-driven society where we want everything now. This is not a sustainable strategy. In nature, it takes time for crops to grow. You don't just plant the seeds and then the next day have a harvest. It takes a season for the crops to germinate and develop; and so it is in business. Short-term gains are not sustainable and eventually the company falls behind.

The recent financial crisis which resulted in the demise of some well-known entities, such as Lehman Brothers, Merrill Lynch and Bear Stearns, is an example of what happens when businesses focus on short-term gains as opposed to longer-term wins.

In our society driven by short-term gains, success is measured in immediate results; this causes leaders to make illogical decisions that whilst viable in the short-term have longer-term consequences for the business stakeholders – environment, team etc. Ego-based leadership drives this myopic view of what is possible. It's all about self and self-preservation rather than about the more collaborative question, "How I can serve others?" Only when leaders, teams and businesses connect to this higher vision of what is possible are they able to access their hidden 90% of human potential and achieve exceptional results.

To achieve the numbers, traditional business leaders often make decisions and take actions that could be harmful to stakeholders. Leaders who put a premium on the numbers over lives are more often than not physically separated from the people they serve. Command and control structures create a system where people are more likely to do the right thing rather then display any initiative and take responsibility. When people feel disempowered, it can hurt their ability to form relationships to a point where self-preservation becomes the primary focus. Short-term gains have led to the destruction of many great companies like General Motors and Sears, and the bankruptcies of Enron, World Com, Kmart and Kodak.

A *Joined Up Leader* takes a stand and shows that there is a different way of doing business, one where when we raise our own consciousness so we can make more deliberate choices that further our personal and organisational development. *Joined Up Leaders* make great decisions, as they understand the impact and consequences – both short and long term – of their actions. They understand that business metrics have a cause and effect relationship.

That said, in business we often think we can control things but in reality we can never really control the outcomes in life. In the face of this, we make the best decisions we can and then focus on the things we can control: our actions and reactions, and trust that right actions will lead to positive outcomes in the long term.

IMPORTANCE OF HIRING PEOPLE WITH ALIGNED VALUES

Joined Up Leaders have the power to create an environment in which people naturally thrive and advance for the good of the organisation itself. Companies and organisations are our modern day tribes. Like any tribe, they have traditions and symbols and language and their own unique culture. And like any tribe, they have a leader. The culture of the organisation will affect the types of people attracted to it. The stronger the culture, the more the "right" type of people are attracted – those aligned with the values of the company.

Zappos is a great example. It is a company with a very strong culture and, as a result, it attracts only like-minded people. As a result of this, it has a very low turnover rate and a waiting list of people who want to work at the company.

Zappos is also a fantastic example of a company that recognises the importance of all team members being aligned to the company vision. According to Tony Hsieh, the CEO, *"Zappos culture embodies many different elements.*

- *It's about always looking for new ways to WOW everyone we come in contact with.*
- *It's about building relationships where we treat each other like family. It's about teamwork and having fun and not taking ourselves too seriously.*
- *It's about growth, both personal and professional. It's about achieving the impossible with fewer people.*
- *It's about openness, taking risks, and not being afraid to make mistakes. It's about being part of a story that never stops unfolding. And it's about having faith that if we do the right thing, then in the long run we will be a part of building something great.*

Our culture is based on our 10 core values:

1. Deliver WOW Through Service
2. Embrace and Drive Change
3. Create Fun and A Little Weirdness
4. Be Adventurous, Creative, and Open-Minded
5. Pursue Growth and Learning
6. Build Open and Honest Relationships With Communication
7. Build a Positive Team and Family Spirit
8. Do More With Less

9. Be Passionate and Determined
10. Be Humble"

So how do Zappos ensure they hire the right people for the job? A tenet that Zappos operates by is *"Hire Slow, Fire Fast"*. Each applicant is required to attend extensive interviews, not just with the human resources department but also with their potential colleagues. They are questioned on their values rather than their skills; after all, skills can be learned, but if the new team member is not aligned to the company culture and values, that could spell disaster. Team members not aligned with the company's values can spread dis-ease within the organisation; hence Zappos' fire fast policy. If someone is not a fit, they need to be quickly removed from the organisation. Much like a rotten apple, if you leave it in a basket of healthy apples, the rottenness spreads.

To support this process, all new Zappos recruits are put on a four-week probationary period. And what do they do if they decide that the new recruit is not a fit, or indeed if the team member no longer wishes to work for the company? Zappos pays them one-month's salary to leave immediately. This quickly removes any "independent" thinkers from the group, restores harmony and so mitigates the silo mentality found in so many organisations.

A PURPOSE-DRIVEN CULTURE DRIVES PROFITS

Operating from a strongly communicated and shared sense of purpose is also a profitable decision. Businesses with a higher sense of social purpose that deliver value experiences get financially rewarded through increased customer loyalty. It makes sense for every business to have a very clear Why and purpose for their existence – the benefits are disproportional. And still, not every company has a Business Promise. Doing well and doing good in society creates a virtuous cycle that is self-sustaining.

DOING WELL

Contributes to organisations

VIRTUOUS CYCLE

Enables organisations to

DO GOOD

The 2014 Deloitte Core Beliefs & Culture Survey revealed that businesses that focused on having a strong purpose rather than building profit were more confident about their growth prospects and also had higher levels of confidence among their key stakeholders. Of thr respondents who worked for companies with a strong sense of purpose, 82% stated they were confident that their organisation would grow in the next year, compared to just 48% of people who worked in organisations without a strong sense of purpose.[21]

Furthermore, according to a 2010 Burson-Marsteller/IMD Corporate Purpose Impact study, a strong and well-communicated corporate purpose can contribute up to 17% improvement in financial performance[22]. And that's in the short term. The longer-term benefits of having employees aligned with a strong sense of purpose are incalculable.

It is worth noting that a company's purpose is never fully achieved. It's not something to be accomplished and then checked off the to-do list. Rather, purpose becomes a true north on a compass, guiding each team members' daily actions.

The real challenge for business becomes truly operating consistently with that purpose, even when billions in revenue is on the line.

FIVE KEY QUESTIONS TO CONSIDER WHEN EMBARKING ON THE PATH TO JOINED UP LEADERSHIP

Leaders who want to embark on this path to a more inspired workforce and purpose-driven results can begin the process by considering these five key questions:

1. Does your organisation have a clear Business Promise?
2. If so, do all the team members really understand it?
3. Do you and others in your company align with the Business Promise?
4. Do your clients and customers clearly understand the Business Promise and what it means to them?
5. Are you willing to make hard decisions to remain true to the Business Promise?

> *"Vision without action is just a dream.*
> *Action without vision just passes the time.*
> *Vision with action can change the world."*
>
> **Joel Barker**

CONDITIONS OF SUCCESS

Having a great Business Promise is of little use if team members do not fully understand the desired outcomes, priorities and clear domains of responsibility. The conditions of success translate the Business Promise into something that can be fulfilled and supported by linking the Business Promise to outcomes and ownership.

In other words, the Business Promise is like the goal and the conditions of success are the strategies and tactics to achieve this goal.

Within a team, individuals are assigned to be accountable for the different conditions of success. Ideally there are a minimum of four conditions of success – one for each of the remaining five elements that we discussed in Chapter Two. (The Business Promise (Why) is represented by the water element.) No one person can be accountable for more than one condition of success to ensure that they stay focused on the task at hand. Additionally, this also immediately creates the need for collaboration and it is highly unlikely that one of the conditions of success can be achieved without consultation with others in the group. Also having four different conditions of success, in addition to the Business Promise, helps ensure that the energies within the business are balanced and in harmony.

Unlike the Business Promise, the conditions of success can change annually. In fact, they can then be used to drive the outcomes that the business wants to focus on during each quarter, and therefore can also provide a GPS of where the business is heading that is fully aligned with its purpose.

Chapter Seven:

Purpose and Values

Takeaways:
- Businesses needs to stand for something bigger and have ambitions to make a real difference in the world.
- When the Business Promise resonates with team members, it allow them to access their hidden 90% of human potential.
- A businesses purpose or Why relates to spirit and is represented within the five elements by water. A business's Why is the lifeblood of the organisation.
- The two performance measures of the primary purpose are: 'How well are we adding value?' and 'How profitably are we achieving this?' Values are defined as the core beliefs by which individuals guide and conduct their lives in a way that is meaningful and satisfying to them. Values are the things against which people measure their choices, whether consciously or not.
- Leaders have the power to create an environment in which people naturally thrive and advance for the good of the organisation itself.
- Hire Slow; Fire Fast.
- The Business Promise becomes a true north on a compass, guiding each team members' daily actions.
- The conditions of success translate the Business Promise into something that can be fulfilled and supported by linking the Business Promise to outcomes and ownership.

Action:
To help you begin crafting your Business Promise and conditions of success, go to *www.on-the-hoof.com/resources* where you can download a series of exercises and templates to get you started.

CHAPTER EIGHT: LEADING WITH COURAGEOUS IMPACT

"No single leader can any longer meet the demands placed on them and there is a growing recognition of the need for highly effective leadership teams."

Peter Hawkins

In the twenty-first century, leadership is not for the faint-hearted. It demands courage and tenacity to create a real impact as a leader, to go where others won't go and do what needs to be done. Leadership is not a rank but rather a responsibility that hinges almost entirely on character. Leadership is about integrity, honesty and accountability – all components of Trust.

Leadership comes from telling team members not what they want to hear, but rather what they need to hear. To be a true leader, to engender deep trust and loyalty, we have to start by telling the truth.

So what does a leader do? With leadership evolving and changing, there is no one solution that fits all. For some people, leadership is all about production and process – it is about what you do, when and where it is delivered, and how it is done. The leader's job is to get team members on the same page so that they can work together effectively. Great leaders know how to get team members aligned around what work they do together and how they do it.

For others, leadership is all about the people. They cite the leader's job is to develop people's sense of belonging to the group. They believe that great leaders should get team members to have a strong shared identity or sense of who they are.

Others say leadership is about purpose, Why the business exists. Great leaders rally team members to have a shared commitment to the goals of the organisation. Great leaders get people to have a strong sense of directional intensity around why they are working together.

Joined Up Leadership=				
Why	**+What**	**+ Who**	**+ Where/When**	**+How**
Purpose	Productivity	People	Production	Process

Joined Up Leadership involves all these five elements – Why, What, Who, Where/When and How – combined with the leader being in alignment with themselves (being authentic and congruent).

Only then can a collaborative culture result where everyone is working for a common purpose in an environment that fosters the release of extraordinary human potential.

Let's be clear, leadership is not the bastion of just those at the top, or indeed those who have the title 'leader' on their business card. It is the responsibility of everyone in the business. Everyone has the responsibility to keep the group safe and this is the philosophy in a herd of horses. Everyone in the herd has a responsibility to protect their fellow herd members from danger, and anyone not fulfilling that role is immediately reprimanded and sent out of the herd. For a prey animal like a horse, being excluded from the herd is just about the worst thing that could happen; alone they are prone to attack from predators. This is why each herd member stays accountable and fulfils his role to protect his fellow herd members.

COLLABORATIVE LEADERSHIP

Leadership that is collaborative ensures that everyone feels included, valued, respected, and involved. Shifting the focus of attention and power from ourselves to the people we are privileged to lead is not what many people have in mind when they think of leadership. Yet, multiple studies have shown that this is precisely the way to incite extraordinary efforts from your followers, to fulfil the vision and objectives of your organisation.[23]

Trust is an *essential* characteristic of collaborative leadership. Collaboration is fostered by building trust and facilitating relationships. It involves leaders combining their heart and mind so they can contribute to the world at large and make a difference.

It also involves leaders having the courage to lead team members where they have never been before; because they, too, are pioneers, willing to step into the unknown.

We expect leaders to protect us and care for us, and, when this doesn't happen, it causes resentment. This is what happened during the recent banking crisis. We weren't upset per se about the amount of compensation that the banking leaders received, but rather the fact that they took the money and perks and did not offer protection to the people and systems entrusted to them. In some cases, they even sacrificed their people to protect or boost their own self-interest.

It is this that offends us because we feel they have violated the very definition of what it means to be a good leader. A leader always accepts responsibility to protect those in their care. A good leader eschews the spotlight in favour of spending time and energy doing what they need to do to support and protect their people. Leaders are the ones who are willing to give up something for us: their time, their energy, their money, and maybe even the food off their plate!

Great leaders understand that it is never about them. There is no ego involved. It's all about the "we" and not the "me". These leaders have realised that their success comes from those they lead. It is all about empowering others to succeed and ensuring that others get into the spotlight. In fact, a great leader is often never seen. They effectively direct their teams from the sidelines, only stepping into the fray when problems or challenges arise that the team aren't empowered to resolve.

Leadership is not a license to do less; rather it is a responsibility to do more. Leadership takes work. It takes time and energy. The effects are not always easily measured and they are not always immediate. Leadership is about caring and being committed to others that you serve.

> *"If your people don't trust you, there is no way they can deliver the type of performance that will grow your business. You are not entitled to the trust of your people – you have to earn it by the way you behave toward them."*
>
> **Bret L. Simmons**

ATTRIBUTES OF SUCCESSFUL LEADERS

Great leaders also recognise that leadership is about who you are (character) rather than what you do (competency). Leadership nowadays is everyone's job. It is about changing our thinking in order to change our behaviour.

In fact, although throughout this book we are proposing a blueprint for evolving a *Joined Up* business with an energised business culture, the fact remains that unless business leaders change their own thinking and that of the team members they lead, systemic and sustainable change will never be possible. *Joined Up Leaders* are aligned in every aspect of their own personal life and how this relates to their business. They model congruency and authenticity.

So what makes a successful leader? Through research and experience, I have distilled 16 attributes that I believe *Joined Up Leaders* must embody in order to be successful and have a courageous impact on their business and in the world.

The 16 attributes are summarised below. They spell the words **COURAGEOUS IMPACT**:

C – CLARITY OF VISION AND CONFRONT REALITY HEAD-ON

Business leaders today can no longer stick their head in the sand like an ostrich and ignore what is happening around them. Even looking at business through rose-coloured glasses can be dangerous. The pace of relentless change means that *Joined Up Leaders* need to continually confront the facts about the state of their organisation and business. Big Data can provide insightful Business Intelligence Dashboards that can help any business owner clearly see what is happening in all areas of the business. Armed with this information, the business owner can make better decisions, and so lead the team and business to even greater heights of success.

A caveat exists though. The business owner must be self-aware and willing to let go of any preconceived ideas they had about how the business would evolve. Data is always right and it's always wrong. You need to ensure that the data is interpreted in context because without this sense check, dire decisions could be made, especially if they corroborate a previous agenda of the business owner.

O – OPEN AND HONEST CONVERSATIONS

As a *Joined Up Leader*, it is imperative that you speak your truth and are comfortable with having open and honest conversations with team members. Authentic communication means saying what has to be said. No one likes confrontation but when left unattended to, negative situations can create a toxic threat to the team or the company's performance. For example, by taking swift action to reassign or exit under-performing team members, you are helping yourself, the team and the business.

U – URGE TEAM MEMBERS TO CHALLENGE THE STATUS QUO

Many business leaders feel the pressure to have all the answers. They feel uncomfortable showing their vulnerability when they don't have all the answers. Ironically, it is this vulnerability that actually magnetises team members to you. By encouraging constructive dissent and healthy debate, you can reinforce the strength of the team and demonstrate that in the tension of diverse opinions lies a better answer. However, unless you have removed fear from the environment, it is unlikely that team members will speak up, for fear of reprimand.

R – RESPECT OTHERS' OPINIONS

All business leaders have blind spots that impact the way they interact with others. Unfiltered 360 degree feedback is not always easy to hear, but it can breathe new life into relationships and your leadership style, if you listen and, importantly, act. The challenge is that quality 360 degree feedback only really occurs if there is a high degree of trust in the organisation and team members do not feel that they will be punished for their honest feedback. An energised and *Joined Up Business Culture* allows and encourages this as an informal and natural structure.

A – ACKNOWLEDGE OTHERS

As a business leader, it is imperative that you let go of the personal need for praise and instead give credit to those around you. At first, your ego may wonder, "What happens if I don't get all the praise? Will I feel irrelevant?" Remember that a good leader takes more than their fair share of blame and less than their fair share of credit. Value others and cheer them on by remembering that success is a team sport. Most *Joined Up Leaders* find that they begin to receive an entirely different level of recognition and acknowledgement, one more about how they are being, not what they are doing, thereby fully establishing their relevance in a new light.

G – GALVANISE CHANGE – GO FOR IT

In fear-based environments, it's all about protecting the status quo and surviving; but as we have already shown, this leadership model will not serve us well as we move further into an era of collaboration. *Joined Up Leaders* acknowledge that the pace of relentless change is fundamentally changing the leadership paradigm. It is time to galvanise change in our teams and business culture. *Joined Up Leaders* need to be solution orientated and lead from the front, setting the direction and encouraging full participation. As with all change, this won't necessarily be easy. Most likely the initial change will be messy as team members seek to adapt, but armed with a unique Business Intelligence Dashboard for your business, you can quickly see when things are drifting off course and course correct in pretty much real time.

E – ESTABLISH A CULTURE OF INNOVATION

Creating a culture where team members don't feel afraid to speak up promotes innovation. It never ceased to amaze me how much creativity my team had and how many innovative solutions they could come up with. Seeing the business from a different perspective from me, they could often find solutions to problems I had grappled with for days. Encouraging team members to speak up when systems and processes aren't working develops a true partnership in business, one where everyone contributes to the success of the business, and where everyone feels engaged and motivated.

Alongside a culture of innovation, it is also important to emphasise that the business is a learning environment, and there can be no learning unless the organisation experiments. Getting things wrong allows the opportunity for team members to grow and develop and for potentially better innovations to emerge. These can lead to growth and profitability. The challenge for business leaders is to ensure that these learning opportunities do not sink the ship, and to maintain a balanced view on what will work and what will not serve the business at any point in time. Again, the Business Intelligence Dashboard can be used to support the efforts of innovation.

O – OPPORTUNISTIC

Given the avalanche of data surrounding business leaders today, a real challenge is "analysis paralysis". The inability to make a decision is as bad as, and in fact may be worse than, making the wrong decision. It leaves the business in a stake of flux with no direction and this is destabilising. A great leader sees the business opportunities and commits to making decisions. This maintains momentum, something all successful businesses need.

U – UNDERSTAND THEMSELVES: THEIR STRENGTHS AND WEAKNESSES

Great business leaders know their strengths and weaknesses and surround themselves with people who are better than they are. They prioritise their team members' time so that the bulk of it is spent on activities they love and that they can be trusted to deliver. This avoids procrastination. Courageous leaders keep the lines of communication open, even when they don't know all the answers. They don't hide behind jargon but rather use straight talk and are not afraid to say, "I don't know".

They share information for the good of the organisation because they know this won't be used to sabotage their own personal performance.

S – SHARE THE LEADERSHIP

Sharing the leadership means acknowledging that, as the leader, you no longer have the answers to everything. Long gone are the days when the one at the top of the leadership pyramid had all the answers. In today's rapid, interconnected world, the leader simply can't know everything. Shared leadership works when everyone is aligned with the same vision for the business and there is no ego in the organisation. Everyone is working for the goal with the same level of commitment. Each team member is focused on working in their specific area of expertise and superior business performance – both in terms of productivity and profitability – results. To create a *Joined Up* business, shared leadership needs to be communicated, demonstrated and encouraged.

I – INTUITION AND INTEGRITY

Integrity is when our words and deeds are consistent with our intentions. The most common display of a lack of integrity in business is when a leader says what others want to hear, rather than the truth. A Business Intelligence Dashboard can help keep focus on what needs to be said; the numbers never lie – assuming, of course, that you are using them in the correct context.

Integrity needs to be a guiding foundation in order for team members to trust that the direction the leader chooses is good for all of them. The importance of telling the truth and being in integrity can safeguard reputations: your own, the teams' and that of the business. People appreciate that mistakes happen; it is how you handle them that makes all the difference.

Intuition is that gut feeling – that inner knowing – of what you need to do. You just feel it, and often there is no rational explanation for your decision. Recent research in neuroscience has demonstrated that we have a brain in our heart and another in our intestines (gut). What we have in each of these, in actual fact, is an extensive mass of neurons that behave in a fashion similar to the neurons contained in the brain, and that appear to function at mega-speeds, often much greater than those of our cerebral neurons. It is for this reason that listening to your gut feeling is so important.

However, many people have learned not to pay attention to the butterflies in the stomach and what the heart is feeling because it is so much easier to let the head lead the way, thus trampling over possibly better choices that might put all of the different sources of intelligence to use. Although I believe things are changing, as a society we have very much undermined and sabotaged the knowing we receive from our feelings and intuition; and yet they can provide us with powerful insights, if we just listen.

M – MODEL THE WAY

The most important personal quality people look for and admire in a leader is personal credibility. Credibility is the foundation of leadership. If people don't believe in the messenger, they won't believe the message. Titles may be granted, but leadership is earned.

Leaders Model the Way by finding their voice and setting an example. Great leaders "do what they say and say what they do". They lead by example from the front and maintain the standards that they expect within the business by embodying the purpose. Great leaders don't expect team members to do something that they would not have a go at themselves.

When leaders fail to model the way and walk the talk, team members feel that there is a lack of integrity. This failure to model can take various forms:

- The organisation asking people to change, yet the top leaders not exhibiting this
- Increased teamwork and cross-organisational collaboration is preached, yet the senior team does not collaborate across divisional lines
- The organisation is seen as cutting back on expenses, yet the senior leaders don't change any of their special perks

Most leaders greatly underestimate the impact they have on other team members simply by their actions and the way they show up. When the top leaders are misaligned (not *Joined Up*), then the organisation is probably unaligned also. For example, if the senior leaders are not seen as a team, then there will probably be silos under them.

P – PRESENCE

Presence is a rare quality in the frenetic 20-second sound bite world we live in. Yet being present in the moment – alert, awake and neutral – has become a leadership imperative. It is an essential attribute: it stops you living in the past or endlessly worrying about the future, both of which are a waste of energy and resources. People with presence have an ineffable quality about them. Being present is simply being attentive and undistracted. This moment-to-moment awareness enables leaders to see everything that is happening around them with peripheral vision, so they never miss any opportunities.

Joined Up Leaders – those with great presence – are masters at Attention Management. They stay focused on the task at hand and don't get distracted by bright shining object syndrome. They keep the business on course, and, as the Chief Focus Officer (CFO), they know exactly what is happening and how to navigate.

A – AUTHENTIC

Leadership depends on our ability to be in alignment, to be wholly congruent, and therefore authentic. This is our natural state when we are feeling at our best, alive and decisive.

With authenticity comes a sense of genuineness, purpose, clarity and focus.

Great leaders are confident in their own abilities and very self-aware. They don't act from a place of ego but rather they live their truth. They show up as themselves rather than a version of themselves that they think others want them to be. As a result, they are congruent and aligned in all that they do – just like my herd of horses.

C – CONNECTION

Great leaders spend time with the people they serve. In the US marines, this is called "eyeball leadership". When leaders don't spend time with the team members they lead, they become disconnected; team members don't feel cared for, and they want and need to feel cared for. This is a basic human need which, when not fulfilled, can cause dissent and "trouble in the ranks"; silo mentalities form, which can sabotage organisational success.

T – TRANSPARENCY

Transparency is the ability to say what needs to be said and do what needs to be done. There is no skulduggery, everyone is clear on what is happening in the organisation and why. Being transparent as a leader often means showing your vulnerability. Whilst some leaders might find this intimidating, a courageous leader realises that by sharing their vulnerability, they will more quickly enlist the support of the team as they are seen as "human".

> **BONUS:** Go to www.on-the-hoof.com/resources where you can take the COURAGEOUS IMPACT Leadership Assessment to see how you compare with these 16 leadership traits and then claim your complimentary leadership breakthrough call.

LEADERSHIP IS A RELATIONSHIP

If the role of a leader is to serve others, it follows that *"Leadership is a relationship"* and this explains the importance of building camaraderie among the people you are leading. When you have a meaningful relationship with another person, you work more effectively together. You have a common goal and a consistent purpose. Your efforts are channelled towards the same outcome.

Effective leaders recognise the importance of building solid relationships. They spend time focusing their efforts in key areas that will build connections with the people they lead. Here are three simple tools that great leaders use to improve their working relationships:

- **Listen**: Leaders let other people talk and pay attention to what they're saying. They remove anything that would distract from their conversations and focus on what people are trying to convey.

- **Understand:** They appreciate what other people do and value their contributions. They know that taking the time to understand where people are coming from will pay dividends in the long run. Leaders are not only open to new ideas, but are also eager to learn new things.

- **Acknowledge:** Leaders acknowledge the contributions of others. They are quick to give credit to others for their successes. They celebrate achievements and delight in the accomplishments of their team. They know that people will be more motivated to work hard and try new things if their leader acknowledges their efforts.

These three traits are very readily recognised in the dynamics of any herd. The horses always pay attention to each other and spend time acknowledging each other's presence by being companionable. The herd members also implicitly understand the contribution that the lead horses and their lieutenants make to the success of the herd. When working with and being a leader for my horses, I, too, have to exhibit these characteristics. I always need to be aware of how my horse is feeling. To do this, I must be present in the moment and not be distracted by my own thoughts. I also know that my horse will perform better if he receives regular positive feedback on how he is doing, and I always acknowledge when my horse tries to do anything I ask or offers of his own free will.

It is this continual positive feedback loop that helps boost my horse's self-esteem and keeps him wanting to deliver more. My corporate experience was just the same. Fail to build relationships and acknowledge and appreciate team members, and you will never gain their commitment to help build a successful business.

Peter Drucker summed up so well why leaders need to pay attention to relationships, and acknowledge and respect each other when he said:

> "Manners are the lubricating oil of an organisation. It is a law of nature that two moving bodies in contact with each other create friction. This is as true for human beings as it is for inanimate objects. Manners – simple things like saying

'please' and 'thank you' and knowing a person's name or asking after her family – enable two people to work together whether they like each other or not. Bright people, especially bright young people, often do not understand this. If analysis shows that someone's brilliant work fails again and again as soon as co-operation from others is required, it probably indicates a lack of courtesy – that is, a lack of manners."

All too often in business, we become stuck in the busyness of the situation and forget to engage and build relationships with other people – and, in my view, these should not just be peer relationships. A good leader builds relationships across the company.

Perhaps because my initial training was in the hospitality industry I have a strong service ethic and really appreciate the value of all team members contributing to my success. Yet when I worked in the corporate world, I often observed managers not engaging with support staff. I'll never forget one day going to pick up some printing from our internal printers. This was something I did regularly as it made sense to me to get to know the people who could help me get my client reports and publications out on time.

During the course of one conversation, the guys in the print room suddenly became aware of the fact that I was a director in the firm. You should have seen the look of horror on their faces; they simply could not believe a director was picking up their own printing. Some may argue that it was not the best use of my time but the guys in the print room always went beyond the call of duty helping get me and my team out of sticky situations when we were running late with deadlines. To me, investing in developing those relationships paid back time and time again as I always had their assistance when everyone else was being told that the deadline was not achievable.

INSPIRING OTHERS TO ACCESS THEIR HIDDEN POTENTIAL

We often think of exceptional human performance in terms of feats of physical strength and agility. However, the reality is that amazing human potential can be reached when we align our emotional and physical state with our vision and passion and purpose. I'm sure you have often heard the phrase, "They're on a mission". When someone is focused completely on accomplishing something of great importance, they appear, as if by magic, to achieve extraordinary results. And when a group of people combine and resonate with a shared common vision and purpose, then the results are magnified. Witness what happens in a disaster zone after a human tragedy, such as a hurricane. People rally together and amazing results are achieved. The job of a courageous leader is to inspire others to step beyond their own comfort zone and, by accessing the other 90% of each individual's hidden potential, to achieve the impossible against the odds.

This concept of *The Other 90%* was introduced by Robert Cooper in his book of that name. It is based on the premise that human intelligence and spirit are two of the most amazing creations known to man, and yet most of us only use a tiny percentage of our brilliance or power. Accessing the other 90% enables us to achieve the impossible. It is based on the premise that life is made up of a series of small choices – practical, emotional and intellectual. These choices are organised in a way that creates either greatness or grief. The outcomes we achieve are based on the small choices we make daily. These choices either drive us towards that greatness, or drag us away from it.

As a leader, will you settle for playing small, or step up and play a bigger game? The only barrier to playing a bigger game is your mindset, following whatever limiting beliefs are blocking you from achieving greatness by accessing the hidden 90%. Operating with the visible 10% leaves you feeling bombarded by stress, change and uncertainty.

Accessing the hidden 90% starts with you taking courageous action, boldly stepping out of your comfort zone to pursue some vision bigger than yourself; when you do this, you give others the permission to do the same. And when we as individuals align with other individuals on the same quest, we create high-performing teams and businesses.

WOMEN, LEADERSHIP AND RELATIONSHIPS

Today, although the number of successful women in senior positions in business is increasing, it is still a small minority. Currently only 4.6% of the Standard & Poor's 500 companies are run by women, yet women are gaining prevalence in more senior business positions. So what traits do these women have that make them successful? In her book *Horse Sense for the Leader Within*, Ariana Strozzi states:

> *"Over 70% of the powerful executives I have met or worked with rode horses as teenagers. Over 30% of them continue to ride in spite of their busy lives. I believe it is because they learned from the horse how to be assertive, confident, declarative and passionate and they translated these qualities into the other areas of their lives naturally and without thought. Most don't relate their present leadership abilities to their earlier years of practising horsemanship. They take for granted that moving a thousand pounds of living mass is not as easy as it looks on the surface, and neither is human leadership."*

What many women understand is that establishing leadership and authority requires trust and respect, and not dominance created through fear and intimidation. They are very clear on what is acceptable and what is not. They know when to say 'No' and mean it. For horses, trust and respect are the cornerstones of any relationship. This does not mean that we can be wishy-washy, but rather we need to show the horses clear, directive and assertive leadership, just like in the boardroom.

Once a horse sees and experiences our assertive leadership and knows that we are serious in our intent, then they will relax, lick and chew, and follow us anywhere. By establishing leadership, the horse understands his position in the herd hierarchy and then relinquishes the desire to challenge this until such time as the leader fails to demonstrate their leadership.

Chapter Eight:

Leading with Courageous Impact

Takeaways:
- Leadership is not the bastion of those at the top. It is the responsibility of everyone in the group.
- Trust is an *essential* characteristic of collaborative leadership. You foster collaboration by building trust and facilitating relationships.
- Leadership is about caring and being committed to others that you serve.
- Great leaders understand that it is never about them. There is no ego involved. It's all about the "we" and not the "me".
- *Joined Up Leaders* embody 16 attributes that enable them to have COURAGEOUS IMPACT.
- Effective leaders recognise the importance of building solid relationships.
- It is only your mindset and limiting beliefs that stop you accessing your hidden 90% potential.

Action:
Go to *www.on-the-hoof.com/resources* where you can take the COURAGEOUS IMPACT Leadership Assessment to see how you are faring with these 16 leadership traits.

CHAPTER NINE: EMPOWER RATHER THAN DELEGATE

"It is better to lead from behind and put others in front especially when you celebrate victory when nice things occur. You take the front line when there is danger. Then people will appreciate your leadership."

Nelson Mandela

Great leaders recognise that business success is a team sport and they cannot do it all for themselves. Given the avalanche of information and data, it is impossible for just one person to know about everything. This is why the old leadership paradigm of command and control structures will no longer be a successful leadership model in the future. There is an unprecedented need to effectively delegate to get everything done. There are various levels of delegation, and, at the highest level, delegation actually morphs into *Shared Leadership*.

In this chapter, we will examine how the *Joined Up Business Leader* acknowledges that control is no longer a viable long-term leadership style, but rather that, to succeed, team members need to be empowered. Great leaders empower others to succeed. They set the GPS for the business and then they rally the troops (team members) to follow. However, team members will only follow if:

1. They are aligned with the vision
2. They feel valued and recognised
3. They recognise and see value in what they can contribute

EMPOWERMENT VERSUS DELEGATION: THE DIFFERENCE

Empowerment and delegation are both important concepts in relation to managing team members, as each involves the leader entrusting team members to take on important roles in the business. Empowerment is intended to serve as a motivational strategy, while delegation is simply a system of assigning work tasks to team members to get them done.

When team members are empowered, they are encouraged to take personal responsibility and make decisions for the situations they find themselves in.

This allows the front line team member, for example, to respond to customer queries and take action to resolve problems without having to escalate the matter to a manager.

This leads to a better customer experience whilst the team member feels a sense of accomplishment to have solved the customer's challenge.

Conversely, delegation occurs when managers assign tasks to team members. The task emphasis of delegation is different to the decision focus of empowerment. When a leader delegates tasks, they typically provide details about the requirements, including the deadline for completion. Effective delegation generally includes a follow-up step. This is where the leader checks in with the team member at predetermined points in the process, and upon completion to gauge results.

The key role of the leader is to recognise what and when to delegate, and what and when to empower team members with. There is a fine line to draw here between micro-managing the situation and abdicating responsibility for the delegated task.

To help explain this better, I like to think of delegation, empowerment and *Shared Leadership* as being on a continuum. At one end, there is delegation, which is task-focused and where there is no decision-making capability and lots of control and monitoring. In the middle, there is empowerment where the team member has some decision-making capabilities within an assigned framework and hence less control is required. At the far end of the spectrum, there is *Shared Leadership* where the team member and the leader jointly share responsibility for the task getting completed and work together in a collaborative and co-operative way, each individual focusing on their own area of expertise.

DELEGATE › EMPOWER › SHARED LEADERSHIP

DELEGATE OR STAGNATE

When a business is just starting out, the idea of relinquishing control to others to help the business leader succeed can seem like an alien concept, although the reality is that the business cannot grow unless this happens. Successful leaders know that the formula for peak personal productivity and business success relies on them systematically investing their time, talent, resources and know-how in the activities they enjoy, find intellectually rewarding and do extraordinarily well, and getting other people to support them doing other tasks that are outside their own zone of brilliance.

The truth of the matter is that there is always someone who can do the activities you hate way better than you. I know in the past I have shunned delegating tasks to team members, thinking they would not enjoy them, simply because I disliked the activity. But what I've come to realise over the years is the things I hate are the things that other people love. For example, whilst I can manage my bookkeeping and reconcile my expenses, it is not a job I relish, and yet my bookkeeper simply loves this task.

The other reason that as a business leader you must delegate to others is that otherwise you are paying yourself a ridiculously high salary to do tasks that someone else could do. This simply does not make for good business economics. With all the technology available today, it is easier than ever to keep track of your time and what you are doing every day. I challenge you to do this for a week and see where you are spending time. I guarantee that this will amaze (and possibly appal!) you.

When I undertook this challenge, I realised that I was spending up to 18 hours per week doing tasks that I could delegate to others such as my bookkeeping, cleaning the house, composing social media posts, formatting a new ezine, and managing my email. I was busy doing £10 an hour tasks and never got to do the £100 an hour jobs, such as marketing and promoting my business. It was easy to find people to help me accomplish the £10 an hour tasks, but way more challenging to find people to effectively market and promote my business. So I fired myself from the £10 an hour jobs and hired reliable team members who could help me instead.

Reflecting back, I encountered the same situation when I was in the corporate world managing a team of 30 people; and I have seen this happen in many other businesses too. In 2005, unexpectedly and within a short period of time, I had a number of people decide to leave my team for a wide variety of reasons, some personal, some professional.

The net result was that we were understaffed. In order to maintain the daily operations, I ended up having to manage client accounts and undertake monthly data analysis. Whilst these were clearly roles I could perform, while I was doing them I really was not delivering any real value to my employer. I was working as a gloriously overpaid data analyst and key account manager and not therefore having the time to perform the department head role that I was hired for.

My skills were not being used to the maximum and, as a result, the business stagnated during this period; I simply did not have the time to engage in any strategic negotiations to grow the business.

POSITIONS OF LEADERSHIP

POSITION 1
Leading from the front

POSITION 2
Leading from the side

POSITION 2
Leading from the side

POSITION 3
Leading from behind

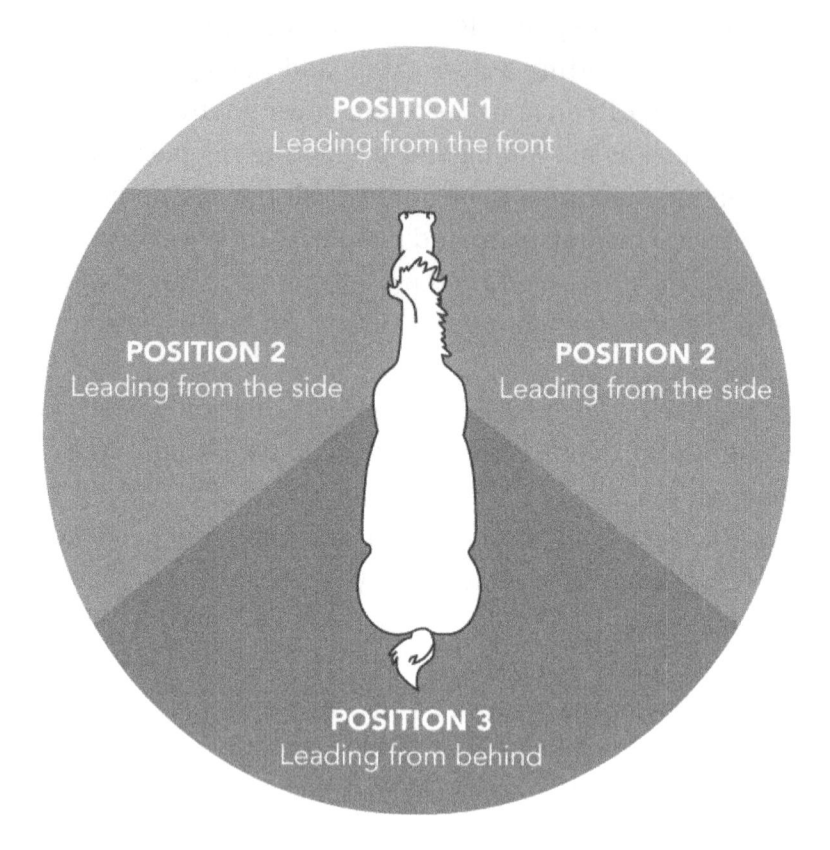

Adapted from Klaus Ferdinand-Hempfling's *Dances With Horses*

Within the natural world, there exists an effective model for how we can lead and empower team members to take on tasks. It is exhibited within a horse herd where there are three different positions of leadership. Any of these three positions can be adopted when leading a horse, or indeed a business. They work on the principle of pull-push leadership with certain styles being more effective in particular circumstances.

POSITION ONE: LEADING FROM THE FRONT

When you *Lead From The Front*, the rest of the team members are supposed to follow. This leadership position is most effective in emergency situations when there is a need to take control because of some threat of danger. In this situation, you just want people to follow and you don't want to negotiate on how and what you are doing – you just need people to trust that you know where you are going and act now as you prescribe. The challenge with maintaining this leadership position indefinitely is that for the leader, it is a very tiring and lonely place to be – up front and alone and constantly on edge looking for the danger.

For team members, this type of leadership is equally challenging; constantly being told what to do becomes demoralising and team members quickly lose focus and engagement, as they do not feel empowered. It does not take much to get them off track and they will wander off in their own direction, doing their own thing, so that they can get some sense of being valued. I often observe this occurring in business and indeed have witnessed it first-hand; by becoming too controlling and micro-managing all aspects of the team, people started to disconnect and lose interest and focus. The net result is less than optimum results for the business as everyone is pulling in a different direction.

POSITION THREE: LEADING FROM BEHIND

Leading From Behind is for me the most powerful leadership position to be in. It relies on setting a course and then inspiring the team members to achieve this. It is an empowering and creative position for both the leader and the team members, as everyone feels engaged, responsible and committed to achieving the goals.

Leading From Behind helps unlock the hidden potential in team members, resulting in significant improvements in productivity, absenteeism, motivation and commitment from team members. The challenge for many leaders using this leadership style is that it involves setting the course and then allowing the team members to get there in their way – which might be a very different way from the one the leader envisaged. Continually nagging team members will not be successful and indeed may result in the team disappearing in another direction. This leadership position involves creating trust and empowering others.

POSITION TWO: LEADING FROM THE SIDE

Leading From The Side might be best described as a supportive leadership position. It is a position of true partnership and equality; in this leadership position, you might go down the pub with your team members – you operate as peers. It is not a position that offers leadership and direction, but is required at times to balance the other two leadership positions. You might use this leadership style when you need to be especially collaborative, consultative and co-operative; however, the challenge when it is used consistently is that nothing gets achieved as no one is leading the process.

LESSONS FROM THE HORSES: WILD HERD LEADERSHIP

Within a herd of horses, we see leading from the front and behind used continually in tandem. Typically, in a herd of wild horses, you will find one stallion (a male horse) and then a band of mares (female horses). Within the band of mares, there will be one horse that is the leader. If you get the opportunity to watch wild horses, you will be able to clearly see the way that the lead mare and stallion work together to maintain the security and safety of the herd.

The stallion is typically found *Leading From Behind*, positioned at the rear of the herd. From here, he can keep an eye out for approaching danger and also influence the direction of the herd by gently pushing them from behind. If he pushes too hard, his herd of mares will disband. Unlike in a business where team members often feel obligated to stay with their employer for income security, the stallion has no such control over his herd. Any inappropriate leadership, and his herd of mares can just run away. He has no fences to keep them in.

The lead mare is typically found at the front of the herd, and her role is to find suitable grazing. She works in conjunction with the stallion, leading the herd to lush pastures and streams so they can stay nourished and refreshed. Whilst grazing, you will often find the lead mare adopting a supportive leadership position, hanging out with the herd and making sure everyone is all right.

Leaders need to provide direction and intent and allow others to figure out what to do and how to get there. Unfortunately, a challenge that many businesses face today is that we have inadvertently trained our team members to comply and not think – this is usually a result of not creating an environment where people feel safe. The problem is that if people only comply, we can't expect them to take responsibility for their actions. Responsibility is not doing what we are told, responsibility is doing what's right, and this will only happen if we have created a high-performance culture fuelled on trust.

WHICH LEADERSHIP POSITION IS OPTIMAL?

According to a study conducted by Dr Natalia Lorinkova, who studies management and leadership at Wayne State University: *"Teams led by a directive leader initially outperform those led by an empowering leader. However, despite lower early performance, teams led by an empowering leader experience higher performance improvement over time because of higher levels of team-learning, co-ordination, empowerment and mental model development".*[24]

This demonstrates that higher-performing teams are a direct result of team members feeling safe and knowing the leader has their best interests at heart; this is also a sustainable approach to adopt, enabling our businesses to survive and thrive over a long period of time.

The answer to the question of which leadership position is optimal is that a leader needs to be able to adopt all these different leadership styles in order to be successful. They need to be adaptable and bring into play the right leadership style at the right time. *Leading From The Front* (directive leadership) works best in emergencies or when the leader needs to clearly show the team where they are heading, whilst *Leading From Behind* (empowered leadership) works best when the direction is clear and team members step up and take responsibility.

The challenge for some leaders, however, is that when they adopt *Leading From Behind*, they have to give up any attachment to the idea that there is only one right way to accomplish the task or project.

The reality is that there are always multiple ways to achieve any outcome and in order to empower people and give them responsibility to deliver the results, you need to trust that their method of achieving the outcome – whilst it might be different to yours – is equally plausible.

For example, I live in Yorkshire and tomorrow I want to get to Birmingham. I might ask my team members for their ideas on how to best get there. There are a multitude of ways I could go, including driving, flying, and taking the train. I prefer to drive but that doesn't make the other methods proposed by my team invalid, since they all get me to the destination on time.

Great leaders recognise that often team members can come up with better solutions to problems and challenges than they can, and they ask for input.

> **There's More Than One Way To Be Right**
>
> This quote from a conversation between Dan Kennedy and Brendan Suhr, the assistant head coach of the Detroit Pistons, during the 1980s illustrates this point succinctly:
>
> *"Do you know how many head coaches there are in the NBA? Well, there are at least that many different ways to be right, because every one of these coaches does things differently, yet they all represent the top 1/10% of the coaching profession. There are 1,000 guys who'd like every one of those jobs. There are at least 100 guys who'd be good candidates for every one of those jobs. So these head coaches all do it 'right', yet they all do it differently."*

THE EMPOWERMENT MATRIX

The leadership positions described previously clearly show that to lead and to empower others, leaders need a mix of both energy and focus. Whether *Leading From the Front* (position one) or *Leading From Behind* (position three), the leader must know where they are going. Clarity of vision is of paramount importance. Without this, team members will lack confidence and security, and may try to take over the leadership position themselves.

This is certainly the case with my horses. When I am uncertain where I am leading them, they step up, concerned for their safety, and take over the leadership position. And when leading my team at Andersen through the fallout of the Enron disaster, this was exactly the challenge I, like many other leaders in the firm, faced. None of us were sure of where the business was going. Our fate was in the hands of the US Federal Court. The business had no direction whilst it waited for the judicial verdict and that is why, like our clients, many team members opted to leave and find jobs where there was more certainty of employment.

The Empowerment Matrix

FOCUS \ ENERGY	Low	High
High	DISENGAGED LEADER	EMPOWERED LEADERSHIP
Low	PROCRASTINATING LEADER	DISTRACTED LEADER

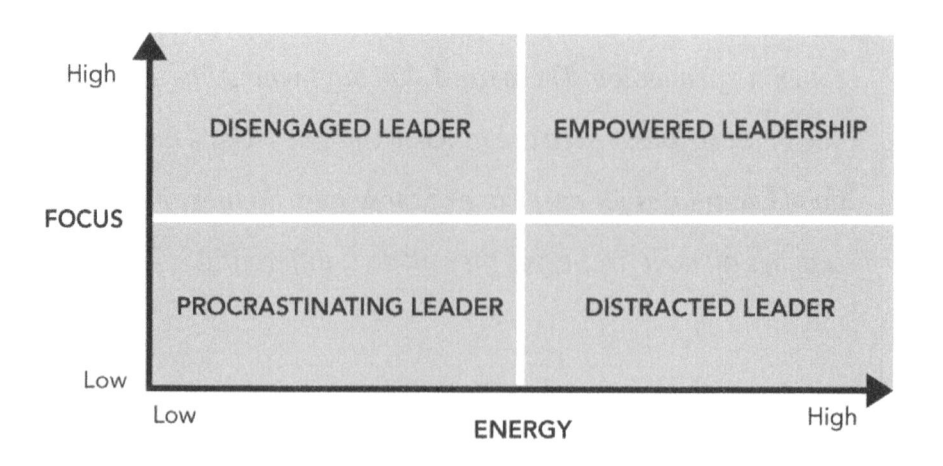

The chart clearly shows the impact of both energy (vigour that is fuelled by intense personal commitment, motivation and desire to do something) and focus (concentrated attention – the ability to zero in on a goal and see the task through to completion) on the levels of empowerment.

Empowered – this occurs when there is high focus and high energy. Leaders and team members are highly effective and purposeful. They are clear on what they are doing and are highly motivated to achieve the outcomes. Team members are in Flow and doing their best work, being highly productive.

Disengaged – this occur where there is high focus but low energy. The leaders and team members are distanced and not emotionally connected to the work at hand. They know what to do but aren't inspired to accomplish the goal. They need motivating and encouraging to see the benefits of this outcome for themselves and the business.

Distracted – sometimes team members have high energy and motivation to accomplish an outcome but they easily get distracted and pre-occupied with other things as they lack focus. They start the project all *gun ho* but then when another project comes along they jump ship and get involved in that without completing the original task.

Procrastinating – when there is low energy and low focus, it is highly unlikely the task will get completed. Team members are hesitant about what to do and often this happens when a leader does not properly explain to team members what is expected or how the project fits into the overall strategy of the business.

The result is that the team members have little motivation and enthusiasm to work on the project, as they can't appreciate the benefits.

> **BONUS:** *You can download your own copy of the Empowerment Matrix at www.on-the-hoof.com/resourcesand then mark on it which tasks you can assign to which quadrants.*

Unfortunately, only about 10% of team members are empowered. The remaining team members, who fall into the other categories, are usually just spinning their wheels. Some procrastinate, others feel no emotional connection to the work, and others are distracted by the raft of other tasks that need completion. So although these team members may look busy, they lack either the focus or energy, or both, to make any sort of meaningful change.

Shockingly, according to the *Gallup Management Journal's* Employment Engagement Index, most employees are not actively engaged at work. According to a 2013 Gallup Survey on the State of the Global Workplace, only 13% of employees worldwide are engaged in their jobs, while 63% are not engaged, and 24% are actively disengaged[25]. With nearly 90% of the global workforce sleepwalking through their daily activities, lack of employee engagement is costing business billions every year.

Furthermore, according to The Corporate Executive Board, those companies that can move employees from low to high engagement can experience increases in productivity of over 21%.[26] So if leaders are to access the hidden 90% potential, it is essential that they help team members become empowered and to get into the state of Flow, where they have high energy and high focus for the activity.

One way to ensure that this happens is to allocate activities to team members which match their own personal strengths and where they are most trusted. In the next chapter, part of the second cornerstone – Empower Others To Act – we will examine how team members can determine their strengths in business.

> **US retail chain Nordstrom has a long believed in empowering their team members to use their best judgement in serving customers. For many years, the text of its one-page employee handbook read, in its entirety:**
>
> **"WELCOME TO NORDSTROM**
> **We're glad to have you with our Company. Our number one goal is to provide outstanding customer service. Set both your personal and professional goals high. We have great confidence in your ability to achieve them.**
>
> **Nordstrom Rules: Rule #1: Use good judgment in all situations. There will be no additional rules.**
>
> **Please feel free to ask your department manager, store manager, or division general manager any question at any time."**

So why don't more leaders empower their team members? My belief is that the current lack of empowerment in many businesses is due to fear. Leaders are afraid of losing control and so they apply rigid command and control structures to help make them feel safe. Leaders lack trust in their team members to do the job and team members become fearful of breaking the rules and being punished.

However, the irony here is that control and creativity are the antithesis of each other. Control stifles creativity and innovation, the thing that can bring companies competitive advantage, and it can dampen passion towards fulfilling the purpose of the business.

Howard Behar, the former president of Starbucks, summed this up well when he said: *"the person who sweeps the floor should choose the broom ... We need to get rid of rules – real and imagined – and encourage independent thinking".* This is especially important in service industries where team members must feel empowered to do what it takes to satisfy the customers.

It is terrible when companies let rules get in the way of satisfying customer needs and yet I expect, like me, you have all too frequently experienced poor customer service, where the customer service representative has been frustrated that they cannot assist you due to company policies and rules.

Chapter Nine:

Empower Rather Than Delegate

Takeaways:
- Great leaders empower other to succeed.
- Delegation, empowerment and shared leadership can be viewed as being on a continuum.
- The three positions of leadership work on the principle of pull-push, with certain styles being more effective in particular circumstances.
- *Leading From The Front* is most effective in emergency situations when there is a need to take control because of some threat of danger.
- *Leading From Behind* is an empowering and creative position for both the leader and the team members as everyone feels engaged, responsible and committed to achieving the goals.
- *Leading From Behind* means giving up any attachment to the idea that there is only one right way to accomplish the task or project.

Action:
Download your own copy of the Empowerment Matrix at *www.on-the-hoof.com/resources*

As we look ahead
into the next century,
leaders will be
those who
empower others.

Bill Gates

CORNERSTONE TWO: EMPOWER OTHERS TO ACT (EO)

Expand The Leader   **TRUST**   Empower Others To Act

JUB

TRUST   TRUST

Engage The Enviroment

JUB = Joined Up Business

"Of all the things I've done, the most vital is coordinating those who work with me and aiming their efforts at a certain goal."

Walt Disney

The second cornerstone of creating a business which is *Joined Up* is **Empower Others To Act**. This cornerstone looks at business through the lens of *Other*. We have moved from the Self-perspective – which is all about how an individual needs to be in business – to how each of us needs to interact – communicate and connect – with one another.

Specifically, here we examine how to create high-performing teams by leveraging all the resources that we have at our disposal. We look at how we can get team members into Flow so that they can access their hidden potential, and how, by empowering team members to take responsibility, they can make more informed decisions to drive the business forward.

In the twenty-first century, we are all aware that natural resources are finite, whilst also realising that there is no limit to our innovative creativity. Imagine what could be possible if the seven billion people on the planet all tapped into their hidden potential – there would likely be no problem on earth that we could not solve, no obstacle we could not overcome.

What John Mackey refers to as *Conscious Capitalism* offers the promise of tapping into human potential in ways that few companies have been able to do. Business must view people as resources, not sources. This energises and empowers people and engages best contribution in service of its higher purpose. In doing so, business can have a profound positive impact on the world.

What do you think about when you read the term *Empower Others To Act*? Many just consider this in terms of their team members, but it is important to appreciate that there are many other people associated with a business who have an impact. These people are often referred to as stakeholders as they have a vested interest in the business.

Examples of stakeholders would be team members, customers, suppliers, preferred vendors, investors, and community groups.

It is essential that all these stakeholders be aligned with the purpose of the business and with each other in order to create sustainable success. If one group of stakeholders succeeds at the detriment of the others, this immediately puts the business out of harmony and into imbalance. And yet this is what happens all the time in businesses where one type of stakeholder's needs – for example, that of the investor – are elevated above the needs of another group – for example, the team members. In this example, the short-term needs of the investor – for profits – are prioritised at the expense of team members whose numbers are cut whilst having to deliver even more. This is a classic example of what is happening in business right now.

A better solution would be for the business to create a system where everyone wins, as the needs of all the stakeholders are respected, valued and integrated into the business. The word "corporate" comes from the word "corpus" or body. All stakeholders form part of the body and, as we know, when the body falls out of balance, it becomes sick and dis-ease is the result.

For business to be successful and achieve peak performance results, it cannot operate from a place of exploitation or coercion. Rather, business needs to operate on the foundation of collaboration and voluntary exchange. Investors, team members, management and suppliers all need to collaborate to create value for customers. Business is a win-win. Stakeholders matter as they embody the heart, soul and lifeblood of an enterprise. And yet too many business leaders don't appreciate the impact their business has on the people associated with the business as well as the environment.

Creating a better world requires teamwork, partnerships, and collaboration, as we need an entire army of companies to work together to build a better world within the next few decades. This means corporations must embrace the benefits of cooperating with one another.

Simon Mainwaring

CHAPTER TEN: KNOW YOUR ROLE IN THE HERD

"TEAMWORK IS THE ABILITY TO WORK TOGETHER TOWARD A COMMON VISION. IT IS THE FUEL THAT ALLOWS COMMON PEOPLE TO ATTAIN UNCOMMON RESULTS."

ANDREW CARNEGIE

In this era of relentless change, business owners are always seeking to get more from less. The most effective way to be able to leverage the resources of team members is to get them operating as a high-performance team, through being in a peak performance state. This is a state that is often called Flow, where you are *Joined Up* and aligned.

Put simply, Flow is the path of least resistance. When team members are in Flow, productivity rises, results increase, occurrences line up, and team members have more fun and feel more connected to the organisation.

It's a state in which a person is fully immersed in an activity, caught in a feeling of energised focus and full involvement. It is focused motivation, where the emotions are not just contained and channelled, but positively energised and aligned with the task at hand. When team members are feeling stressed, overwhelmed or anxious, it's a fairly good indicator that they are out of Flow.

The opposite is true when they are in Flow; they feel joy and even rapture whilst performing the task; they are fully engaged.

When experiencing Flow, there can be a distortion of time. Often people's internal clocks don't seem to match the external clock, either sped up or slowed down. Within this phenomenon, people immersed in their task (in Flow) often look up at the clock thinking only a short time has passed, only to find it is many hours later than they thought it was.

In the workplace, Flow can be seen where an individual's challenges and skills are equally matched, thereby creating a harmonious environment.

When team members are in Flow, the following occurs:

- Complete involvement in what they are doing – focused and concentrating
- A sense of ecstasy – a sense of being outside everyday reality
- Greater inner clarity – knowing what needs to be done, and knowing how well they are doing
- Knowing that the activity is doable – that their skills are adequate to the task
- A sense of serenity – no worries about oneself, and a feeling of growing beyond the boundaries of the ego
- Timelessness – thoroughly focused on the present, hours seem to pass by in minutes
- Intrinsic motivation – whatever produces Flow becomes its own reward

The Flow experience is surprisingly consistent across activities, whether the person thinks the activity is play or work. The research on Flow across wide-ranging samples and diverse activities shows how positive the experience is. People in Flow experience effortless concentration, enjoyment and satisfaction.

They want to be doing what they are doing. They feel that something is at stake in the activity and feel the activity is important to their future goals.

Their self-esteem grows and they feel in control of their situation. People in Flow also feel happy, strong, active, involved, creative, free, excited, open and clear.

The conditions required to get into Flow are:

- High perceived challenge level
- High perceived skill level
- Knowing what to do
- Knowing how to do it
- Knowing how well you are doing
- Knowing where to go (where navigation is involved)
- Freedom from distractions
- Aligned with your expertise

When team members are in Flow, they don't necessarily have to understand in detail the vision of the business, but they do need to know where the business is going and what they must do next from moment to moment to achieve this. If you take rock climbing, for example, you have to know the next piece of rock to move your hand or foot to – it's not about reaching the top of the mountain.

You have to know what to do; you also have to know how to do it. If navigation is involved, you also have to know where to go. Concentration is essential, so you must also be free from distractions that would interrupt your attention. When the Flow conditions have been met, team members are able to engage in a series of challenging tasks that are neither too difficult (not overwhelming) nor too easy (not boring).

Every step of the way, it is obvious what to do next, how to do it, where to go next, and how well they are doing, so they can continuously adjust their performance based on continuous, immediate feedback. In this way, the Flow conditions create a Flow loop: an unimpeded loop between action and feedback that allows for continuous and effortless tuning of performance while taking action. Flow loops make an activity worth doing for its own sake.

RECALIBRATE
Applying the learnings to improve performance

LEARNING
Asking for and receiving feedback

GROUNDWORK
Deciding what to do and getting into action

In this state, people effortlessly go from one task to the next, continuously adjusting their performance to tackle the challenges they face. Action and awareness merge as all of their attention is taken up by the activity with no attention capacity left over to experience boredom, anxiety, self-consciousness, to ruminate about the past or future, or even to notice bodily discomfort. This is the experience of Flow; so when designing Business Intelligence Dashboards, it is imperative that they are easy to use and understand for the team members to give appropriate feedback.

If they are not clear and relevant, they won't add to the overall Flow of business, but rather distract from it; and this in turn will hamper the creation of a high-performing team.

WHY TEAMS?

> *"Not finance. Not strategy.*
> *Not technology.*
> *It is teamwork that remains*
> *the ultimate competitive advantage,*
> *both because it is so powerful*
> *and so rare."*
>
> **Patrick Lencioni**

Before we examine how you figure out your role in the 'herd', let's look at why we need teams and the benefits that they can bring to businesses. The great feature of being part of a team is that it enables us to achieve more. I just love this acronym for TEAM:

- **T – together**
- **E – everyone**
- **A – achieves**
- **M - more**

I often use the phrase that "success is a team sport" because I truly believe this; can you recall a time in history when one act of genuine significance was achieved by just one man or woman? On all occasions, a team has been involved.

This is why President Lyndon Johnson once famously said, *"There are no problems we cannot solve together, and very few that we can solve by ourselves."*

The importance of teamwork is paramount in any business and all good leaders must realise that they cannot be successful without the support of team members. Jonny Wilkinson might well have been the best rugby fly-half that England has ever seen and, indeed, his spectacular drop goal in the final minute that won England the 2003 World Cup is legendary, but Jonny could not have achieved that success without the support of his teammates.

Individuals play the game, but teams win championships. The same is true in business: great leaders play the game, but only committed, motivated teams achieve great financial success. Success is a team sport, however you look at it.

BENEFITS OF BEING IN A TEAM

There are a number of benefits of being in a team, and these include:

- Teams involve more people and therefore make more resources – time, ideas and energy – available than one individual would have
- Teams allow a leader to maximise their potential and minimise their weaknesses
- Teams provide multiple perspectives on how to reach the goal, as each individual will see the problem in a different light. This allows for the creative flow of ideas and the stumbling blocks that one person might see can easily be navigated
- Teams share the credit for victories and the blame for losses. This fosters genuine humility and authentic communication
- Teams keep leaders accountable for the goals
- Teams can simply do more than the individual

So why, then, do people sometimes want to do things by themselves? Some reasons might include:

- Ego – not admitting that you can't do everything. As Andrew Carnegie once declared: *"It marks a big step in your development when you come to realise that other people can help you do a better job than you could do alone."*
- Insecurity – leaders feel threatened by their team members. By failing to promote teamwork, the leader undermines their own potential and erodes the best efforts of the people with whom they work. They would do well to listen to the advice of former US President Woodrow Wilson who said: *"We should not only use all the brain we have, but all that we can borrow."*

- Naiveté – underestimating the difficulty of achieving big things
- Temperament – some people are not very extrovert and it simply does not occur to them to think in terms of working with others. They never think to enlist the support of others; however, ironically, working alone creates huge barriers to their own potential. As Dr Allan Fromm noted: *"People have been known to achieve more as a result of working with others than against them."*

The harsh reality is that success cannot be achieved alone. Today's current economic climate has meant that more and more people are setting up their own businesses. In 2014, just over 4.6 million people in the UK were self-employed and running their own small businesses. What I witness time and time again with my clients is many of these businesses struggling to succeed. According to Statistic Brain, 25% of new businesses fail in their first year, only 50% make it to year 5, and just 25% survive 10 years. So why is this? It is not because the business owners don't have great ideas or don't know what to do; quite simply, many people suffer from what I call "the Lone Ranger syndrome", the isolation of working alone, with no one there to motivate, support, provide feedback and offer accountability. Even the Lone Ranger had his faithful companion, Native American Tonto, to support him on his journey.

THE TALENT DYNAMICS FRAMEWORK

Every person has a unique blend of energies in their profile, like ingredients within a recipe. These Energies give us our primary characteristics and the value we bring to others. Whilst some of us have just one dominant Energy, others can have a more blended profile with two or sometimes three Energies with equally high percentages. Those who have a single dominant Energy tend to be simpler to understand, with fewer contradictions, whilst those with a more complex configuration can at first appear to be more complex with the different Energies potentially at odds with each other.

What is important to recognise is that your dominant Energies give you your focus, emphasis and the value you deliver. They determine how you feel and respond, and are at the root of not only your greatest successes, but also your biggest challenges or failures. Your dominant Energies give you a particular focus, a way of viewing, interpreting and responding to the world; they create the feelings, thoughts, values and beliefs you hold. Your dominant Energies are like your personal window into the world, ultimately determining what really matters to you and what drives you. Your dominant Energies determine why you are naturally interested, talented and gifted within certain areas of life and work, determining your contribution and value to others.

The dominant energies within your unique Energy dynamic determine your natural talents, and when working in these Energies, you will excel, be in Flow and access the hidden 90% of your potential. Conversely, the Energies that have a very low or zero percentage tend to be where you will have your blind spots or where you have little focus or interest.

Talent Dynamics, developed by Roger Hamilton, is an excellent assessment tool for helping get teams aligned, with all team members in the roles that best suit their talents. However, it achieves way more than this. It is probably best described as a business development system that empowers an organisation to grow its profit and productivity dramatically. It does this by measuring and increasing the trust and Flow in its leaders and teams.

A unique feature of the Talent Dynamics assessment tool is that it measures the level of trust and Flow through an organisation at different scales: at company level (How is the company valued in the market?), at team level (How is the team valued in the company?), and at individual level (How is the individual valued in the team?), Talent Dynamics profiles allow team members and business leaders to see others in context, and also recognise the team in context of the growth stage of the company.

The system gets to the heart of the business by getting to the heart of each team member. What are the conditions under which each team member performs at their best with effortless ease? How can team members empower those around them to perform at their best? It begins with the principle that each team member has an underlying talent that, when allowed to shine, creates extraordinary results.

Talent Dynamics goes beyond being simply a psychometric test; the system differs from others in that:

- It relates natural talents to eight intuitive profiles that are easy to remember and explain to others, each with its own set of role models today that we can relate to.
- It links each profile to a set of strategies that, when followed, lead to a 'Flow' state. So rather than seeing each profile as a box to sit in, each is a game to be played and mastered.
- A unique facet of Talent Dynamics is the link of the eight profiles to the seasons and phases of company life cycle – so you can see not only who should do what, but when they should do it. In times of rapid change, knowing when your winning formula becomes your losing formula is critical.
- The invisible thread that links us to each other and the performance of our company results in a meaningful link between nurturing our own personal well-being and the well-being of the company.

195

When you get team members aligned in the roles that best suit their talents, they are able to deliver real value to the business. And when other team members can leverage this value, then productive, profitable *Joined Up* businesses result.

THE TALENT DYNAMICS SQUARE

The foundation of the Talent Dynamics Square is the four Energies – wood, fire, earth and metal. These form the basis of a pyramid with water energy forming the apex. Within the Talent Dynamics philosophy, water is not given its own profile – water is the source of all other frequencies, the foundation of flow, and therefore is inherently present within the other four elements. Within Talent Dynamics, the water element is defined as Spirit.

Depicted this way, the Talent Dynamics Square clearly shows two pairs of opposites in the way team members think and act. Some people think more with their 'head in the clouds', are more 'creative' and use their imagination. This is represented by the 'Dynamo' energy at the top of the square. Some team members think more and act with their 'ear to the ground'. They are more 'sensory' and depend on what they see around them. This is the 'Tempo' energy at the bottom of the square.

The other pair of opposites are introvert and extrovert. Some team members act more through people and are more extroverted. This is represented by the 'Blaze' energy on the right side. Other team members act more through analysing data, and are more introverted.

This is represented by the 'Steel' energy on the left side.

Talent Dynamics Square

DYNAMO — Wood - What
CREATOR
MECHANIC
STAR

INNOVATION — Intuitive

STEEL — Metal - How
LORD
MULTIPLY — Introvert

MAGNIFY — Extrovert
SUPPORTER
BLAZE — Fire - Who

TIMING — Sensory

ACCUMULATOR
TRADER
DEAL MAKER

TEMPO — Earth - What/When

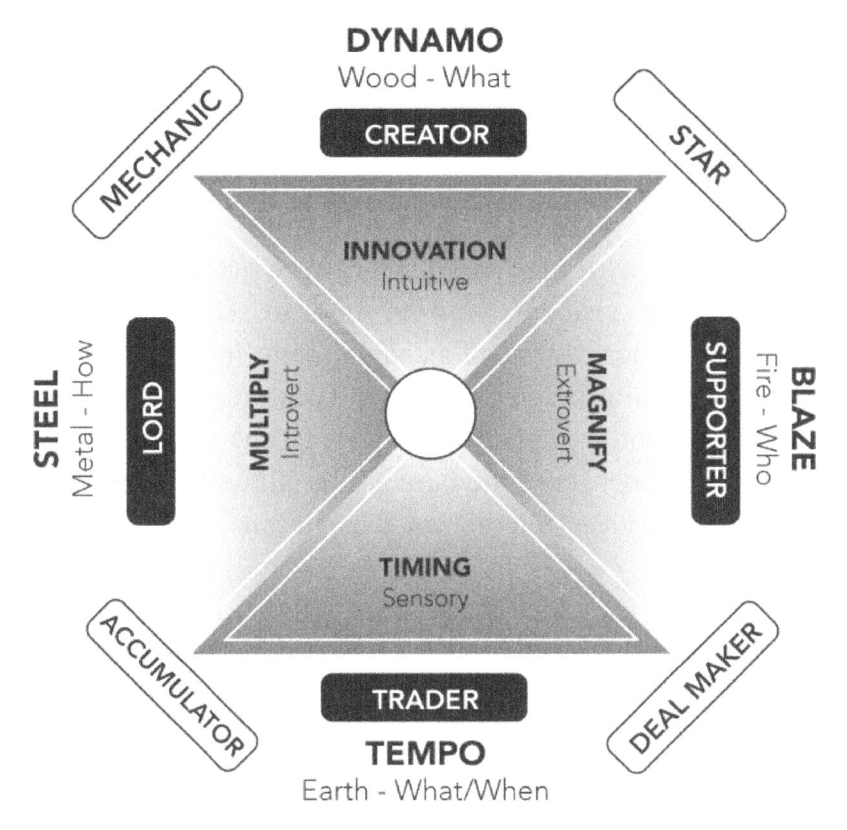

Talent Dynamics Square

As a result of these five Energies, all teams will have a collective frequency that sets the environment for everyone in the team. New product development and strategy require a Dynamo team. Sales, marketing and networking require a Blaze team. Service, troubleshooting and scheduling require a Tempo team. Financial management, analysis and systems require a Steel team. Vision and setting culture and values require a Spirit team.

One of the challenges that I often come across in organisations is that there is an overabundance of one frequency in the team. This can become a problem as the team is not balanced and therefore starts operating dsyfunctionally. Often, simply adding individuals with the missing frequency can propel the team into Flow, with the resulting shift increasing the effectiveness of everyone in the team.

FIVE ENERGY TYPES AND THE VALUE AND CONTRIBUTION THEY BRING TO A HIGH PERFORMING TEAM

WATER ENERGY: SPIRIT

Team members with high water energy are great at sensing the future. They are visionary and are able to see the big picture and are sometimes described as having their head in the clouds. Always questioning, they learn from the past, seeing mistakes and then seeking a better alternative. They have an ability to reflect on the past and almost sense the future. This allows them to improve products and services and the world we live in.

Team members with high water energy are fearless, are able to make risk assessments, and are reassuring, authoritative, and powerful.

WOOD ENERGY: DYNAMO

Team members with high wood energy are often highly creative and innovative, using their imagination and strong drive to push things forward their way. They are a well of ideas and creativity. Their team members trust them to share what should be done next and create exciting new ideas and plans. They are the people who get things started with pace and with energy, but can often struggle to get projects completed.

FIRE ENERGY: BLAZE

Fire Energy team members are talkative, passionate, fun-loving and enthusiastic. They have a seemingly endless amount of energy and both a desire and an ability to share and communicate a message. They make others feel at home and people naturally warm to them. They effortlessly build relationships and manage people. Their colleagues trust them to network and build rapport. They are the people who inspire others to work with passion and drive.

EARTH ENERGY: TEMPO

Earth Energy team members have a desire to understand and be understood. They are well grounded, with an attention to detail and a natural ability to look after the needs of others. As such, they work well in teams and deliver great customer service. Their colleagues trust them to get things done on time and in order. They are the people who effortlessly collaborate with others. They keep the show on the road with everything and everyone looked after and on board.

METAL ENERGY: STEEL

Team members with high metal energy are efficient, clear-headed and hate waste. They spot details others miss while creating systems and structures to improve efficiency. Their team members trust them to complete tasks with accuracy and measure results effortlessly. They often live with a sense that something is missing or still needs to done, and with this constant search, they are brilliant at spotting everything that hasn't been done, taken care of, or finished.

The different energies combine to create eight different Talent Profiles – think of it like an eight-sided mountain, where there are different rivers flowing down each side. Each of the team members has their own Flow, with natural ways in which they think and act based on the balance of their frequencies. Everyone is born with a different mix of the frequencies

When you take the Talent Dynamics profiling test, you identify how much of each frequency you hold. The balance determines which of the eight games you play most naturally. This is the profile that creates the greatest resonance and harmony with your natural frequencies. The more time team members invest in their strongest frequency, the sooner they get into Flow.

THE EIGHT TALENT PROFILES

There are eight Talent profiles depicted on the Talent Dynamics Square. Everyone has a mix of the different energies and the profile reveals the dominant energy type that someone has. It would be a mistake to assume that all Creators are the same, and to use the assessment as a way to label people, because the mix of the different energies means that everyone is unique.

For example, Richard Branson and James Dyson are both Creators, but they are very different. James Dyson, with more steel energy in his profile, is more introverted and physically creates products, whereas Richard Branson is more extroverted and is an ideas person. He comes up with great ideas for companies and then lets someone else run them for him.

Let's briefly review each of the profile types starting at the top of the Talent Dynamics Square with the Creator with their Dynamo energy and then moving clockwise around the square through the Blaze, Tempo and Steel energy.

> **BONUS:** *Want to discover your Talent Dynamics Profile? Simply go to www.on-the-hoof.com/resources where you will find a an additional special bonus to get you started on learning where your strengths lie and how you add value to your business.*

Creator Profile: Creators are the best initiators. Although they can be quick to create chaos, they can also be surprisingly innovative at finding ways out of chaos. Put them in charge of new projects but move them on to the next creation once their job is done.

Star Profile: Stars are the best promoters. They need to lead from the front. Give them the chance to shine and give them the space to deliver results without tying them down. Give them the systems and support to enable them to focus on building new business.

Supporter Profile: Supporters are the best leaders. Don't expect them to come up with the plan. Build a plan and set the goals with a Supporter and then let them lead the team towards the plan. Let them set their own management style and their own agenda.

Deal Maker Profile: Deal Makers are the best peacemakers. They will leave everyone feeling good. Don't expect them to go out cold calling as they thrive on building the relationships they have. Work with Deal Makers to nurture existing customers and relationships.

Trader Profile: Traders are your best negotiators. They always know what systems and which people will provide the service and support to cement a satisfied and loyal customer relationship. They work best when given clear parameters to work within.

Accumulator Profile: Accumulators are your best ambassadors. They are reliable, get things done on time and are not prone to making rash decisions. Accumulators make the best project managers when a specific result needs to be delivered reliably.

Lord Profile: Lords are your best analysts. Give them the space to study the detail and to deliver the data. Don't ask them to go out and network, spend time building relationships or in negotiations, as they are strongest when focused behind the scenes.

Mechanic Profile: Mechanics are your best completers. They will wrap up the process and find smart ways to do it better next time. Don't ask a mechanic to start from scratch, but give them an existing process or product to improve on.

COMMON TEAM ROLES FOR EACH OF THE FIVE ENERGIES

As we saw in Chapter Two, certain energies have an aptitude for different roles within the business. Broadly speaking, new product development and strategy require a team with lots of wood energy. Sales, marketing and networking require a team with fire energy. Service, troubleshooting and scheduling require a team with earth energy. Financial management, analysis and systems require a team with metal energy. Vision and setting culture and values require a team with lots of water energy.

Each of the different energies therefore clearly has a different area in which they excel. The role of the *Joined Up Leader* is to figure out the dominant energy of each team member and align him or her to roles that harness these strengths in order to achieve optimal performance. The more all the team members are working from their natural strengths (i.e. in Flow), the more team engagement, productivity and profitability will increase.

In the following table, we examine what would be business heaven and hell. Business heaven occurs when we have the right people with the right skill sets in the right roles. Business hell is when we have the wrong people with the wrong skill sets in the wrong roles.

Team Heaven	Team Hell
Strategy is led by a Spirit Energy Team	Strategy is led by a Tempo Energy Team
Product creation is led by a Dynamo Energy Team	Product creation is led by a Steel Energy Team
Marketing is led by a Blaze Energy Team	Marketing is led by a Spirit Energy Team
Customer Service is led by a Tempo Energy Team	Customer Service is led by a Dynamo Energy Team
Finance is managed by a Steel Energy Team	Finance is managed by a Blaze Energy Team

TEAM DYNAMICS: KNOW YOUR ROLE IN THE HERD

'THE LAW OF NICHE'

It is my belief that every team member has a role where they add the most value to the team; however, often in business we "promote" people to roles that they are not suited to. The resultant consequences can be dire for the business.

David Ogilvy summed this up well when he said, *"A well-run restaurant is like a winning baseball team. It makes the most of every crew member's talent and takes advantage of every split-second opportunity to speed up service."*

Having the right people in the right roles is essential to a team's success and the dynamics of a team can change according to the placement of people:

- Regression – having the wrong person in the wrong place
- Frustration – having the wrong person in the right place
- Confusion – having the right person in the wrong place
- Progression – having the right person in the right place
- Multiplication – having the right people in the right places

It does not matter what kind of team or herd you are dealing with, the principles are the same: all team members have a place where they add the most value and when each person does the job that is best for them, everybody wins. Often the best team selection is not the person who can be most effective, but the person who enables the existing team to become more effective.

In 2003, Jonny Wilkinson's role was that of fly-half for the England rugby team. What would have happened if Sir Clive Woodward, the then England coach, had asked Jonny to play hooker for the important World Cup Final against Australia? He would have been out of position and unable to shine, and morale would have dipped in the team as they would not have been playing to their capability. The team would have become resentful, realising that they were not living up to their potential, and Steve Thompson, the hooker, would have become despondent that his skills were not being utilised. The team would have lost confidence and the opposite team – in this case, Australia – would have benefited from the chaos that ensued. Too often I see this happening in companies – people placed in roles they are ill-equipped to handle. The effect on the team and the business can be immense.

Case Study:

The Power of Having People Working in Their Niche

In the highly competitive world of Real Estate, a high-functioning sales team is vital, followed closely by quality listings to satisfy their hunger to sell. One high profile South East Queensland agency turned their struggling sales team into a high-performance sales team within months, using the guiding principles of Talent Dynamics and getting the right people into the right roles.

Sluggish sales and unmet sales targets were early warning signs that the team were falling out of step, despite a strengthening property market. The General Manager knew every individual had the qualities of a great salesperson, yet somehow their motivation was lagging their ability. He needed to decipher the cause of their failing performance.

Each sales rep took a Talent Dynamics Profile test. The General Manager had assumed all profiles would be Stars – known for their prowess as promoters and delivering results, or Supporters – able to reap sales with their Blaze energy leadership. But the Talent Dynamics profiling results proved different. From the eight reps, only three were Stars and one a Supporter, complemented by a Deal Maker, two Traders and one Accumulator.

By understanding how their Talent Profiles powered their performance, the team identified changes that would take them into rapid Flow. What quickly turned their team into a "dynamic dozen" was working together to change how each person went about selling so that they also complemented the others.

Their new goal: to increase revenue by $100,000 over the following 6-12 months.

The Stars came up with the strategies to help the Deal Maker, Traders and the Accumulator, instantly inspiring and reducing competition between them. Each eased into action – and their natural Flow.

Over the following weeks, the sales team completely changed their focus and responsibilities. The Deal Maker shifted to partnering with other agencies and financiers in the region. The Trader took over the 'walk-ins' and incoming phone and website enquiries. The Accumulator concentrated on telesales and follow-up sales, as well as reporting weekly sales figures. The Supporter took over the Office Manager role and recruited a small team of three commission-only sales agents who worked closely with her – running information evenings, connecting with the local Chamber of Commerce, promoting their office, and running monthly events.

The three Stars continued with traditional listing strategies by marketing direct to homeowners. They also featured at the monthly events, each one in turn, which further developed them into their particular area of expertise: one in apartments, one in standard priced houses, and the other in executive homes, and house and land sales.

Within six months, the team had exceeded their initial $100,000 target! They are now set to increase their bottom line by $500,000 by the end of this year. This dynamic real estate firm has propelled their motivation and their performance to new levels by embracing Team Dynamics at its best.

FINDING THE RIGHT MATCH

As we start to grow the business, it is imperative that we bring on board the right people: people aligned with the vision and passion of the company, and also people who bring the right strengths to their role. The new hires also need to be an energetic fit in the team. It is important that we trust them to do a good job; this is something that takes time to nurture, and some people who on paper we thought would be great hires simply fail to deliver.

It takes time to get to know someone and build the trust to sustain a relationship, whether personal or professional. This is why some of the best business relationships are those borne out of friendships with former colleagues we have got to know, like and trust very well. Our society is one of instant gratification and we are impatient. We can now find the answer to almost any question online with Google; we can watch TV on demand; we are used to getting what we want now, with no waiting. The challenge is that, whilst this approach is great when it comes to purchasing consumer goods, it does not work when building relationships. It takes time to form the bonds of trust that can withstand the storms of business, and without these bonds in place, team members will bail when the going gets tough.

> *I experienced this situation when leading my team at Andersen through the aftermath of the Enron saga. My IT manager operated very peripherally to my business unit. Although he worked exclusively for my team (and was the only person who fully understood how my unique benchmarking tools were programmed), he was, on paper at least, part of another team. As such, I was guilty of not including him in all my team activities and sharing with him the vision of the business unit. On reflection now, I realise I somewhat excluded him from our team and I certainly spent very little time getting*

to know him. Consequently, with the possible threat of job losses hovering over us as Andersen fell rapidly into demise, he jumped ship and found another job. This had a devastating impact on the business, with his critical knowledge of my bespoke computer systems. It was a tough lesson for me in the importance of shared responsibility and mitigating business risks by ensuring that multiple people understand different aspects of the business.

Thankfully, I found a great replacement who managed to save the day; I am eternally grateful to them for getting me out of a very difficult situation, which could have literally killed my business unit overnight.

Interestingly, in the years since this incident, my horses – in particular Bracken – have taught me the importance of patience and taking the time to get to know someone.

Bracken came to me as a six-month-old rescue pony who was found abandoned on the motorway. She was terrified of people and very wary of anything. In those early days, when she would not approach me, all I could do was sit with her and wait. We call this Sharing Territory and it is based on the premise that when the horse finally approaches you, they will do so of free will, because they want to be with you. When this happens, it is easy to connect and engage.

It took many months for Bracken to really connect and I had to be very patient. My natural achiever instinct was to do it all now, but deep down I knew for certain that whilst I might get some short-term gains, they would not be sustainable.

The only way to build her trust was to wait and be there for her when she was ready.

This, too, is what we need to do with our team members and our clients. They must know we care and are there for them and then when they are ready, they will start interacting with us, on their terms. Only then we can start shaping the interaction; but we can't do this until the relationship is in place.

OPTIMAL TEAM SIZE

Is there an optimal team size? Bill Gore, the founder of W.L Gore & Associates, the company that came up with GORE-TEX, believes that there is. The point of discovering this came the day he realised that his company had grown so large that he no longer knew his team members' names. After doing some counting, he concluded that in order to maintain camaraderie and teamwork within the factory, each unit should contain only 150 people. Bill Gore's gut instinct as to this magic number of 150 is borne out by the work of Robin Dunbar, a British anthropologist and professor in the Department of Experimental Psychology at Oxford University, who figured out that people cannot maintain more than 150 close relationships.[27]

Interestingly, the hunter/gathers tribes of our ancestors also used to live in groups that maxed out at 150, and the Bushmen of Southern Africa and Native American tribes also live in groups that cap out at 150. Even the size of a company of marines is 150 people, and recently I learnt that the size of some of the wild mustang horse herds in Wyoming is 150 head. It appears to be that 150 is the number where we can naturally manage all the close relationships. Above this level, social interaction starts to break down and silos emerge, as people do not feel safe and secure in the masses.

This is why it is important that senior leaders trust mid-level managers to manage their teams – because, quite simply, a leader cannot effectively manage large groups of people and still create a strong sense of trust and co-operation.

WHAT MAKES 150 SUCH A MAGIC NUMBER?

There are two aspects that make 150 such a magic number: time and brain power. Given that time is finite, if we are part of a group of more than 150 people, we simply don't have the time to connect with all of them. There are only 480 minutes in an eight-hour workday. At 150 people, that is less than four minutes contact with each person per day (and, of course, we need to make some time for work too!)

Also, our mental capacity means that many people struggle to remember more than 150 names. I'm sure you've all experienced meeting someone and then bumping into them some days, weeks or even months later and not being able to remember their name. Imagine how the other person feels. If you were the business leader and they were the team members, do you think they would feel inspired and motivated to work hard for you? I suspect not, as they probably wouldn't feel valued.

This is corroborated by Dunbar's study, which revealed that when the group is more than 150, then people are less likely to work hard and less likely to help each other out. Furthermore, Dunbar observed that in larger businesses, if the team members were not allocated into groups of 150 or fewer, then team members tended to have more friends outside of their job than inside, as the larger the group of people we work with, the less likely we are to develop any kind of trusting relationship with them. This has significant implications for how we set up and manage our teams if we want them to work at optimum efficiency.

VISIBLE RESULTS

As social animals, it is imperative for us to see the actual, tangible impact of our time and effort; for our work to have meaning and for us to be motivated to do even better. When we are able to physically see the positive impact of the decisions we make or the work we do, not only do we feel that the work was worth it, but it also inspires us to work harder and do more. This is why shared Business Intelligence Dashboards are so important in business. They help our teams see immediately how they are doing and, importantly, how the entire business is performing. Armed with this information, combined with an alignment to the vision of the business, corrective action can be taken when necessary and successes celebrated. This helps boost superior performance and enables us to access the hidden potential in the business.

SHARED LEADERSHIP AND TEAMWORK

We alluded earlier to the fact that the current leadership paradigm has to change and that nature and wild herds of horses have the answer. Their way of collaborative and co-operative teamwork has served them well for many millions of years. So what can we learn from the herd structure that can help us in business?

Typically, in the wild, a herd of horses is led by two leaders: the lead mare, who positions herself at the front of the herd, and her counterpart, the resident stallion, who positions himself at the rear. The lead mare and stallion work in tandem to keep the herd organised and safe; one does not lead over the other but rather they co-ordinate within their respective roles. The stallion's main role is that of protector, keeping the herd safe from impending danger, whilst the role of the lead mare is to set the direction and decide what to do, where to go and how quickly to move.

When chaos erupts, the stallion defers to the lead mare in setting the direction of travel, and assumes the role of sweeper, pushing the entire herd forward. The stallion also keeps the younger horses in check and trains future stallions in the physical prowess they will need to defend their own herds.

The mare and the stallion partner together to lead the herd, assuming the different leadership positions of *Leading From The Front and Behind* respectively, as described in Chapter Nine. However, in addition to this shared leadership of the herd, the lead mare and stallion typically rely on some important lieutenants to ensure their success. Often it is one of the other mares that senses danger first and then communicates that to the lead mare who decides what to do. These lieutenants provide the lead mare with feedback on what is happening in the ever-changing environment. They also assist her in the day-to-day running of the herd, making sure that the younger horses are taught acceptable behaviour. The herd's success rests on this premise, just as the success of any team rests on each team member understanding how they contribute to the overall success and results of the team.

Given the continued changing environment business operates in and the deluge of data, this model of leadership is perfect for businesses to operate more effectively. Imagine how much more productive and effective an enterprise could be if everyone was committed to the success of the business; if everyone shared the values of the firm and if an entrepreneurial spirit of innovation and calculated risk taking existed. The leader would feel supported, no longer overwhelmed by the vast array of decisions to be made, and the team members would feel empowered, knowing they had the remit to make decisions that could impact the future of the business.

Chapter Ten:

Know Your Role In The Herd

Takeaways:
- High-performance teams arise when every team member is operating in Flow and following their natural talents.
- Having the right people in the right roles is essential to a team's success and the dynamics of a team can change according to the placement of people.
- All team members have a place where they add the most value and when each person does the job that is best for them, everybody wins.
- Each person has a different balance of energies and how they most naturally think and act. Everyone in your team has a profile and a natural path to success.
- The optimal team size is 150 people.

Action:
Go to *www.on-the-hoof.com/resources* to unlock your special Talent Dynamics Assessment bonus gift.

There are only

two mistakes

one can make

along the road

to truth;

not going all the way,

and not starting.

Buddha

CHAPTER ELEVEN: THE POWER OF COURAGEOUS CONVERSATIONS

"It takes two to speak truth
— one to speak,
and another to hear."

Henry David Thoreau

As leaders, we all know that we need to sometimes have difficult conversations – I like to refer to them as courageous conversations. These are conversations, which, if they took place, would improve life for us and everyone else in the team. The problem is that fear often causes us to put this off and, as a result, the offending team member continues to provide sub-standard performance, miss deadlines, engage in interpersonal conflicts and exhibit "toxic" behaviour.

Honest communication is essential to the success of any business and therefore it follows that if there is good communication between team members, productivity will increase and people will feel more valued and motivated. They will become more connected to the business. Communication creates interaction and it is this interaction that creates results.

This connection to results was shown clearly in the McKinsey & Co. study *The War for Talent*, which compared the top performing quintile of companies with the mid-quintile (not the lowest performing quintile). This study found that there was a dramatic difference between the two in terms of openness and candour in meetings.[28] Furthermore, a CPP, Inc. study of workplace conflict revealed that team members in the US spend roughly 2.8 hours per week dealing with conflict and a study by Accenture revealed that, even in the recent challenging economic climate, 35% of team members left their jobs voluntarily mainly because of internal politics[29].

Yet time and time again, I find that business leaders and team members are not very adept at communication and are worse still at having what I call courageous conversations, especially when it is necessary to address a difficult topic such as poor team member performance.

Many leaders shy away from these conversations for fear of "rocking the boat" but this ostrich-like approach never works and, in my experience, only comes back to haunt at a later date.

The best teams have free, open, respectful and yet challenging conversations in their meetings. In far too many meetings, however, the team leader is conflict averse, so no one wants to bring attention to *the elephant in the room*. This results in superficial, information exchange-type meetings rather than honest dialogue.

One of the companies surveyed by McKinsey & Co. was Home Depot. They have a great motto regarding meetings: "Say what you think in the room, not after the meeting." Likewise, 'Yum! Brands' David Novak team's motto is, *"Team Together, Team Apart."* To them, that has a special meaning. Everyone openly dialogues and shares different points of view in meetings but once a decision is made, they speak with one voice to the business in owning and implementing the decision.

"*Team Together, Team Apart*" at Yum! Brands also means that they support one another outside the meeting, helping each other be successful and never speaking negatively about one another. This mindset has kept Novak's company successful through many challenges over the years.

Interestingly, a Gallup poll in 2013 called *State of the American Workplace* revealed that when a boss ignores team members, 40% disengage from work, but if the boss criticises team members on regular basis, only 22% disengage[30]. The implication is that if team members get criticised, they are actually more engaged, as at least it shows that someone is acknowledging them.

There are benefits in communicating and connecting with team members, however, that happen beyond this, as courageous

217

conversations provide everyone with clarity about what is happening and this avoids even more difficult situations further down the line.

For many self-employed business leaders I work with, the area where they most struggle to have courageous conversations, apart from with team members, is around money and how to price their products and services. For some reason, having a conversation with a potential client around money seems "dirty", and so the issue is avoided. The result is that both parties end up feeling uncomfortable: the client is not sure whether or how much they have to pay and the business leader does not know when to bring up the issue. No one wins and in fact everyone is confused, which raises stress.

I remember making this mistake when I first entered into a joint venture partnership to co-deliver a workshop to a client. At the time I was embarrassed to bring up the discussion of how the profits would be split and I just made an assumption that a 50:50 split would be agreed. But I never verbalised this and so I entered into the contract with no definitive knowledge of what I was going to get paid. I abdicated responsibility in this instance and became the ostrich sticking my head in the sand. The net result was unpleasant for all of us. My joint venture partner had a completely different perspective on how the fee should be split and I became resentful when she took more than a 50% share. It was a powerful lesson in the fact that whilst honest conversations may be difficult to have, they provide everyone with clarity and avoid misunderstanding. Rest assured I have never made this mistake again!

ACCESSING THE OTHER 90%

One of the key skills in having courageous conversations is being able to access the other 90% of information that is not in the words being said.

According to the work of UCLA psychology professor Albert Mehrabian, face-to-face communication can be broken down into three components:

- Words
- Tone of Voice
- Body Language

When verbal and non-verbal messages are not consistent, what people see us do and the tone we use far outweigh the words we say. He also noted that when feelings and attitudes are being communicated:

- What we say accounts for only 7% of what is believed
- The way we say it accounts for 38%
- What others see accounts for 55%

Amazingly, this means that more than 90% of the impression we convey has nothing to do with what we say with our words.

I'm sure you have experienced the situation when you have walked into a room and know instinctively that something is wrong, even though everyone is professing that things are alright. There is just something about the way the people are acting – their body language and tone of voice – that lets us know all is not well.

Often even when we challenge people, they continue to say that everything is fine when their body language is screaming something else at us. This is a classic case of the person's words not being aligned (*Joined Up*) and congruent with what they are feeling in their body. Often this occurs when people feel under pressure.

The gap between what people feel and what they say is huge and can be very costly to business. A national survey in the US suggested that 70% of employees were afraid to speak up at work, and in other cultures this might be even higher. Imagine if we could measure the lost productivity and stress generated through unexpressed fears and concerns. I expect the results would be shocking and galvanising.

The power of having courageous conversations is in being able to stay present to what is happening around us and learning to read body language and understanding nuances enough to notice the inconsistency in what is being said. Having honest conversations relies on the power of great listening. Often what is not said is more important than what is said.

If we pay attention and listen to our intuition, we can read each other with consummate ease. This was demonstrated at a seminar by Tony Robbins I attended when we were discussing body language and how it was the global currency of communication. There were over 7,000 people in the audience, from different countries, backgrounds and walks of life, and yet we could immediately connect with how each other was feeling by reading the other person's body language. For example, if someone was shy and timid, their body posture would include bent-over shoulders, head down, eyesight averted, short slow steps, whereas someone who was happy and joyous would be standing tall, shoulders and head back, body open, invariably with a smile on their face.

Recognising that the words that we say have less importance than we give them merit for was an important insight for me when I was leading teams and having to have courageous conversations. It highlighted how important it is to approach courageous conversation from a place of calm and curiosity. If we approach the conversation from a place of anger and resentment, the person we are speaking with will be able to read it in our body language and this is when these types of conversations can inadvertently escalate. Clear, coherent and congruent communication is essential for creating a successful working relationship that has positive results and outcomes.

POSITIONS OF PERCEPTION

So how do we moderate our emotions and approach a conversation with calm and curiosity? One of the best tools I use to help my clients get perspective on any challenging conversation they need to have is to examine the conversation through three different lenses using the positions of perspectives (the same viewpoints that we are assessing the *Joined Up* business Cornerstones through).

As a reminder, the three positions of perception are:

- Self
- Other
- Observer

Firstly, we look at the situation through our own lens (from the position of self) and notice how we feel and what emotions come up for us. Then we examine the same situation through the lens of other (the person we are having the conversation with). We note how they could be feeling in this moment and what the rationale for their actions might have been.

Thirdly, we take the stance of observer and look at ourselves and the other person through the lens of a third party. This gives us another perspective on what else might be happening.

Then, armed with this information, we are able to have an honest conversation in a calmer manner as we appreciate the different perspectives on what is happening. No longer are we seeing just through our own lens – which, quite frankly, might be cloudy – and we are able to make much better informed decisions.

It is also important to consider which leadership position to adopt when having a courageous conversation. Do you need to be leading from the front, from behind, or the side? This will depend on the desired outcome for the conversation.

If you need to have an honest conversation with someone regarding their work performance, for example, and the likely outcome is that you will possibly have to let them go, then you'll likely feel you need to have this conversation by leading from the front. You must set the direction for the conversation and bring the team member along with you. There is no opportunity for negotiation here.

Contrast this with a conversation where you are examining why a project failed. For this type of conversation, you may well be leading the conversation from behind. You want to have a collaborative dialogue and examine the factors that impacted performance. Leading the conversation from the front would not work in this moment, as it would presuppose that you knew why the project failed and there may well be issues that you had no idea of and need to learn about.

HOW TO PREPARE FOR A COURAGEOUS CONVERSATION

As you go through this process of examining the conversation from the different perspectives, consider asking yourselves these questions:

1. What is the purpose for having the conversation? What exactly is the behaviour that is causing the problem? What impact is this behaviour having on the team and the business? Having clarity on the problem is crucial to ensuring that the conversation stays on track and does not get derailed by sabotaging ancillary issues.

2. What are you hoping to accomplish? What would be an ideal outcome? What is non-negotiable? Be aware of your hidden purpose as this might unconsciously sabotage the conversation. For example, your tone of voice could make a team member feel reprimanded when what you in fact wanted was to support them.

3. What assumptions are you making about this person's intentions? Adopt a curious and inquiring mindset. Be open to hear first what the other person has to say before reaching any conclusions in your mind. You may feel intimidated, frustrated, ignored or maybe even disrespected, however be cautious about assuming that this was the speaker's intention. Often the impact of what people say does not match their intent.

4. What is being triggered for you? What are your needs and fears? Are there any common concerns? Are you more emotional than the situation warrants? Take a look at your "story" – what in your past history is being triggered? If you recognise this you will go into the conversation owning that some of the heightened emotional state has to do with you.

223

5. How do you imagine the conversation will play out? If you think this is going to be difficult, then it probably will be. If you truly believe that whatever happens, some good will come of it, that will likely be the case. Adjust your attitude for maximum effectiveness, and always focus on a positive outcome.

6. Who do you need to have this conversation with? What might they be thinking about this situation? Are they even aware of the problem? If so, how do you think they perceive it? What are their needs and fears? What solution do you think they would suggest? If you find yourself thinking that the courageous conversation might turn into a fight, like with an opponent, then reframe the situation to see them as a "partner", that you are seeking to get a resolution with.

Finally, consider if you are in someway responsible for this situation. What could you have done differently that may have resulted in a different outcome.

6 C'S TO A SUCCESSFUL COURAGEOUS CONVERSATION

When challenged with having a difficult conversation, many people simply do not know how to approach the situation. This is why I have developed a framework that I call *the 6 C's To Successful Courageous Conversations* to provide you with a road map for navigating the conversation.

CENTRE

It is key that you stay in charge of yourself, your purpose and your emotional energy throughout any courageous conversation. Breathe, centre and notice when you become off-centre, and choose to return to centre again.

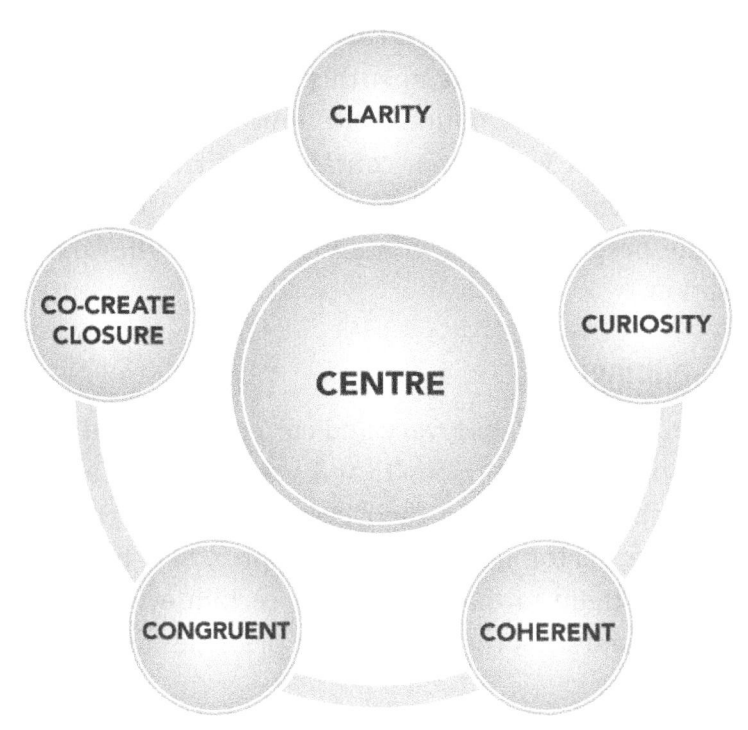

The 6 C's To Successful Courageous Conversations

This is where your power lies. By choosing the calm, centred state, you'll help the person you are speaking with to be more centred, too. Centering is not a step; centring is how you are as you take the steps. Grounded and in the moment.

> **BONUS:** *For more on Centering, go to www.on-the-hoof.com/resources and download the free guide and the 6 C's To Successful Courageous Conversations Template*

STEP #1: CLARITY

Be clear on the reason for the conversation and the outcome that you desire. Most courageous conversations falter because there is a lack of clarity about the real issue. Get to the root cause and focus on this matter rather than the symptoms that might be showing.

Consider how the behaviour you are addressing is impacting the team and the business. Remember this is not about you, so ensure that you control your emotions and approach the conversation in such a way that you do not contaminate it with unconscious feelings or mixed body language. (For most people, this means doing some preparation work in anticipation of the courageous conversation.)

STEP #2: CURIOSITY

Cultivate an attitude of discovery and curiosity. Pretend you don't know anything (you really don't) and learn as much as possible about the other person and their point of view. Pretend you're entertaining a visitor from another country, and find out how things are for them in that place; how certain events affect the other person, and what their values and priorities are.

Watch for their body language and listen for unspoken energy as well. What do they really want? What are they not saying? Let the person talk until they are finished. Don't interrupt except to acknowledge. Whatever you hear, don't take it personally. It's not really about you. Learn as much as you can in this phase of the conversation. You'll get your turn, but don't rush things.

STEP #3: COHERENT

Coherent means showing that you've heard and understood. Try to understand the other person so well you can make their argument for them. Then do it. Repeat back to them what you heard so you can ensure you fully understood what they said. They will not change unless they see that you see where they stand.

Acknowledge whatever you can, including your own defensiveness if it comes up. Acknowledgement can be difficult if we associate it with agreement, however keep them separate.

Saying, "this sounds really important to you," doesn't mean that you're going to go along with their decision but it does make the other person feel listened to.

STEP #4: CONGRUENT

When you sense the other person has said all they want to, then it's your turn. What can you see from your perspective that they've missed? Help clarify your position without minimising theirs. Seek clarity from the other person on how they came to the conclusion they did. And why that was not what you intended.

STEP #5: CO-CREATE CLOSURE

Now you're ready to begin building a new solution. Brainstorming and continued curiousity and inquiry are really useful here. Ask the other person what they think might work. Whatever they say, find something you like and build on it. If the conversation becomes adversarial, go back to inquiry. Asking for the other's point of view usually creates a sense of safety and encourages them to engage. If the other person feels they are being listened to and can shape the outcome, they are more likely to feel inspired to offer solutions.

I urge you to use this framework for any difficult conversations that you need to have rather than sticking your head in the sand and avoiding the issue and hoping it will go away.

Communication is essential in business and the latest 2015 Employee Engagement Trends Report by Quantum WorkPlace reveals that one of the biggest areas of uncertainty for employees remains the fact that there is not often honest and open communication with managers.[31] So simply by addressing this issue head-on, you should start to see trust and employee engagement levels increase.

Case Study:

The Power of Honest Communication: Continental Airlines

Gordon Bethume, who changed the fortunes of Continental Airlines, demonstrated an extreme example of how communication can turn a business around. When Bethume joined the company in 1994, it was a mess; it had gone through bankruptcy twice and had ten leaders in as many years. The company had not made a profit in a decade and flight schedules were erratic. It was reported that the company had three times as many complaints as any other airline. There was massive distrust within the company and a massive lack of co-operation between teams.

Bethume set about changing the culture of the business and whilst this did not happen overnight, his policy of engaging with team members and sharing his plans for the company's turnaround and his accessibility to team members to answer any questions they had, contributed massively to getting people back on track. Team members began to trust their leader for the first time in decades and, as a result, the company turned around from posting a loss of US$204 million in 1994 to generating a profit of US$202 million in 1995.

What Bethume's approach clearly demonstrates is that team success is dependent on the quality of leadership. Would General Electric (GE) have gained the respect of the corporate world without Jack Welch? Would the US have sealed victory in the Gulf War without the leadership of Generals Norman Schwarzkopf and Colin Powell? Whatever team you are part of, its success is dependent on the leadership. So whether you are leading a company of thousands of employees or a team of just ten people, or even seeking to be a leader for your horse or your own life, the outcome of that relationship will be due in large part to your leadership capability and your ability to communicate.

Chapter Eleven:

The Power of Courageous Conversations

Takeaways:
- Avoiding having honest conversations, however difficult, is a recipe for disaster.
- Team members value clarity of communication and knowing where they stand. There is nothing worse than finding out on the "grapevine" about your performance.
- Be clear on the outcome you want from the conversation, whilst always being open to hear the other person's point of view.
- Before the conversation, look at it through the three different lenses of self, other and observer. Experience how that changes your emotion about the situation.
- Always centre yourself before any difficult conversation.
- Having honest conversations requires courage.
- The power of having courageous conversations requires you to stay really present to what is happening around you.
- Learning to read body language and listening to notice any inconsistency in what is being said are essential skills for having courageous conversations.

Action:
For more on Centering, go to *www.on-the-hoof.com/resources* and download the free guide and the *6 C's To Successful Courageous Conversations Template*.

In any moment of decision,
the best thing you can do
is the right thing,
the next best thing
is the wrong thing,
and the worst thing
you can do is nothing.

Theodore Roosevelt

CHAPTER TWELVE: PURPOSE-DRIVEN DECISION-MAKING

"Command and control is not the future — it's about collaboration: you make better decisions through collaboration."

Jim Chambers

We all have to make difficult and challenging decisions throughout our life and these decisions often impact the future direction of our lives. Where do I live? Who should I marry? These are life-changing decisions. In business, too, we have to make strategic decisions all the time. Should we launch this programme or that programme? Joint venture with this person or that person? Enter this market or that one? These decisions can impact the success or failure of a business.

Yet have you ever stopped to think about how many trivial decisions you make every day? A 2011 study by K. Douglas reported in the New Scientist revealed that we make up to 10,000 trivial decisions every day.[32] Often these decisions are so trivial that we don't fully think about their consequences but over time a number of these trivial decisions can magnify to have a great impact on our lives.

As a business owner, you might make a number of decisions to spend small amounts of money on, say, domain names. Each transaction value is small, less than £10 in many cases, but over time you can find that you have amassed over 40 domain names totalling close to £400 per annum, most of which are not being actively used in the business. (This is a situation that I recently found myself in.) This is why it is important to have a Business Intelligence Dashboard to help flag to you where the monthly expenses are being spent.

Making better decisions is a matter of self-empowerment and we need to get better at collecting, processing and filtering the information we base our decisions on. Whilst establishing who to trust and whose recommendations to take on board, it is also important to recognise that emotions, feelings, mood and memories play a huge part in decision-making. This is why it is imperative to establish a culture in business that rewards decision-making, which supports the vision and the purpose of the business rather than the ego of the individual. Without this clarity, poor decisions will result, as personal agendas and opinions get in the way.

DATA DELUGE

A *New York Weekly Times* edition contains more information than the average person in the seventeenth century would have come across in their entire lifetime[33]. In 2008, we consumed three times as much information as in 1960, and by 2020 it is estimated that we will be generating 44 times more data than we are producing today. This data deluge brings opportunities, too, as we can now get access to raw, unedited source data rather than having to rely on third-party interpretations of the results. And yet when the sources of the data are so disparate and often supply conflicting information, which data source do you believe?

Aligned to this is the Continuous Disruption of data. Like a dripping tap, data is being drip-fed to us every minute of every day via the plethora of social media sites and email. Specifically, email is Mental Enemy Number 1 as our phones and mobile devices now continually ping with updates. It has become like a drug that is addicting society. In 2014, more than 204 million emails were sent every minute of every day.[34]

Our data addiction causes us to live in a constant state of disruption. It is extremely difficult to stay present and in the moment with all these distractions. We need to create ways for team members to have the mental and physical space, devoid of distractions, so that they can improve decision-making. In fact, our state of constant distraction is causing business an enormous loss of productivity and efficiency. A Microsoft Research study, which tracked over two thousand hours of employee computer activity, found that once distracted by an email alert, computer users take an average of 22 minutes to return to the suspended task with the same level of focus[35]. In 27% of cases, it took them more than two hours to return to the suspended task with the same level of focus.

So not only is there a loss of productivity for the business, there is a loss of energy for the team member, as changing tasks requires a lot of energy, just as in nature it takes considerable energy for water to be converted to steam and then condensed back again. Similar amounts of energy are wasted every time someone interrupts one task to focus on another.

Most of us are going through life without interrogating whether our decision-making processes are fit for purpose. We need to take more control of our decisions to become empowered thinkers. We need our team members to recognise they are empowered to make decisions. Plus we need to determine whether we have the right team around us to support us making the best decisions for the business. What type of environment have you created? Do "yes" men and women surround you, or do you have an inner circle that challenges you and your assumptions? Data can help us make better decisions, but only if we look objectively at the data and see what it is really saying, rather than what we want it to say.

With all this data surrounding us, it is important to make sure that we focus on the entire picture that the data is painting and not just one aspect. There is a need to view the data with peripheral vision or else we focus on one aspect and fail to appreciate the full consequences of our decisions.

In 2005, Professor Richard Nesbitt began an extraordinary experiment involving both American and Chinese students. He showed each group a set of varied images for just three seconds each to see how they viewed them. The results were demonstrably different. The American students focused on the focal object and barely looked at the background, whilst the Chinese students took longer to focus on the focal object and once they had, their eyes continued to dart around the image taking in the background information too.

For example, if there was a snake on the ground next to the focal object, the Chinese students would be more likely to see it than the American students. This raises an important point – that it is imperative to be able to see and understand all the data before making a decision. Failing to do this could result in you missing something really important that could seriously impact the business. The information that glitters the most brightly may not be what actually serves us best.

INATTENTION BLINDNESS

There is so much data out there that inattention blindness – the inability to be present and see the wood from the trees – is becoming a real problem[36]. There is a real need to take the blinkers off when making decisions, to improve the powers of attention and perception. We should also include non-quantifiable measures in our decision-making processes. Just because something can't be measured does not mean it should be ignored. By devaluing that which cannot be measured, we risk poor decision-making and distorted priorities. As was once said:

> *"Not everything that counts*
> *can be counted*
> *and not everything*
> *that can be counted*
> *counts."* [37]

THE DOPAMINE RUSH

Once we find data that supports what we want, we get a dopamine rush (this is the chemical that makes us feel good). We get a further dopamine rush every time we find data that supports that decision. As a result, we focus on information that supports it and ignore everything that contradicts or doesn't conform to our initial analysis. We must force ourselves to actively search for information that challenges our pre-conceived ideas. Often the CEO needs to become the Chief Challenge Officer. In today's society, where things are changing so fast, the past is not a predictor of the future; decision-making today needs to take this into account.

Just because that is how we did it in the past does not mean that it's what will work in the future. This is the tough lesson that Finnish communications giant Nokia experienced in 2007. From the 1990s onwards, Nokia dominated the mobile phone industry (I know; I was a big fan and would only use Nokia phones) and in 2007, at its peak, the company had a market value of $303 billion and Nokia manufactured approximately four in ten handsets bought globally[38].

However, when Apple introduced the game-changing iPhone in 2007, Nokia was caught sleeping. Ironically, the company had piled $40 billion into creating an iPhone-style device with colour touchscreens, maps and shopping but the product never hit the shelves as management killed the idea, thinking it would not appeal to the mass market. How wrong they were? In the five years after the iPhone was introduced, Nokia lost over 90% of its market valuation, whilst in 2012, Apple's share price peaked, making it the most valuable company in history.

The lesson is not to get so attached to past success or failures that they inhibit the ability to think clearly and to assess the present challenges with an open and objective mind. One way we can avoid basing decisions on the past is by giving ourselves more time to gather and consider information. It is a case of slowing down in order to speed up. Time pressures encourage tunnel or distorted vision, whilst the best ideas often emerge after a reflective pause.

US President Barack Obama reportedly advised UK Prime Minister David Cameron that *"The most important thing you need to do is to have big chunks of time during the day when all you're doing is thinking. Without that you lose the big picture"*[39]. And without the big picture, you miss the opportunities.

GIVE AUTHORITY TO THOSE CLOSEST TO THE INFORMATION

If the business is going to produce better decisions and use Big Data in the way it is meant to be used – to give us better visibility on what is happening in the business so that we can avoid the blind spots and become *Joined Up* – then we need to give authority to those closest to the information. This is what Nobel Prize Winning Economist, Friedrich Hayek, described as "local" knowledge – the dispersed wisdom of those on the ground.[40] We need to empower people who can make real-time decisions and take corrective action. It is not until those with the information relinquish their control and delegate decision-making to team members on the front line that a business can run better, smoother and faster, and reach its maximum potential.

The problem is that in the past we have created business structures that do not empower team members to make decisions; everyone believes they have to be compliant and this can have disastrous implications for the enterprise. In businesses where only 13% of team members on average are engaged and therefore caring about the consequences of their actions, at some point something bad is going to happen – something that was probably highly preventable.

It is the leader's job to take responsibility for the success of the team, to ensure they are well trained and feel confident to perform their tasks and to give them responsibility and hold them accountable for achieving targets. This means that team members must be empowered.

THE JOINED UP BUSINESS DECISION MAKING FRAMEWORK™

You might be surprised to learn that each of the different elements – water, wood, fire, earth and metal - influences the way people approach decision-making. People with high Wood Energy tend to be decisive, results orientated and firm in their decision-making. They often make decisions based on intuition and go with their gut feel about something. They are often considering what will be achieved, or what will happen if I make this decision. Since they can get inspired by many different things, the downside is that they can decide to do too much.

When making decisions, people with a lot of Fire Energy are always considering how the decision will impact their relationship with others. Who will be affected is a key criteria for them in the decision-making process.

People with a lot of Earth Energy are caring, patient and calm. They make decisions based on whether it feels right. They are typically considering how the timing of the decision will impact the team, customers and other stakeholders. They approach decision-making very practically and logically, considering the impact on others.

People with high Metal Energy can be slow to make decisions, as they like to analyse all the permutations. They tend to be pessimists, focusing on what happens if things go wrong and evaluating the potential risk and damage to the business in the event the initiative fails.

Lastly, people with high Water Energy have a natural ability to reflect and they tend to make decisions based on whether the outcome is likely to uplift others in a positive way. If they sense it will do that, then they, too, can make decision quickly.

One of the challenges that many of my clients have is how to make the right decision for the business. The art of great decision-making is to ask yourself great questions. Often when we are unable to make decisions, it is simply because we are asking the wrong questions.

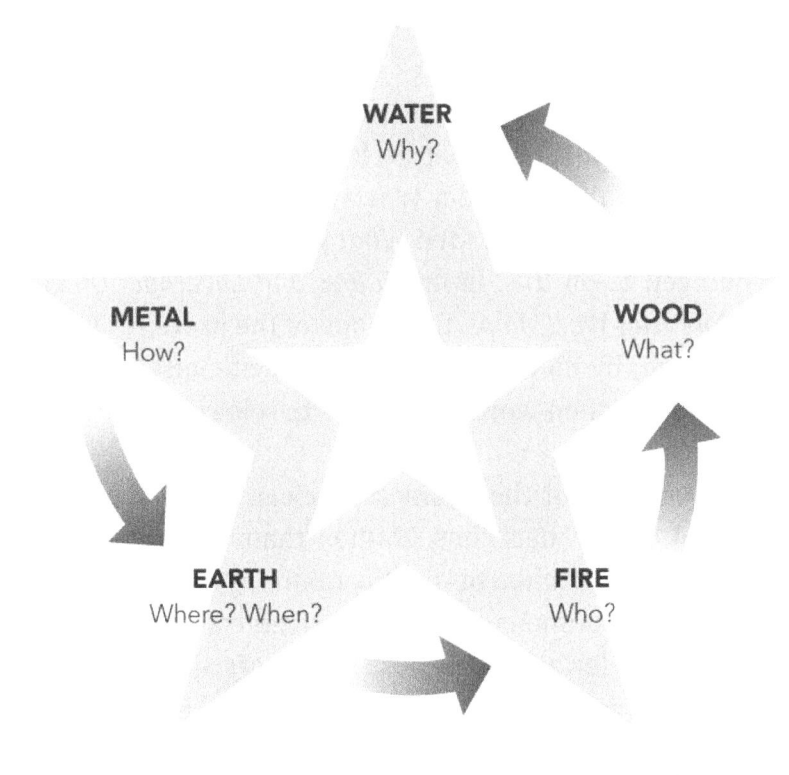

WATER — Why?
WOOD — What?
FIRE — Who?
EARTH — Where? When?
METAL — How?

The Joined Up Decision Making Framework

The *Joined Up Decision Making Framework™* in the previous diagram provides a great system for helping identify which question to ask. If you follow the natural flow – as we referred to in Chapter Seven – every great decision starts with being clear on *Why* you are doing what you are doing. Once you have established the *Why*, then you can start getting clear on *What* needs to be done, with *Whom* and *When* and *Where*. Finally, only once these decisions have been made can we get into the *How*.

> **BONUS:** *You can download your own copy of the Joined Up Business Decision Making Framework™ at www.on-the-hoof.com/resources*

All too often, however, we jump from *What* to *How* and miss out the other steps. If you are ever stuck in making a decision, I strongly suggest you ascertain where you are on the framework and then move backwards around the circle; for example, if you are stuck on *How* to do something, consider *When* you need to do the task, *Who* you need to do it with, and then *What* you need to do – and finally *Why* you need to do this. In my *Values and Leverage: Unleashing Hidden Potential Workshops*, this is one of the exercises that I take teams through; by identifying where a specific task is blocked in the cycle, we can then work backwards to release it.

When the purpose of the business is clear, this leads to bolder, quicker and better decisions. Rather than adjusting decisions according to the winds of public opinion or changes in the competitive environment, a purpose-driven company takes these things into consideration while also being informed by something more soulful and worthwhile. This leads to superior overall performance. Purpose informed decision-making is a critical connection between clarity of purpose and superior performance, financially and otherwise.

The US pharmacy chain CVS Health is a great example of a company that made a strategic decision to walk away from billions of dollars a year in revenue because a product was at odds with the company's purpose. So what was the product and what was the situation? CVS Health's purpose is "to help people on their path to better health". When CEO Larry Merlo realised this, he also appreciated that "the sale of tobacco products was inconsistent with our purpose." So he voluntarily decided to forego a source of $2billion a year in revenue. The decision was an easy one for him to make because of the clarity of the purpose of the company; a classic case of purpose informed decision-making in action.[41]

IN THE DATA JUNGLE WHICH METRICS SHOULD YOU FOCUS ON?

With the myriad of data out there in the data jungle, how do you know which metrics to focus on to help you make decisions? If we liken the data variables to wild animals roaming the African bush, then in my experience we tend to focus on the predators. In business, that means the metrics everyone knows and are familiar with, such as turnover and profit. Because of their gravitas, they often seem to hold a disproportionate importance in what we see. The metrics businesses typically use to measure, manage and communicate results – often known as key performance indicators (KPIs) – include financial measures such as sales growth and earnings per share (EPS) in addition to non-financial measures such as customer loyalty, team turnover and product quality.

The challenge is that these metrics often have only a loose connection to the primary purpose of business, which is to create value. And, because the connection is not sufficiently informative or connected, business leaders rely on their gut instinct of what other metrics are relevant and fail to notice where their intuition may be flawed. This is not to say that intuition is not required in decision-making; it is. It is required to sense check that the data is being provided in the correct context; data can easily be manipulated when its context is misunderstood.

I had first-hand experience of this when I was running Deloitte's HealthClub Benchmark Survey. In collaboration with the business leaders in the privately owned health club sector – the likes of Esporta, Cannons, David Lloyd and Fitness First – we devised the first ever benchmarking survey for the industry, designed to collate monthly data on the industry's performance, in terms of numbers of members, performance and profitability. It was an 18-month project and to start with, all the operators had to agree the same industry definitions of the metrics so that the data could be compared 'apples with apples'.

Once agreement had been reached and the data collected and processed, Deloitte, as the industry aggregator, released data to the UK health and fitness industry on the trends that were reported in terms of growth in membership numbers, attrition rates, and profitability statistics. However, the challenge was that the data was widely misreported in the press. For much of 2006 and 2007, the numbers showed that there was a decline in membership levels for this market sector, however many sources reported there was a decline in the use of health clubs across the UK, and therefore the implication was the UK public were not staying fit.

What the reports failed to mention is that these statistics related only to the privately operated health clubs and no reference was made to what was happening in terms of membership levels of publicly run health clubs, pay-as-you-go venues, or indeed what exercise individuals decided to do at home. Out of context, the results appeared to show the UK population becoming "couch potatoes" who never exercised. Whether this was true or not, we will never know, as the corroborating statistics are not available, but it shows how powerfully data can misrepresent what is happening if cited out of context.

When choosing which metrics to track, it is imperative to ask these questions:

1. What is the objective?
2. What factors will help achieve that objective?

In other words, you need to seek to track metrics that help you reveal cause and effect. The statistics should be both *persistent* (showing that the outcome at one time will be similar to the outcome of the same action at another time) and *predictive* (in other words, that there is a causal relationship between the action and the statistic measures and the desired outcome).

INTUITION V LOGIC

When making decisions, it is imperative that a balance is achieved between relying blindly on the data (logic) and relying blindly on intuition and gut instinct. For effective decisions to be made, both aspects need to be aligned and considered. In the table below, we set out the downsides and upsides of relying on logic and relying on intuition.

Relying only on logic	
Downside	**Upside**
Can get overwhelmed with conflicting data	Easy to explain decision
Dependent on external opinions or advice	Sounds rational
Can prolong research and delay decision	Appears to minimise risk
Relying only on intuition	
Downside	**Upside**
Hard to explain decision	Feels right
May not have data to back it up	Can be backed up by personal history/experience
Can be mistakenly confused with fear or excuses	Quick

For many business leaders, challenges occur when they blindly and (maybe overconfidently) believe that their judgements and abilities are correct, even though the data is pointing to something else. For example, if the business leader believes that employee turnover is a key metric to track because it impacts the customer experience, they may fail to stop and realise that not all employee turnover impacts the customer experience; rather it is the turnover of the team leaders, for they influence how the team members perform. Looking critically at the data, better decisions can be made and focus can be aimed at improving the retention of team leaders, which will impact the business more in terms of customer satisfaction and profits.

Similarly, business leaders tend to rely on the familiar and overestimate its importance relative to other metrics. Take the example of the data jungle again. Business leaders focus on the familiar "lions" they regularly see and fail to notice the impact of the "hippos". Hiding in the waters, just out of sight, hippos are in fact the most dangerous mammals on the African plains because they are extremely unpredictable. (Interestingly, *Hippopotamus* is Greek for *"river horse".*) I wonder what hippos you are ignoring in your business at your peril!

For those in the know, it is ironic that hippos are the most unpredictable mammals on the African plains because HiPPOs (the highest paid person's opinion) are also a real danger in business right now. When data is scarce, expensive to obtain, or not available in digital form, it makes sense to let well-placed people make decisions on the basis of experience they have built up and patterns and relationships they have observed. However, with data more available than ever, those highest paid people need to appreciate that often the best decisions can be made by those closest to the situation. Successful, real time, data-based decisions can be made on the front line, but only if those team members feel empowered to make the decisions without fear of retribution from senior leaders.

Business leaders often prefer to stay with the status quo than face the risks that come with change. Change is constant now in business; however, only businesses that adapt will survive and this means continually changing the metrics being monitored to reflect where the business is in the product life cycle.

When a business is starting out, tracking the number of new customers and the channels they are attracted by is usually a key metric to understand; then as the business grows and expands, a focus on customer service and retaining existing customers becomes a better priority to focus on. The reason is simply that it is cheaper to keep existing customers than attract new ones, and if a more mature company focuses entirely on new customer acquisition, it might fail to realise that as many customers are leaving as are being attracted, and this will have serious implications for the profitability of the business.

In conclusion, the business environment needs to enable team members to act, to make decisions and take risks without fear. It is only by making decisions and taking action that we realise whether the course of action that was chosen was the best one. Given the complexity of business today, there is simply no way to anticipate the outcome of business decisions. Often the decision that you felt was a slam-dunk turns out to be exactly the opposite. Only by trying something can you assess its success and then calibrate your actions to get a different result. The key is to set up metrics at the start, evaluate the impacts, and calibrate as you make changes.

It is important that team members feel it is acceptable to "get things wrong" because only by them making these decisions ("mistakes") can they learn and the business prosper by altering its course of action. (As the business leader you do, of course, need to manage the risk of the decision-making process to ensure that the decisions taken aren't of a magnitude that could permanently kill the business.)

As discussed, we need a Business Intelligence Dashboard to help us steer through the seas of relentless change but we cannot focus solely on these metrics. We need to create a data-driven business culture where there is collaboration and co-operation, and this can only happen if we keep our teams small and focused in an atmosphere of trust. All levels of management need to feel empowered and everyone needs to act like a leader, having a caretaking responsibility for those in their charge. Then, and only then, will team members feel empowered to make data-driven decisions that benefit the entire business, and not just themselves and their department.

> *"Sometimes it's the smallest decisions that can change your life forever."*
>
> **Keri Russell**

Chapter Twelve:

Purpose-Driven Decision-Making

Takeaways:
- We make up to 10,000 trivial decisions every day. Often these decisions are so trivial that we don't fully think about their consequences, but over time a number of these trivial decisions can magnify to have a great impact on our lives and businesses.
- Making better decisions is a matter of self-empowerment and we need to get better at collecting, processing and filtering information.
- There is a need to take the blinkers off when making decisions to improve the powers of attention and perception.
- Use the *Joined Up Decision Making Framework™* to avoid overlooking key decisions and to help you when you get stuck.
- When making decisions, it is imperative that a balance is achieved between relying blindly on the data (logic) and relying blindly on intuition and gut instinct.
- Always look at data variables in context and be prepared to challenge your own thinking.
- Give decision-making responsibility to those closest to the data.

Action:
You can download your own copy of the *Joined Up Decision Making Framework™* at *www.on-the-hoof.com/resources*.

CORNERSTONE THREE: ENGAGE THE ENVIRONMENT (EE)

Expand The Leader   **TRUST**   Empower Others To Act

JUB

TRUST   TRUST

Engage The Enviroment

JUB = Joined Up Business

"PERFORMANCE WITH A PURPOSE IS BASED ON THE BELIEF THAT COMPANIES CAN — AND MUST — ACHIEVE BUSINESS SUCCESS WHILE ALSO ACHIEVING A LASTING AND POSITIVE IMPRINT ON SOCIETY."

PEPSICO CEO INDRA NOOYI

You are a product of your environment. So choose the environment that will best develop you toward your objective. Analyze your life in terms of its environment. Are the things around you helping you toward success - or are they holding you back?

W. Clement Stone

In this section, we look at **Cornerstone Three: Engage The Environment** and the role the environment plays in developing a high-performance culture within business – a place where everyone is engaged and enjoys work and, as a result, the business and all the stakeholders thrive. In terms of the positions of perspective, this view is from position three – that of the *Observer* – the neutral stance on what is happening and the place from where we can get perspective on what is happening to the *Self* and *Other*.

Often the environment is a highly neglected part of business, and yet it has an integral impact on business success. This is because everything is interwoven together and is interdependent. A business cannot exist a vacuum. It needs living people, natural resources and places to exist.

The business environment is comprised of:
- *Micro environment or the internal environment*
- *Macro environment or the external environment*

The combination of internal and external factors influence a company's operating situation. The business environment can include factors such as: clients and suppliers; competition; improvements in technology; laws and government activities; and market, social and economic trends. In addition, the environment within the business – company culture and atmosphere – will also impact performance. You simply won't have an engaged team and motivated leaders if the environment does not support this. If there is any fear in the environment, decision-making will be impaired. Team members will not challenge the status quo for fear of reprimand and, as a result, innovation will be stifled. It is important that the environment encourages decision-making and taking calculated risks.

This was beautifully summed up in 2006 by Anne Scoular when she noted on the Corporate Research Forum:

"The tendency [is] for people to over-emphasise personality-based explanations for behaviours, while under-emphasizing the role and power of situational influences. In other words, people assume that what a person does is based more on what kind of person he or she is, rather than the social and environmental forces at work on that person. It is what surrounds managers that has such a powerful influence – internal social and environmental forces in the organisation's culture, systems, policies, climate and protocol."

As in nature, the business environment supports all the other aspects and to ignore this area can be the downfall of a business. The environment sets the standards and the ethos for the business and so the tone for how activities occur in the workplace.

If the conditions in which we work meet a particular standard, then everyone is capable of the courageous action, above and beyond what you have expected of them. People are driven by the desire to serve and will sacrifice (even their lives) in pursuit of what they believe in and what is aligned with their values. This is why it is imperative to ensure that the business has a clear vision and purpose and that this is articulated to the team members.

When the right conditions create an inspiring, harmonious, trust-based environment, team members excel and go beyond what is expected. When this happens, strong bonds are formed, the type of bonds that can't be broken by fear. People give everything to protect what they believe in and people look out for each other. There is a real spirit of collaboration and this drives business success.

Within a herd of horses, this spirit of collaboration and connection is easily observable. The horses stay within the environment of the herd in order to stay safe. The leadership is shared, with every herd member having a role in ensuring the safety of the herd. When any team member senses danger, they immediately alert the others and everyone quickly starts moving to escape the danger. Herd members that don't pay attention and fulfil their role are reprimanded immediately because their lack of focus could jeopardise the safety of the entire herd. In this way, the herd stays engaged and attentive because every herd member has a role to play in ensuring the safety of the group.

> *"We begin to see, therefore, the importance of selecting our environment with the greatest of care, because environment is the mental feeding ground out of which the food that goes into our minds is extracted."*
>
> **Napoleon Hill**

THE ONLY WAY FORWARD,

IF WE ARE GOING TO

IMPROVE THE QUALITY

OF THE ENVIRONMENT,

IS TO GET

EVERYBODY INVOLVED.

RICHARD ROGERS

Chapter Thirteen: Is the Business Environment Killing You?

"Our environment, the world in which we live and work, is a mirror of our attitudes and expectations."

Earl Nightingale

THE HIDDEN DANGERS IN BUSINESS TODAY

Unlike our ancestors, we don't have to cope with the fear of being killed by a sabre-toothed tiger on a daily basis; however there are a myriad of dangers in business that can harm us. They pervade our life – sometimes real and sometimes perceived. Examples include the ups and down of the stock market, which can affect companies' financial performance and valuation. New technology can make products obsolete overnight. Competitors are a threat, trying to steal customers. Other external factors, such as government regulation, contribute to the constant threats that business face. These work together to hinder growth and profitability.

Internally, there are dangerous forces at play as well, some of which we can manage. Leaders can mitigate the stress that team members feel from these internal threats by minimising intimidation, humiliation, isolation, rejection and staff just feeling dumb, or useless.

A recent study showed that when people feel safe at work, they perform better. This is due to our natural biology. The human body is designed to survive and thrive. We are intrinsically wired this way. Our internal mechanism protects us from danger and we are wired to seek out safety. Just like my horses, when we perceive there is danger (whether real or not), our defences go up. We go on high alert and default to doing anything to protect ourselves. I see this happening all the time in business and it is often a contributing reason to businesses not operating at optimal performance. When in a state of fear, it is impossible for team members to access the 90% of their hidden potential and turn that into productivity and profitability.

The converse is also true. When everyone feels safe amongst their own tribe, they relax and are more open to trust and co-operation. It's just a question of biology and anthropology. If certain conditions are met, people feel safe and work together to achieve extraordinary results.

A feeling of belonging, of shared values and deep sense of empathy, dramatically enhances trust, co-operation and problem-solving, and this in turn improves team performance and therefore business results. It is not skills per se that enhance team performance but rather the ability of people to pull together to get something done; just like a wild herd of horses pulls together to stay safe from predator attack.

The goal of leadership is to foster an environment free of danger by giving team members a sense of belonging, the power to make decisions and offering trust and empathy. Simon Sinek refers to this as a *Circle of Safety*[42].

The team members, just like my herd of horses, create the *Circle of Safety*. They decide who they let in and who they keep out, based on the balance of the circle. You only have to watch what happens when a new horse is introduced to the horse herd to see this in action. The existing herd members decide whether or not to welcome the new horse in. How the new horse behaves significantly impacts the outcome. Usually, the new horse is accepted because his fear of being rejected is so high that he complies with the rules that the herd set out. As a prey animal, not to be accepted into the herd could lead to death from predators.

If a team member is excluded from the *Circle of Safety*, this can create real challenges and yet it is something that I often observe and have personally experienced in business. The problem is that when people are kept outside of the circle, they create their own circles, which then act as silos. Office politics result and mistakes are covered up rather than exposed; the spread of information slows and unease replaces a sense of co-operation and security. This happens too often in business and the consequences can be devastating. In the worst case, the business leader can be forced to resign their position.

This, too, is seen in a herd of wild horses. The wild horse herd is comprised of one male horse (a stallion) and a bunch of female horses (mares). When young male horses reach the age of about three years old, they are expelled from the herd and have to fend for themselves. The young males form bachelor herds and effectively create their own silo. This enables them to live safely as a group; safety in numbers based on all members of the herd being aware of predators and impending danger.

The challenge for the stallion in the original herd is that as he gets older, those bachelor horses will come back and challenge him for his leadership position. The silo comes back to haunt the *Circle of Safety*; and if the stallion loses the fight, he gets expelled from the herd and the winning bachelor horse takes over his herd.

When team members exist within a *Circle of Safety*, they feel valued by colleagues and cared for by superiors. They feel confident in their leaders, and when they know management care for them, this creates an environment where there is free exchange of information and effective communication. This is fundamental to driving innovation and prevents problems escalating. It helps the business be more prepared for the dangers from outside and allows it to seize opportunities. When everyone shares freely what is on the Business Intelligence Dashboard, every member of the business knows what to do and how to respond to the prevailing winds of change.

Trust, innovation and co-operation and collaboration are the result of feeling safe and trusted amongst people we work with. When the *Circle of Safety* is strong, we naturally share ideas, intelligence and the burden of stress. Every strength within the team is amplified, enabling the business to reach its full potential.

YOUR BOSS CAN SERIOUSLY HARM YOUR HEALTH

In 2011, a study by the University of Canberra in Australia concluded that having a job you hate is bad for health and sometimes worse than having no job at all. The study revealed that levels of depression and anxiety amongst people unhappy at work were the same or greater than those who are unemployed.

Stress and anxiety at work have less to do with the work we do and more to do with weak management and leadership. Your boss can seriously harm your health. When team members know someone cares for them, levels of stress decrease. This is why so many people in poorly led teams and departments change jobs; team members have no loyalty to the leader and have no sense of belonging.

Compare this to the industrial age where people had jobs literally for life. There was a real sense of community in business – everyone knew everyone. High levels of trust existed and co-operation was the norm. Team members felt cared for and made a positive contribution to the business.

However, as extended family units have broken down – in part due to improved transportation links and communications – communities have become torn apart. People no longer know their neighbours. Many people live in isolation, their primal basic need for social interaction unfulfilled, feeling alone and out of a *Circle of Safety*. To compensate, we have become dependent on technology in the form of social media for virtual friendships. Social media helps people feel like part of the community, and yet, as many of us have experienced, this is just an illusion; these virtual friends rarely step up to the plate and care for us when things get tough.

Similarly, researchers at University College London in 2011 found that people who did not feel recognised for their efforts were more prone to heart disease. Feelings of control, stress and our ability to perform at peak potential are all directly tied to how safe we feel in the business.

When we are part of a *Circle of Safety* with a group of people whom we trust, then there exists a collectively responsibility to co-operate to face outside challenges and threats. However, when there is no sense of belonging, team members are forced to invest time and energy to protect themselves from each other. With their focus on inward issues, they miss outside opportunities – i.e. for growth. This is bad for business. Internal fighting wastes resources and can blind the business to upcoming threats as well as opportunities.

The success or failure of a business is based on expanding leadership excellence and empowering team members combined with creating a supportive environment. Leaders need to be focused on their team members – they have to create a strong culture, encourage shared values, understand the importance of teamwork, create trust among the members, maintain focus, and understand the importance of people and relationships to success. Team members enable the success of business and *Joined Up Leaders* are those who create an environment where they can care for their team members and place the team members' needs above their own.

OUR HUMAN MAKE-UP

People have a natural instinct to co-operate and care for one another – although sometimes when you look at business, this is hard to believe! Everything in the human psyche is designed to help us survive. Our bodies employ a system of positive and negative feelings to promote behaviours that will enhance our ability to get things done and co-operate e.g. happiness, pride, joy, anxiety.

THE FEEL-GOOD CHEMICALS: ENDORPHINS AND DOPAMINE

Our bodies also have a system designed to help us repeat behaviours that are in our best interests. Endorphins and dopamine make us feel good when we accomplish our goals. These are the chemicals of progress.

Endorphins, released in response to stress and fear, also mask physical pain. It is endorphins that give us a rush to keep us going, for example, when running a marathon or when we need to complete a piece of work before a client deadline. I personally experienced this recently when I was writing a white paper on *7 Simple Strategies To Boost Profits Without Busting Your Bank Account*. Although the print deadline was Monday, which I was prepared for, I omitted to realise there was also an online delivery deadline of Friday. I discovered my oversight late on Thursday afternoon so I had to work very late into the night to get the report completed earlier than planned. I was beyond tired but I kept going, and when at 2am the report was complete, I was on a real high. I realised how much I loved that feeling.

In fact, the release of these endorphins can almost become addictive as many people crave the buzz they get when this chemical is released into the bloodstream. Endorphins are what keep runners going and people feeling that they have to work out each day at the gym.

They become addicted to feeling, and when they don't receive it (because they don't engage in the activity), they become anxious and agitated.

Endorphins are also responsible for laughter release and since we can't be afraid and laugh at the same time, they provide a great mechanism for us to overcome fear. This is why laughter is often described as the best medicine there is. Laughter is a powerful antidote to stress, pain, and conflict. Nothing works faster or more dependably to bring your mind and body back into balance than a good laugh. Humour lightens your burdens, inspires hopes, connects you to others, and keeps you grounded, focused, and alert.

Laughter is also infectious. The sound of roaring laughter is far more contagious than any cough, sniffle, or sneeze. When laughter is shared, it binds people together and increases happiness and intimacy. Laughter also triggers healthy physical changes in the body. Humour and laughter strengthens your immune system, boosts your energy, diminishes pain, and protects from the damaging effects of stress. Best of all, this priceless medicine is fun, free and easy to use.

Dopamine is the reason for the good feeling we get when we find something we're looking for or do something that needs to get done. It is responsible for the feeling of satisfaction e.g. crossing something off the 'to do' list. The positive feeling of progress or accomplishment is primarily because of dopamine. Dopamine makes us goal-focused, and when we achieve a goal, we get a mega kick of dopamine – which is why we keep going and why it feels really good to work hard to achieve something difficult.

The way the human psyche works, there is no biological incentive to do nothing. This is why people can get depressed when they don't have a job or any focus in life – their life becomes devoid of dopamine. The downside of this chemical is that dopamine can become highly addictive and can cause alcoholism and binge eating. These are examples of dopamine working to reward behaviour but in an unproductive way.

These feel good chemicals don't always produce the results nature intended, however. A big challenge occurs in business when dopamine is the primary means of reward – hit the goal, get the money. It can become addictive and, as with gambling, people strive to make the numbers. This can erode the *Circle of Safety* as everyone becomes self-centred and ego-driven rather than considering their impact on other team members. To my mind, this is exactly what happened during the 2008/9 financial crisis. The bankers, driven by their dopamine rewards, lent more money than was prudent, and gambled big time on stocks that were doomed to failure. There was an ego-driven short-term view of business: "So long as I get my bonus cheque this quarter or this year, I don't need to worry about what will happen in the future".

Endorphins and dopamine work together to ensure our survival in terms of food and shelter. They help us get things done so that we can earn a salary and pay for housing and food. It is no joke when we say we need a job to survive. We really do feel that way. Without endorphins to give us the edge, we would not keep going when we are tired and exhausted. Dopamine provides the chemical rush when we've accomplished something, making us want to do it again and again. The challenge, however, is that success manifests best when you are working in a team. It's harder to do all these things alone, especially the big things – which is why we also need to have a balance of serotonin and oxytocin.

THE SELFLESS CHEMICALS: SEROTONIN AND OXYTOCIN

Serotonin and oxytocin have been described as the 'selfless chemicals', as they help keep the *Circle of Safety* strong and enable us to feel valued. They bring us feelings of belonging, trust and inspiration. Unlike some species who are just concerned with self and have no desire to co-operate, humans are designed to live in tribes and co-operate with one another. This is an integral part of our DNA and it has helped humankind survive for thousands of years.

Serotonin and oxytocin help us forms bonds of friendship and encourage us to look out for each other, which in turn enables us to create high-performance businesses. When team members co-operate and protect each other, serotonin and oxytocin operate to develop the bonds of trust and friendship. Oxytocin and serotonin effectively grease the social machine and when they are missing, friction results. When a business culture is created where these two chemicals are absent, it sabotages the business, its team members and their level of happiness. This is because a business simply can't exist without social interactions amongst the team members.

Serotonin gives us a feeling of pride. It's the feeling we get when we perceive that others like and respect us. We feel strong and confident and it raises our sense of being. As social animals, people want and need the approval of other herd members. Everyone wants to feel valuable, which is why team members value awards, ceremonies and company recognition. Team members want to know the work they do is valuable.

Oxytocin creates the feeling of friendship, love or deep trust. It's the feeling we get when in the company of trusted colleagues and close friends. It's that warm fuzzy feeling that is needed for empathy. We know that there is someone there to cover our backs. Oxytocin enables us to trust others and help us build relationships, feel human connections and like being in the company of others. Oxytocin makes us social.

When *Joined Up Leaders* create an environment that promotes teamwork, it is not surprising that more gets done. In groups, everyone can contribute their strengths and so every aspect of work and projects can get covered more easily and quickly. Just like in my herd, when we are working in a group, no one person has to be vigilant alone to ensure the group's safety – it becomes a shared responsibility. This enables us to rest and do and be our best, just like the horses.

Finally, oxytocin directs how vulnerable we can afford to make ourselves. It is a social compass that determines when it is safe to open up and trust someone or when we should hold back. Different from dopamine, which creates instant gratification, oxytocin is long lasting. It helps develop the bonds in teams as we learn to trust each other.

TRUST YOUR GUT FEELING: CORTISOL

We have all experienced that gut feeling that something is not right. It is this feeling that keeps us from danger and acts as an early warning system. Cortisol is the chemical that activates this gut feeling and is responsible for the stress and anxiety we experience. It puts us into a heightened state of awareness, alerting us to potential danger and preparing us to take extra measures to protect ourselves and raise our chance of survival.

This is best illustrated in nature where one herd member senses danger, alerts everyone else and then the herd runs away. I witnessed this many times in Africa with the zebras and gazelles grazing on the plains. When one of them sensed danger, they would alert the herd and then, as if by magic, the whole herd would enter a state of heightened awareness and, if appropriate, flee. This synchronisation of the "system" is scientifically referred to as entrainment and it occurs when energy aligns and everyone and everything starts moving in unison, as one.

We often witness the same situation in an office, where one person suspects something, shares that with someone else and then a rumour spreads like wildfire.

I personally experienced this phenomenon when I was leading the HotelBenchmark Team at Andersen after the collapse of Enron. At the time there was a lot of uncertainty as to the future of Andersen, but rumours abounded that the UK division would probably be bought by one of our competitors. I remember one day walking into our office to find my team members all learning the KPMG company song, as they believed we were going to be acquired by them. In fact, Deloitte eventually acquired the Andersen UK division so that time spent learning the KPMG song was wasted time. This is one of the challenges when cortisol levels start running so high; it is difficult for team members to focus and, as stress levels increase, they become more and more distracted, thereby further impacting productivity.

The problem is that cortisol is not supposed to stay in the bodily system. It is designed to fire off when we sense a threat and then fade when the threat has passed. However, if the threat (or the perception of threat) continues and we end up living in a constant state of anxiety and stress, this can cause long-lasting damage to our internal systems.

In the wild, after the threat has passed and danger has been outrun, the herd has physically run off the cortisol and are back in harmony. Humans, with our sophisticated neocortex, try to evaluate the cause of the stress e.g. the boss at work or a colleague, and can keep the sense of threat alive; thus the cortisol stays in our bodies. Regardless of whether the danger is real or perceived, the physical stress effect is real. Our bodies are not rational like our minds, they just respond to the chemicals flowing.

This means that when we work in an environment where our team members and bosses don't care for us, this can create ongoing low-level anxiety; because humans are social animals, we feel stressed when unsupported. When we feel we are responsible for ourselves and we recognise that our colleagues only care about themselves – i.e. are ego-driven – this is quite scary for the primitive part of our brain. The problem is not with the people, but the environment.

In the herd, everyone cares for each other, but in business most of us work in environments which are self-serving and where members of the group don't care much about each other's fate. This means impending danger is often kept a secret and, as a result, the bond of trust among employees or between leaders and workers is weak. This is exactly what transpired at Andersen in the wake of the collapse of Enron.

Biologically this becomes a problem as the cortisol inhibits the release the oxytocin, the chemical responsible for empathy, creating a negative spiral which sends people more into stress and fear and makes them less inclined to engage in connected behaviour. The impact on the business is considerable in terms of lost productivity and profitability.

In the case of Enron, it was devastating. Not only did Enron end up filing for bankruptcy but Andersen, its auditor, got caught up in the web of deceit and was indicted and had its license to practice revoked. Consequently, Andersen had to cease trading as an accountancy firm.

In one fell swoop, one of the largest accountancy firms in the world vanished, its reputation in tatters as its credibility destroyed.

A constant flow of cortisol is not only bad for business health but also team members' health as it wreaks havoc with our glucose metabolism. It increases blood pressure and impairs cognitive ability, making it harder to concentrate. Another side effect of high cortisol release is that the immune system shuts down; when we work in an environment where trust is low, relationships are weak and functional, and stress and anxiety are the norm, we become more vulnerable to illness. This translates into more sick days and absenteeism – and all of this impacts the bottom line.

In contrast, good work environments encourage people to release oxytocin and serotonin, which lead to trust and co-operation. These are great for creating positive results for the business.

THE RIPPLE EFFECT OF THE BUSINESS ENVIRONMENT

It is important to realise that the business environment is not a stand-alone concept but is integrally related to all other aspects of the business and the greater community. When a business environment is created that has an unbalanced focus on short-term results and money (at the expense of the other stakeholder needs), this impacts society at large.

Conversely, when a collaborative and co-operative environment exists at work, team members are happy and this translates to them being happy at home; this in turn means an improved society. It is the role of the business leader to create an environment where people feel fulfilled and engaged at work. It is this ability to grow one's team to do what needs to be done that creates lasting success, both for the business and for society.

So how can we assess the type of environment that we are creating within the business? Is it one that promotes collaboration and co-operation, or does it instil fear and trepidation in our team members? The Deloitte Shift Index indicated that 80% of people are dissatisfied with their job[43]. This is a great example of how the Big Data metric of employee engagement can be used to highlight blind spots in business and enable us steer the business towards a successful outcome. Without this data point, the business may not fulfil its potential to create a high-performing enterprise.

HERD DYNAMICS

A horse herd provides a perfect example of how to create a business/team that does not "kill" its members. Living in herds to ensure their safety and for companionship with rigid rules for how the group operates to maintain the harmony, every horse has their role in the herd and every horse knows their responsibilities. There is absolute clarity and, as a result, no pointless arguments or destructive internal politics. There is trust between herd members and acceptance of the hierarchy of leadership. Compare this with society, where the cohesiveness of groups of people – whether they be teams, family units or business entities – are often fuelled by fear and mistrust. We can learn much from horses about how to run our businesses and boardrooms more effectively.

Horses can show us how to work as a team if only we let them. Like us, horses have a natural desire for companionship and to be part of a herd. This is their survival mechanism. Being a Lone Ranger out on the plains would mean a very high probability that they will come under attack by some predator, maybe in the shape of a mountain lion. Being alone and trying to keep yourself safe from danger 24 hours a day is daunting; and yet it is a situation that many small business owners, in particular, have to face. Devoid of any support, they feel like they are on a never-ending roller coaster that they can't get off, because, if they do, their business might fail. This is why it is imperative that all business leaders seek to form teams around them to support them and help avoid the Lone Ranger syndrome.

The physiological aspect of the environment is something that is not often considered, and yet it has enormous impact. Without creating the right environment, one that nurtures our innate human needs for connection and support, we can literally be killing our team members' commitment to the business. When team members don't feel safe and valued, they don't just not contribute – in many instances, they end up actively sabotaging the success of the business.

Chapter Thirteen:

Is The Business Environment Killing You?

Takeaways:
- The goal of leadership is to foster an environment free of danger from each other by giving team members a sense of belonging. This means creating a *Circle of Safety*.
- Exclusion from the *Circle of Safety* results in silos forming within the business. This leads to distrust.
- Endorphins and dopamine make us feel good when we find something we're looking for, build something we need or accomplish our goals. These are the chemicals of progress.
- Serotonin and oxytocin – the selfless chemicals – help keep the *Circle of Safety* strong and bring feelings of being valued, belonging, trust and inspiration.
- If cortisol stays in the body too long – because we perceive we are in danger – this causes stress and can cause long-lasting damage to our internal systems.
- The Deloitte Shift Index indicated that 80% of people are dissatisfied with their job.

Action:
Download my complimentary report on *7 Simple Strategies To Boost Profits Without Busting Your Bank Account* at *www.on-the-hoof.com/resources*.

You must take
personal responsibility.
You cannot change the
circumstances, the seasons,
or the wind,
but you can change yourself.
That is something you have
charge of.

Jim Rohn

CHAPTER FOURTEEN: HARNESSING NATURE'S NATURAL RHYTHM

"SELF-DISCIPLINE IS AN ACT OF CULTIVATION. IT REQUIRES YOU TO CONNECT TODAY'S ACTIONS TO TOMORROW'S RESULTS. THERE'S A SEASON FOR SOWING A SEASON FOR REAPING. SELF-DISCIPLINE HELPS YOU KNOW WHICH IS WHICH."

GARY RYAN BLAIR

The primary goal of any system is balance – and the business environment is no different. In nature, there are natural laws that get evoked to get systems back in balance. Everything in nature has a natural rhythm. We know that every day the sun will rise and set, and that during each year we will experience four different seasons. It is this rhythm and flow that keeps nature in balance. One of the challenges we face in our technological age is that we've lost our sense of rhythm. Unlike the farmer whose priorities change with the seasons, we have become impervious to the natural rhythm of life and business and, as a result, we have our priorities are out of balance.

Let me illustrate what I mean. For a farmer, springtime is his most active time. It's then when he must work around the clock, up before the sun and still toiling at the stroke of midnight. He must keep his equipment running at full capacity because he has only a small window of time for the planting of his crop. During the summer, the farmer harvests the winter wheat and straw and, whilst the crops grow, he prepares for the autumn. When the days start to get shorter, there is lots to do harvesting the crops and planting the winter wheat. After the harvest, some of the fields are fertilised to create the best environment for the next year's harvest. Eventually, winter comes and there is less for him to do; this is a time for planning and for repairing equipment and machinery ready for the spring.

The lesson here is to stay present and aware and learn to harness the seasons of life. Decide when to pour it on and when to ease back, when to take advantage and when to let things ride. It's tempting to keep going from 9 a.m. to 5 p.m. year in and year out and lose a natural sense of priorities and cycles. Don't let one year blend into another in an endless parade of tasks and responsibilities. It is important to keep your eye on your own seasons, or else you can lose perspective on what you are accomplishing.

THE SEASONS OF BUSINESS

If everything is composed of energy, it follows that there is a natural ebb and flow to all activities, with times of contraction and times of expansion; we can only be aware of these by being present and mindful. We can see this in the seasons. Spring and summer are times of expansion whilst autumn and winter are times of contraction. People, too, have an ebb and flow to their lives and, to be successful, it is important that we recognise when our bodies need to rest and honour that time. In fact, most people resist the period of contraction and try taking more action, which ironically often leads to even more contraction in their lives.

During periods of contraction, we feel weak, restricted, suppressed, frustrated, unhappy and tired. We don't feel like doing much and this is a signal from the body that we need to get clarity on what to do. Contrast this with periods of expansion when we want to take action as we feel energised, happy, joyous and have self-belief.

If you were to compare these two time frames to a set of traffic lights, periods of contraction are the red "Stop" light whilst periods of expansion represent the green "Go" light. The challenge is that most businesses and people are so disconnected from what is happening around them that they fail to see these changes in seasons and keep going through the red or contraction time; then things become difficult as they are fighting against the natural flow of the environment. With their foot continually on the gas pedal, the business flat lines. (There is no inconsistency here that a heartbeat has a regular beat (ebb and flow) and yet when we die the heartbeat just flatlines!)

Businesses also follow cycles, which is why it is rare to find the same companies being the best performers, year on year.

Businesses, like people, need to recharge and refocus their efforts. They need a period of reflection.

The cycle of business exactly matches the natural patterns of nature as illustrated below:

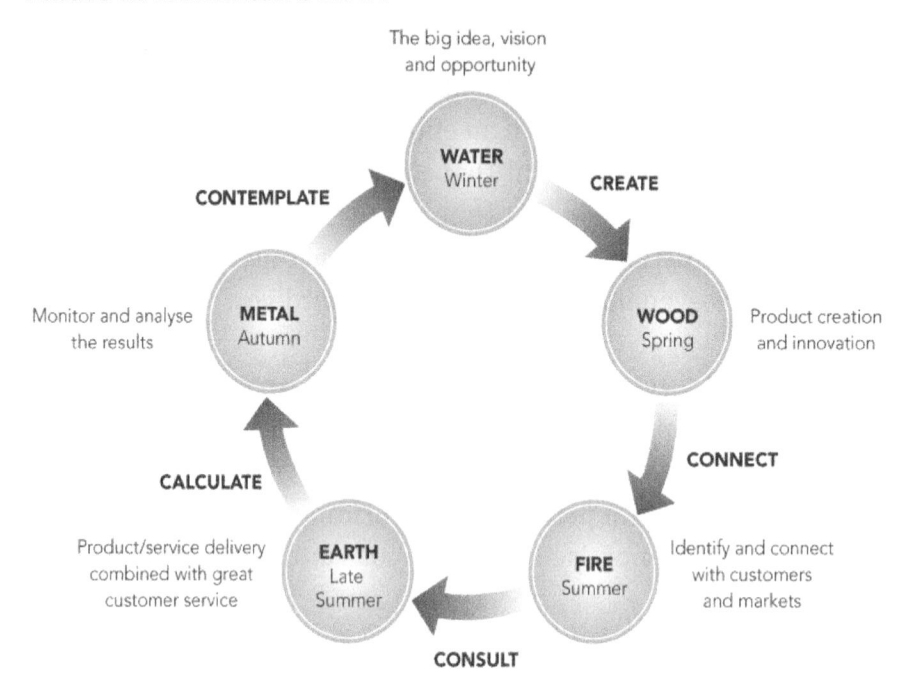

The Natural Cycle of Business Creation

Reviewing and expanding on the model of business "seasons" covered earlier, when a business is just starting out, it needs lots of Water Energy to help get clarity on the real purpose and raison d'être of the business. Then the Wood Energy comes into play creating the vision and coming up with the strategy. Wood energy is spring-type energy; it gets things moving. Then the business moves into a phase of growth, represented by summer and Fire energy. Here you find companies acquiring market share and presence by connecting and collaborating with others. Next, business moves into the late summer phase of consultation, represented by Earth energy. This is a time when a business is established in its niche and looking after customers is an imperative. Then the business moves into autumn (Metal energy), which is all about consolidation and calculation – getting more from the business by closely monitoring the numbers. Lastly, the business moves into winter and Water energy again. This is typically a time of reflecting back on what has and hasn't worked, and looking for ways to expand the product offering with product extensions; and so the business moves back into creation mode and the spring energy. It's a virtuous circle.

An example of the cyclical nature of business can be seen in the DotCom crash of the late 1990s into the early 2000s. In 1998, graduates rushed to Silicon Valley to take up the huge number of positions available in fledgling Internet companies. Billions of dollars were loaned to start-up companies and in 1999, most of the 457 Initial Public Offerings (IPOs) were Internet and technology related. Of these ventures, 117 doubled their share price on the first day of trading, yet the rapid growth and expansion of the industry meant that it overstretched itself. Many of these companies, whilst innovative, were not financially viable and so by late 2002 the entire market had imploded, resulting in massive job losses. The industry needed to take time to reflect and refocus. The survivors of the DotCom crash, such as Amazon, are now thriving businesses, with Amazon founder Jeff Bezos now reportedly the 15th richest man on the planet.

Black Tuesday (29th October 1929) is another example of a system getting back into balance. In the time before that date, the system had been overvalued and a small correction was not going to rectify the situation – the imbalance was too extreme. The correction was so significant that it started the Great Depression; the stock market lost nearly 90% in value and rising unemployment left as much as 25% of the country jobless. The Depression lasted nearly a decade and did not end until America joined World War II.

Knowing what business season you are in is vital to ensure success. The best way to figure this out is to examine which season you have just passed through. If you have a great product that has proven itself in the market, you are out of spring and into summer, where you will be focusing on building your market. If you have many new customers and sales are coming in easily, you are out of summer and into late summer, with a focus on serving your customers well. If your customers are happy and your team members are settled, you are out of late summer and into autumn, where your focus will be on analysing and measuring how the business performed. Then you move into winter, reflecting on what has occurred and seeking ways to enhance performance before moving back into spring.

The big error that many business owners make is that they fail to realise when they have moved from one season to the next, and continue with the same strategies when a new approach is needed. Often the wrong type of leader is running the business in the wrong season. If this coincides with team members being in the wrong roles, the results can be disastrous.

My own personal experience of not fully appreciating the seasons of business occurred when I was leading the HotelBenchmark Team at Deloitte. As someone with high wood energy, I delivered great value to the business during its creation stage: coming up with the plan, devising the business strategy, creating the product offering and figuring out a way to deliver this innovative benchmarking tool to the industry in a totally new way. With my Dynamo, Innovation energy, I was the natural leader for the business during this phase of evolution.

However, as the business grew and firmly established itself as the market leader in its niche, moving through the summer season into autumn, I continued to lead the business. This was a mistake. I was out of "Flow", not enjoying my job and, quite frankly, not delivering the best value to the business. As the business moved through the seasons, it really needed a leader with that season's energy to match in order to achieve optimum results.

It is not just businesses that follow the cycle of the seasons; industries run through cycles and different industries run through different cycles in different countries. For example, Richard Branson created Virgin Australia Airlines (formerly Virgin Blue) at a time when the budget airline industry in Europe was in the winter season, but in Australia the budget airline industry was in the spring. Rupert Murdoch launched his US operations when the media industry there was in the autumn season because the media industry in his native Australia had moved to the winter season.

BALANCED BUSINESS SYSTEMS

Within a business system where dopamine is the primary driver, much is achieved, but the team feel lonely and unfulfilled no matter how rich or powerful they get. Life is led by a series of quick hits, looking for the next rush. Dopamine simply does not help us create things that are built to last. Conversely, in a hippie-type commune where everyone is connected, there are rushes of oxytocin, but without any measurable goals or ambitions, people can feel lacking in accomplishments. No matter how much love there is, people can feel like failures due to the lack of balance.

When the system is in balance, superhuman results can be achieved as courage, inspiration, foresight, creativity and empathy become the norm. As a result, team members can deliver extraordinary results, which translate into superior business performance.

When individuals have less, they tend to be more open to sharing what they have. Bedouin tribes, such as the Maasai in Kenya, don't have much, and yet they are happy to share because it is in their interest to do so. They welcome people into their homes and hospitably share their food even though it is scarce. Their survival depends on sharing because one day it might be them seeking food and refuge.

Ironically, the more people have, the bigger their fences, the more sophisticated their security to keep people away and the less they want to share. Many of today's working environments frustrate rather than foster our natural inclinations for trust and co-operation. Current values and norms in business and society encourage dopamine-driven performance and reward individual achievement; there is no balance of the serotonin and oxytocin rewards of working together and building bonds of trust and loyalty.

This imbalance in the corporate culture affects the stability of large business and in the worst extremes causes them to crash. Some examples include Enron, WorldCom and Lehman Brothers. The same imbalance perpetuates the situation, creating a greater imbalance of chemicals and the vicious cycle continues – team member health is at risk, the stability of companies is at risk and the economy is at risk.

We have unintentionally created a world quite out of balance and whilst many realise that this imbalance needs to be addressed (if we don't do something, nature will create a natural correction for us), few leaders today have the confidence and patience to do what needs to be done. Their desire for instant gratification and the culture of "results now" mean that many leaders are still focused on themselves rather than leading the people. There is a lack of empathy and humanity in the way we do business.

THE INTEGRATED PERFORMANCE MODEL

The relationship between our physiology and our performance is summed up well in the following diagram, modified from the Integrated Performance Model. What is relevant here is that our environment – not only the physical building but also the people and objects in it – has an impact on our physiology and therefore our state of being.

As an analogy, it is difficult to meditate in a busy supermarket – the environment is just not conducive to being still; there is too much happening. When people meditate, they typically go to a quiet place and sit down. Maybe they light candles. Their actions are designed to create an environment that is peaceful so their mind can slow down.

I know well the importance of environment to my performance. If my office and my desk are full of papers strewn all over the place, I find it difficult to concentrate and my productivity subsequently decreases. There is something about the serenity and calm of a tidy office that helps me keep my energy focused and concentrated and so I deliver better results. It is the same when I train horses. When I train my horses in a quiet place, particularly one they are familiar with, the training seems effortless. But put them in a noisy environment, especially one they are unfamiliar with, and their mind wanders. They simply can't focus on the task at hand because of all the distractions and frustrations that result for me and them.

PERFORMANCE

BEHAVIOUR

THINKING

FEELING

EMOTION

PHYSIOLOGY

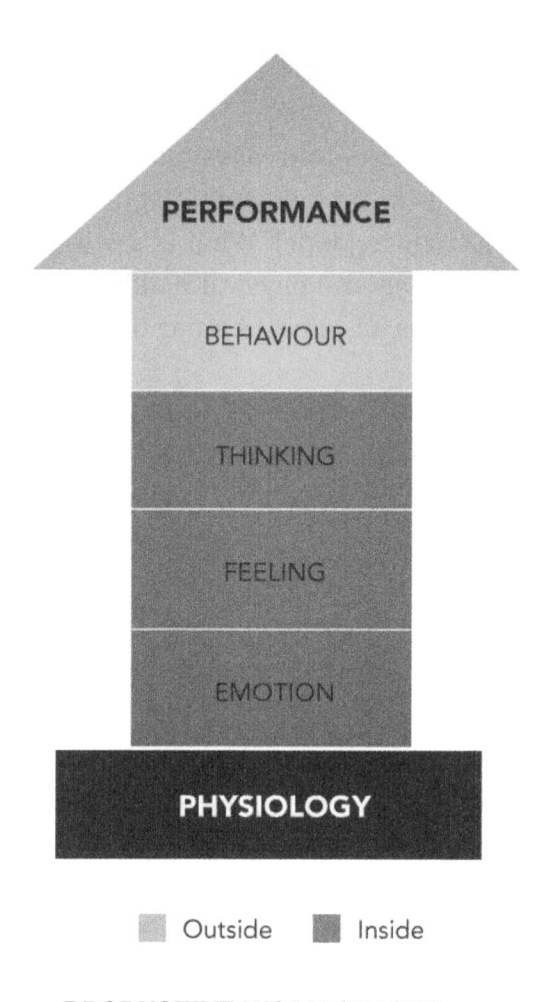

Outside Inside

PRODUCTIVE WORK SPACES

The trick to achieving more with less is to realise that where team members do a specific task is as important as *when* they do it. Too many office environments are set up so that all the daily activities are done in the same place. Stress and overwhelm are created by mixing different energies together.

Many hours per week are potentially wasted in moving from one activity to another. When we try to accomplish everything in the same place, we end up unfocused as we jump from one task to another. Worse still, we just become reactive to our environment: one moment we are working on our accounts (a metal energy activity) then the phone rings, so we speak to a customer (earth energy activity), and then revert back to working on the spreadsheet. Every time we change between these different activities, we move out of Flow wasting valuable time and energy. Focus and momentum on the initial task is lost and it requires energy to build them up again.

Another analogy: every time you start a new task, it is a bit like taking off in an aeroplane – lots of energy, in the form of fuel, is expended getting the plane off the ground. Once the plane is in the air, there is momentum and the amount of fuel used is disproportionately low. It's the same in business. Each time you change activity, it is like the plane taking off again in terms of how much energy you use. How much more productive could we be if we limited the number of times per day our plane needed to take off?

By working with nature's natural frequencies, you can create a schedule and a work location plan that matches your natural rhythms. There is an energy to working environments just as there is to life and if we can harness the right environment for the right task, then the energy will flow and the task will be much easier to accomplish.

Creative Space (Wood Energy): this is the space for innovation and creativity. It is the place to brainstorm, write creatively, come up with new ideas and answer the question *"What?"* Great activities to do here include product development, strategy and branding. Make this a space where you can pin things up and see the big picture. Make the space quirky and change it frequently to spark creativity and bold action. Don't take phone calls here, answer text messages or use any kind of social media. In this innovative space, you don't want to get stuck in details or distracted by others.

Connective Space (Fire Energy): this is the space to create your sales and marketing environment, and have conversations, take questions, answer emails and answer the question *"Who?"* This space should be bright, open and vibrant, set up to ensure you have everyone's contact information close at hand; this is a space of conversation, where there is no room to daydream or procrastinate.

Consultation Space (Earth Energy): this is your service environment and a great place for both customer and team care. It is a space to be calm and grounded and to sit with team members to plan or with clients to listen. This is where everything has a *"When?"* and *"Where?"* Element. This isn't a place to promote or sell, but rather a place to provide care and service and a place of smaller people-related activities. Don't let any overly strong energy (positive or negative) into this space.

Calculation Space (Metal Energy): this is your control environment, a space for documentation and measurement. This is a place to concentrate on the detail, get quiet time and focus clearly on the *"How?"* This is where you keep all your accounts, financial information, spreadsheets and Big Data metrics. It is a clear, clean, organised and disciplined space that leads to precision and clarity; this is where all your detailed files can be easily accessed. Keep out all interruptions and have no phone, email or other distractions in this space. Be wiling to be critical and take criticism from here.

Contemplative Space (Water Energy): this is the bridge environment where everything comes together and where leadership is aligned to the primary purpose; it is the heart of the enterprise. This is a place that inspires you and allows you to reflect on your higher purpose and bigger mission; it is the space of clarity and certainty and is a great place to start off each day.

> **BONUS:** You can download a worksheet to help you identify the right place for you to conduct each type of activity at www.on-the-hoof.com/resources

Many companies are beginning to realise the importance of environment to the productivity of their team members. When I worked at Andersen, we had a few rooms designated as creative space areas, where team members could brainstorm on new ideas away from the traditional workspaces.

In her book, *I Wish I Worked There: A Look Inside the Most Creative Spaces in Business,* Kursty Groves examined 20 well-known companies, including the LEGO Group, Oakley, Bloomberg and Urban Outfitters, and provided insights into how these firms use space in ways that promote creativity and collaboration, increase satisfaction and decrease employee turnover.

In particular, she distinguished between *stimulating spaces* (that tell stories or enable people to access different information), *reflective spaces* (where people can go to focus or relax, as an individual or as a team), *collaborative spaces* (where people casually connect with one another, i.e. the cafeteria), and *playful spaces* (where people can bond through playing games, e.g. football).

If it is not possible to change your environment, then one way to feel more energised is to move your body, i.e. change your physiology. If you have been sitting for long periods of time, simply getting up and stretching your arms in the air can make a massive difference to how you feel. One summer I attended the National Achievers Congress in London and Tony Robbins was the keynote speaker.

He spoke for nearly four hours to over 7,000 people at the Excel Arena and managed to keep us all engaged and motivated throughout his entire presentation. How did he do this? One way he kept us all energised was by continuously changing our state. Tony would talk and then get us up out of our seats and give the person next to us a shoulder massage. Half an hour later, he would get us to jump up and down. He understood that in order for the audience to stay interested in his material, we needed to stay engaged and one way to do this was to ensure that everyone's energy levels stayed high. I am not suggesting that you go around giving your colleagues shoulder massages (although you may choose to) but rather that you plan on doing short, focused bursts of work and then take a quick five minute break and go for a walk. Although this can seem counterintuitive, it actually boosts team member productivity and increases levels of focus.

Horses, too, are very sensitive to the energy of the environment that they are in, with the result that their entire temperament can alter if they are in an energy state that does not resonate with them. Two of my friends have experienced this phenomenon when they have stabled their ex-racehorses on yards that are noisy and busy with activity. On both occasions, their respective horses started to exhibit all kinds of stable vices like weaving (rocking back and forth), crib-biting, wind-sucking and box-walking. However, when the horses were moved to smaller, quieter yards, these behaviours (which are typically deemed undesirable in the equine world) disappeared.

If the horses are so sensitive to the energy of the environment, it stands to reason that they are super-sensitive to the different energies people emit; hence the fact that they are "energy barometers". They read the energy and intent behind all our actions and can therefore challenge us when we are incongruent in what we are asking of them.

TEAMS UNPLUGGED

Just as business follows the energy of the seasons, it follows that team members who are part of the business also have a rhythm. This is called their *personal rhythm*. Everyone has certain times in the day when they are most productive. I do my best work first thing in the morning – that is when I'm most creative. My low point is usually around lunchtime and then I tend to get a burst of energy in the evening. *Joined Up Leaders* appreciate that each team member has their own rhythm and so allow flexible working hours. This means that if you are a morning person, you can come in early and leave early, or if you are more of an evening person, you might not come into work until lunchtime and then work later into the evening.

Operating a flexible work schedule means that there must be trust between all parties that the work will get completed. Also, good communication is required by team members to ensure that there is always sufficient coverage within the team to meet the customers' needs.

With business becoming more global than ever, there is a competitive advantage to having office coverage for more than just the traditional work hours, as you can then more easily service the demands of clients across borders.

In addition to the personal rhythm to each day, there is also a personal rhythm to the year. Just like nature goes through the seasons, our body passes through the seasons – having times when our energy level is high and times when it is low. Vacations are designed to help team members unplug, rest and recuperate. They are the equivalent of the winter season on the farm and are required so that team members can come back with more energy and focus.

Yet according to a March 2012 survey of 952 employees for the job and career site Glassdoor, some 15% of US employees who were entitled to paid vacation time haven't used any of it in the past year. [44]

Ignoring vacations is a deadly short-term tactic, harming long-term business health.

Chronic focus on the short term always has negative long-term implications. A division of Computer Sciences Corp. (CSC) lost 80% of its revenue and employees as burnout drove people away. Unused vacation days is a simple metric of a company culture that values short-term benefits over long-term performance, and a culture that supports fear over results.

The ill effects of not taking vacation, documented in research, include fatigue, poor morale, heart problems and reduced productivity. Vacation resistors cause problems for the entire office; often they refuse to delegate duties and they make colleagues feel guilty. Many fear that if they go on vacation, they will be seen as weak. Somehow there seems to be a badge of honour for not taking vacation and yet when team members get an opportunity to truly unplug (no email or office phone calls during vacation), they come back more creative, innovative, motivated and happy.

Recently, Richard Branson, founder and chairman of the Virgin Group, instigated a "non-policy" for paid time off.[45] This decision means that all of Virgin's team members in the company's main offices in the US and the UK now have open-ended access to vacation time. Branson got the idea from Netflix, another early adopter of the vacation non-policy, along with several other tech firms like Zynga, Groupon, Evernote, VMware, Eventbrite, and HubSpot.

However, even when this policy is in place, some team members still do not take vacation time. This is why Evernote pays its team members $1,000 to get away, disconnect from work and "come back with a stretched-out mind".[46] Team members have to go away for at least one week to get the cash. When in 2012 FullContact started offering each of its team members $7,500 a year to help finance a non-working vacation, the use of vacation time rose sharply, with team members taking on average about 10 days vacation each.[47]

Here are three reasons why team members actually get more done when they have open-ended access to vacation time:

1. **It makes them less anxious.** With our ageing population, now, more than ever, team members have elderly relatives they might need to care for. When life throws up a curveball that doesn't fit within the standard vacation framework, team members can respond without feeling stress and anxiety about using all of their vacation time caring for others or, indeed, recovering themselves from an illness. Special circumstances like these emphasise the point that the right number of days off for each person will vary from year to year based on circumstances. An open policy makes it possible to accommodate individual needs as they arise. Periodically, too, we should all be able to relax and take a well-deserved break for no good reason – even (or sometimes especially) if we've run out of our fixed number of vacation days.

2. **It implies trust, which breeds responsibility.** Many employers are concerned that team members may take advantage of the organisation by taking too much time off, damaging business results. However, if you've hired the right people and trust them to manage their own calendars,

they won't abuse the non-policy. In fact, most will likely take less time off than if you had a formal policy. With freedom comes great responsibility, and effective team members are living proof of this principle.

3. **It makes people happier and inspires them to work harder.** *Joined Up Leaders*' faith that team members won't abuse the policy generally is linked to their culture. If part of the company culture and values relate to team members always having the business' best interests at heart, the team members are committed to doing right by the company and productivity actually increases. This is because, in addition to being very thoughtful about their workload versus vacation time, when team members do decide to take time off, they work even harder beforehand to make sure that they're not leaving other team members in the lurch.

In conclusion, the environment directly impacts productivity and therefore profitability, so how can you change the environment to boost performance? Whilst you might not be able to implement all the ideas in this chapter and have separate areas for conducting each of the different activities by energy type, you can recognise your own personal rhythm and those of the team members working with you. Simply acknowledging this and working with a rhythm that suits you will immediately experience improve performance as will batching activities together that have the same energy type.

Chapter Fourteen:

Harnessing Nature's Natural Rhythm

Takeaways:
- The cycle of business exactly matches the natural patterns of nature, experiencing spring, summer, autumn and winter energy.
- When business gets out of balance, it self corrects – witness the ups and down of the stock market.
- Industries run through different cycles and industries run through different cycles in different countries.
- The big error that many business owners make is that because they fail to realise when they have moved from one season to the next, they continue with the same strategies when a new approach is needed.
- The trick to achieving more with less and becoming more productive is to realise that where team members do activities is as important as *when* they do them.
- Plan your schedule and work location to match your natural rhythms.
- Encourage team members to unplug from the business for vacation. They will come back more creative and motivated, seeing things from a different perspective.

Action:
You can download a worksheet to help you identify the right place for you to conduct each type of activity in your business at *www.on-the-hoof.com/resources*.

I hate to speak
about individuals.
Players don't
win you trophies,
teams win trophies,
squads win trophies.

José Mourinho

CHAPTER FIFTEEN: CREATING A WIN-WIN SITUATION

"TRUST IS THE GLUE THAT HOLDS EVERYTHING TOGETHER. IT CREATES THE ENVIRONMENT IN WHICH ALL OF THE OTHER ELEMENTS — WIN-WIN STEWARDSHIP AGREEMENTS, SELF-DIRECTING INDIVIDUALS AND TEAMS, ALIGNED STRUCTURES AND SYSTEMS, AND ACCOUNTABILITY — CAN FLOURISH."

STEPHEN M. R. COVEY

The macroeconomic conditions of business are tough. Today more than ever, success in business is about so much more than the financial numbers which, as we have already seen, focus the business on one stakeholder's needs at the expense of another. Instead, it is about creating win-win situations. Only then can all aspects of the business be in balance. A conscious business empowers, collaborates and decentralises – resulting in continual innovation and creation of multiple value for all stakeholders.

The harsh fact is that businesses often fail because they don't have a high enough degree of innovation, co-operation and collaboration. Inevitably, a competitor comes along with a superior teamwork, co-operation, collaboration and interdependency, and eventually the less effective business is unable to compete. Take Southwest Airlines as an example. They used to be a small, inconsequential airline operator and yet today, through taking an innovative approach to their business, they have now become one of the most profitable and valuable airlines in the United States.

For business to be successful in the twenty-first century, it is imperative that it fosters an entrepreneurial spirit amongst team members. Long-term, sustainable competitive advantage is achieved through out-innovating the competition in ways that enhance efficiency and create greater value for customers. To achieve this, team members need to be unleashed and allowed to tap into their own genius. Imagine the impact if every single person working for a company were able to create and innovate. Imagine how much more intellectual capital would be available to the business, as each person would be accessing their full potential, making a real contribution and be in Flow. It would be a win-win situation for everyone.

Contrast this with the traditional control and command structures where the message to team members is typically something like,

"We don't pay you to think: we just pay you to do your job". As a result, great opportunities to be creative and innovative are lost because the team members interfacing with the customers do not feel empowered to make decisions and challenge the status quo. Ironically, the one thing that the command and control structure seeks to achieve in fact hampers business growth as resources are not optimised and business opportunities are wasted.

Whole Foods is a great example of a company that has managed to empower their team members by creating a workplace based on love and care and that is also fun, where team members aren't afraid and collaboration reigns. It is this release of creativity and innovation that has enabled the company to improve and evolve rapidly.

Without a collaborative culture, this innovation and creativity would have been of limited value. It is no good for one business unit to come up with a great idea and then not share it with the rest of their colleagues. A culture of collaboration enables successful ideas and innovations to be shared and spread rapidly throughout the business. The great thing is that technology can help rapidly disseminate the information so new ideas can be almost instantly put into action. With even more Big Data metrics than ever before, businesses can effectively monitor and track how these new initiatives are impacting business performance.

This continual review process creates the opportunity for continual learning and improvement within the business. In this set up, business truly becomes a living system that learns, grows, evolves, self-organises – and even self-actualises – on its own. The right degree of decentralisation, empowerment, love and care in the workplace enables business to adapt, innovate and evolve faster enabling them to enjoy strong, sustainable competitive advantage.

BALANCING ENTREPRENEURSHIP WITH BUREAUCRACY

As businesses grow, the challenge for business leaders is to strike a balance between fostering the spirit of entrepreneurship and innovation and having some stability, order and control in the form of bureaucracy. Business processes and systems are required to make everything function smoothly.

Within nature, we have the perfect model for any business to create this balance and harmony. There are systems everywhere but none are so oppressive that they take the system as a whole out of balance. In fact, nature is consistent over time and this helps us feel secure and safe.

We know that every day the sun will rise and then set – but there is fluidity in this. It is not rigid and fixed; sunrise and sunset times vary with the seasons.

The sun, as the centre of the solar system, provides light and warmth. Weather systems and ecosystems supply ongoing food and water. Our bodies give us many years of service thanks to 11 continuously operating internal systems – digestive, nervous, circulatory, muscular, and so forth. Each of these systems is responsible for a very specific result, and each must perform consistently to maintain the health of the body.

Business systems provide the framework for creating successful businesses. They streamline operations and save companies time, energy and money. They ensure consistency of service; and yet these systems are adaptable and can be changed to respond to changing market conditions.

Here are some examples of great businesses that have all built their success around innovative and powerful systems:

- McDonald's restaurants introduced a system of fast and convenient food. They've now built over 36,200 stores worldwide that systematically produce the same menu utilising low-cost labour.

- Federal Express created a revolutionary system to deliver packages overnight by using a central hub.

- COSTCO sells merchandise at cost (plus about 11% administration) and makes their profit on a system of membership fees.

- Walt Disney amusement parks have rides (fun systems) that move large numbers of people quickly and efficiently to prevent long waits. The parks are also immaculately clean. Disney has thousands of systems that give customers a happy and memorable experience.

- Amazon.com is an Internet system that provides the most inexpensive, easy to evaluate, easy to buy and complete selection of books (and other products) found anywhere.

- Wal-Mart has built an unmatched logistics system that efficiently moves vast quantities of merchandise to and from regional warehouses all over the world.

These businesses, and many others, have built their fortunes on remarkable systems that serve customers better than anyone else in their target market. Their systems are innovative and creative and most likely came into existence because team members were empowered to speak up and come up with ideas that helped them serve the customer better. Great companies are made on great ideas, and great ideas come from those closest to the customer.

PUTTING THE CART BEFORE THE HORSE

Systems provide a way to help *Joined Up Leaders* know if the business is on track – but only if the systems and the processes within them align with the business strategy. For far too long, technology has been driving business strategy rather than being an enabler.

> *"Make technology the enabler, not the driver, of your Joined Up Business Strategy."*
>
> Julia Felton

The real fact of the matter is that today we have more systems collecting more data than ever before, so intuitively we should be better at managing businesses and taking decisions to course correct when required; and assuming that everyone has bought into the company vision and purpose, this will result in a win-win for everyone.

As businesses become more decentralised and collaboration increases between team members (some of which will be geographically remote), business dashboards provide a way to easily and quickly communicate to everyone how a project or business process is working. Dashboards enable accountability and show the team how they are performing. There is nothing more demoralising for team members than to be given a project and then have no visibility on how they are doing. Access to regular business metrics helps team members see their contribution to the project and the business. And as we discussed in Chapter Seven, feeling valued and knowing you are playing a part in the success of the business is a big driver for team member engagement and productivity.

> *"We treasure what we measure. The secret of success is when we measure what we treasure."*
>
> **Roger J. Hamilton**

SYSTEMS FAILURE

Even though the premise in business is to create a win-win and have a business ecosystem that is in balance, just like in nature there are times when it fails. When the natural ecosystem fails, it is put back into balance – sometimes by cataclysmic events such as tsunamis and earthquakes.

A business as an entity can suffer systemic failure too. This typically occurs in the whole system or high-level system, where there is a failure between and within the system elements that need to work together for overall success. Factors in systemic failure may include confused goals, weak system-wide understanding, flawed design, individual incentives that encourage loyalty to subordinate (rather than superordinate) goals, inadequate feedback, poor co-operation, lack of accountability, etc.

Whole system failure may co-exist alongside functional success. The leadership of silos may individually be successful but not be sufficiently integrated into the whole system owing to a shortcoming of systems design, management or understanding. In cases of systemic failure, individual executives who operate at a lower sub-system level may be free of responsibility and blame. They may argue (correctly) that it was the wider system that failed. They may claim that particular systems that integrate with their own work let them down. However, responsibility and accountability for the successful design and running of the (integrated) "whole system" should rest somewhere.

Whole system success requires a performance management system that is pitched above the level of individual systems and their functional leadership. Features may include group or team-level goal setting, development, incentives, communication, reviews, rewards and accountability. The aim is to focus on what binds individuals together and what binds systems together, rather than functional silo performance. A whole system can succeed only through managers collaborating in and across a number of functional systems. The whole system can fail only if leadership at the level of the whole system fails, and where several senior managers are involved, hence such failure may be labelled a systemic failure of leadership.

Understanding and anticipating how the whole system is intended to work, how it actually works and how it may buckle under pressure, can practically elude and defeat many executives. To avoid censure for this tough challenge, they sometimes seek recourse to the often hollow mantra "lessons will be/have been learned". They also try to divert attention and reassure investors by referring to a single bad apple (e.g. a 'rogue trader') behind which usually lurks a systemic failure. The leadership challenge is accentuated by the realisation that for every legitimate, official or consciously designed system (which is intended to be, and is supposedly, rational), there is a shadow system. The shadow system is where all the non-rational issues reside e.g. politics, trust, hopes, ambitions, greed, favours, power struggles, etc.

The system can confuse, overpower, block and fail leadership. But leadership can also fail the system. When a major failure of leadership occurs within, across or down an organisation, it's referred to as 'systemic'. This is what we are experiencing in business today. Many leaders just aren't up to the job of leading through relentless change, as they have not been given the opportunity to develop the emotional capabilities required to lead a business in the twenty-first century. Our existing leadership programmes are flawed as so many focus on developing leadership competencies rather than leadership character traits.

The stark reality is that leaders who are not emotionally agile cannot deal with the plethora of situations thrown at them and leaders who have any degree of being self-serving will tend to block opportunities for shared leadership and the creation of a collaborative and co-operative culture, one where team members are empowered to access their hidden potential and be in flow delivering value to the business. Emotional agility is as essential trait for a successful leader in today's world of business.

Chapter Fifteen:

Creating A Win-Win Situation

Takeaways:
- Unleashing the entrepreneurial spirit amongst team members creates a win-win situation.
- Innovation and creativity without collaboration is of limited value to the business as ideas get stuck in silos and are not implemented.
- Strike a balance between fostering the spirit of entrepreneurship and innovation and having some stability, order and control in the form of bureaucracy.
- Business processes and systems are required to make everything function smoothly.
- Dashboards provide a way for the business to share key metrics with team members and so improve communication and accountability.
- Appreciate that systems failure can happen and when it does, step up and intervene promptly.
- Leaders need to be emotionally agile and work with the system to prevent blockages.

SECTION THEE:

OVER THE FINISH LINE

"A Joined Up business evolves when the people, processes and playground (environment) are aligned. The result is a purpose driven, productive and profitable business."

Julia Felton

> When a team outgrows individual performance and learns team confidence, excellence becomes a reality.
>
> Joe Paterno

CHAPTER SIXTEEN: ENERGISING A HIGH-PERFORMANCE CULTURE

> "OUR JOB IS TO PROVIDE A CULTURE IN WHICH PEOPLE CAN FLOURISH AND REACH THEIR DREAMS — IN WHICH THEY CAN BE ALL THEY WANT TO BE."
>
> JACK WELCH

Culture is made up of the collective habits and behaviours of all the teams and individuals involved in the business and a high-performance culture can only result when all the three foundational cornerstones intersect to evolve a *Joined Up* business. At the point of overlap where leadership meets the team and a supportive environment, extraordinary results can occur. And in today's data-driven society, this is the place from which empowered decisions, based on data, can be confidently made.

Decisions can be made confidently because all the stakeholders are actively engaged in the success of the enterprise and are empowered to do what it takes to create success. There is no fear of redress for making a bad decision so long as lessons are learned and corrective action is taken. As a result, team members do not try to sabotage the success of the business (knowingly or not); they are instead invested in creating open, honest communication where everyone collaborates and co-operates as this ensures everyone wins.

The culture of a business describes the character of a group of people and how they think and act as a collective. A company with a strong character will have a culture that promotes caring and treating all people well, regardless of rank and role in the business. Team members will feel protected within the company and know that colleagues have their back. This contrasts with a culture of weak character, where people feel that any protection they have comes from their ability to manage politics, promote their own success and watch their own backs.

The purpose of a healthy, high-performance culture is to support the long-term success of the business. Culture drives business results and a healthy culture creates a fulfilling place to work. In shaping culture, it is important to know what strategies, business goals and initiatives the business's behaviours are there to support.

In their book, *Corporate Culture and Performance*, John P. Kotter and James L. Heskett document the connection between strong cultures and exceptional results. After following a number of companies over a ten-year period, they concluded that *"businesses that better lived their value statements were more effective, because their managers and leaders consistently exhibited the behaviours needed to win. Shared values create a template for both corporate and individual behaviour. When these values are clearly stated and accepted by all members of the business, they set guidelines and standards for making decisions, determining priorities, solving problems and addressing competitive pressures."*[48]

CULTURAL EROSION

One of the challenges in business is that culture is not permanent.

I was fortunate (!) to witness cultural transformation and experience both these sides to business culture whilst working at Andersen. When I joined the firm in 1996, it was aspiring to be one of the top accountancy firms in the world. It had a great reputation and people really wanted to work there. There was a lot of kudos to say you worked for what was in those days Arthur Andersen. Everyone had pride in their job, and for me personally it was an honour to be headhunted into the company to set up their specialist hospitality research and business intelligence team.

For the first four years or so, things went really well. Business was booming, my team was growing and everyone was inspired to achieve great things. The business unit I was leading was growing fast and expanding rapidly across the world. Things were good.

I don't know exactly when the cultural transformation started. At the time, the company had some 85,000 employees worldwide and the business was strongly managed from its US headquarters in

307

Chicago, where Arthur Andersen had set up the business in 1913. Ironically, the founder Arthur Andersen had been a zealous supporter of high standards in the accounting industry. A stickler for honesty, he argued that accountants' responsibility was to investors, not their clients' management. As mentioned earlier, during the early years it is reputed that Andersen was approached by an executive from a local rail utility to sign off on accounts containing flawed accounting, or else face the loss of a major client. Andersen refused in no uncertain terms, replying that there was "not enough money in the city of Chicago" to make him do it. For many years, Andersen's motto was "Think straight, talk straight."

So it is ironic that Andersen's demise should be caused by alleged complicity as an auditor for the energy giant Enron. On 15th June 2002, Andersen was convicted of obstruction of justice for shredding documents related to its audit of Enron, resulting in the Enron scandal. Although the conviction was later reversed by the Supreme Court, the impact of the scandal combined with the findings of criminal complicity ultimately destroyed the firm.

It was during the ten months from October 2001 to August 2002 (from when the Enron scandal was announced to the time that Andersen agreed to surrender its CPA licenses) that the cultural shift clearly began to emerge in the UK firm. With the underpinning character of the business in tatters, impersonal dopamine-driven measurements took over. Team members' results-driven chemicals fell out of balance, and trust and co-operation became diluted. It was a tough time to lead a business unit, when there was so much fear and uncertainty. Would we all lose our jobs? If not, who would take over the company? Anxiety and stress levels were high, and not unsurprisingly many people jumped ship, not waiting to see what might happen.

Goldman Sachs is another company that has seen the character of its culture change significantly in the past decade. Once a revered place to work, in the late 2000s a former Goldman's employee referred to the company as having an atmosphere of ruthlessness, with managers pitting one team against the next as they fought for a project or client. He described the environment as having no trust, no mutual respect and no accountability when things went wrong. The environment was one of "win at all costs". The result was that this employee and a number of co-workers left. It was just too much for a human being to put up with, maintain their sanity and be happy.

The editorial by Greg Smith, an executive director of Goldman Sachs, in the *New York Times* on 14th March 2012, revealed the extent to which this toxic character had infiltrated the business:

"The culture was the secret sauce that made this place great and allowed us to earn our clients' trust for 143 years. It wasn't about making money; this alone will not sustain a firm for so long. It had something to do with pride and belief in the organisation. I am sad to say that I look around today and see virtually no trace of the culture that made me love working for the firm for many years. I no longer have the pride, or the belief. Leadership used to be about ideas, setting an example and doing the right thing. Today, if you make enough money for the firm (and are not currently an axe murderer) you will be promoted into a position of influence."[49]

BEYOND THE CALL OF DUTY

Business success is inextricably linked to corporate culture, which in turn is a combined result of leadership, teamwork and the environment (the three foundational cornerstones). When team members feel unsupported and are not connected to the purpose of the business, then inferior results occur. The contrary is also true. In a corporate culture that encourages and rewards people for helping and sharing everything they learn, collaboration and real innovation is possible. Team members excel and go beyond the call of duty.

One of the most poignant examples of team members going beyond the call of duty happened at the Taj Mahal Palace Hotel in November 2008 after terrorists attacked the hotel with automatic weapons. Team members risked their own lives to save the guests. There are stories of telephone operators who, having got out safely, went back into the hotel to help guests, and of kitchen staff who formed a human shield to protect the guests. The hotel general manager, Karambir Singh Kang, who lived in the hotel with his family, calmly supervised the evacuation of hundreds of trapped guests, even though his own family, trapped within the confines of the hotel, were in mortal danger.

On that fatal day, 31 people died; 11 of them were team members, in addition to the general manager's wife and two sons. So why did the team members act so bravely? The reason is the culture the leaders had instilled in the business. As one of the finest hotels in the world, the Taj Group insists that their team members put the interests of the guests before that of the company, and they are often rewarded for doing so.

True to their word, after the event the Tata Group, owners of the Taj Mahal Hotel, recognised the sacrifice of the team members; Ratan

Tata and other senior company leaders attended all 11 funerals and visited the families of all 80 team members who were killed or injured. Within 20 days, Tata had established a new trust to provide assistance to all those who were injured and to the families of those who were killed. Tata provided compensation to the families for every deceased member ranging from $80,0000 to $187,000, and in addition they:

- *Guaranteed that deceased team members' residences would be provided to the family through the lifetime of the next of kin*
- *Waived all loans and advances, regardless of amount*
- *Committed to paying the team members' last full salary for life*
- *Took complete responsibility for the education of children and dependents through college – anywhere in the world*
- *Provided full health care coverage for all dependents for the rest of their lives*
- *Provided a counsellor for life for each person*

The actions of all parties involved in this tragedy – the team members and the business owners – clearly demonstrated the symbiotic relationships that everyone had with each other. There was no "me" happening at this time but rather everyone rallied around collectively to support each other. There was camaraderie, collaboration and co-operation, which resulted in a level of performance and commitment that surpassed what anyone else thought was possible.

By demonstrating great leadership (expand the leader), empowering others to act and having engaged the environment, the Tata Group had energised a culture where individuals accessed their hidden 90% of potential and went beyond what could have reasonably been expected of them. Through the creation of a purpose-driven business, they had aligned individual and business needs and fostered a spirit and culture that in the face of adversity could not be destroyed. This is truly an example of a great Joined Up Business. [50]

IMPROVED CULTURE: IMPROVED RESULTS

A company's culture can be a severe constraint on its success or a source of strength and sustained competitive advantage. It takes effort to keep all three foundational cornerstones aligned and operating interdependently and yet when companies do this, success can be significant. As James Heskett of the Harvard Business School noted: *"A strong culture can help or hurt performance. Culture can account for up to half the difference in operating profit between two organisations in the same business. Shaping a culture is one of the leader's most important jobs; it can be ignored, but only for so long and at one's peril".*

Trust and transparency are the two main characteristics of a business culture that directly impact results. As can be seen in the following graph, when there is high trust and high transparency in business, high performance results as the business is in Flow. When there is low trust and low transparency, fear and suspicion result. In this environment of fear, the "me" attitude kicks in and individual engage in business sabotage in a misguided attempt to protect themselves.

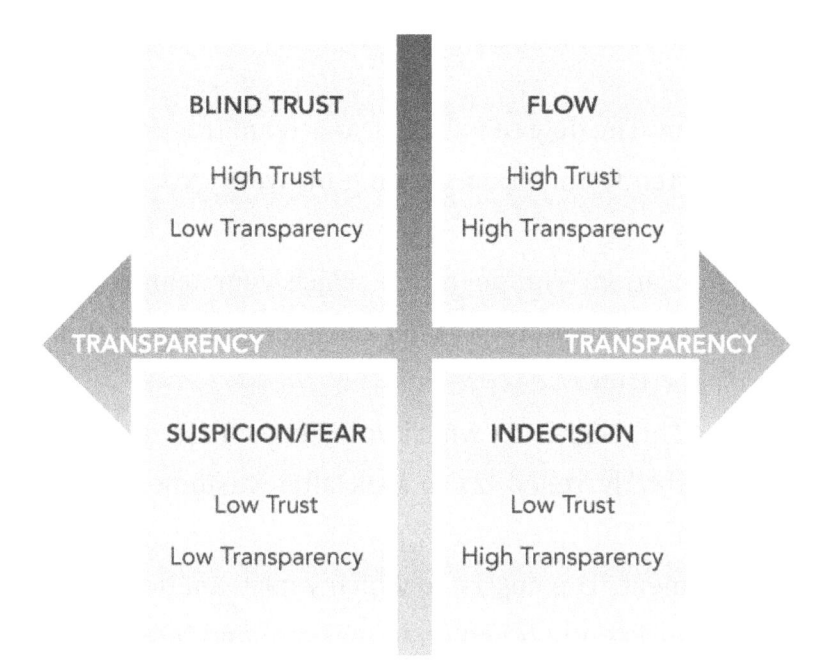

BLIND TRUST	**FLOW**
High Trust	High Trust
Low Transparency	High Transparency
SUSPICION/FEAR	**INDECISION**
Low Trust	Low Trust
Low Transparency	High Transparency

← TRANSPARENCY — TRANSPARENCY →

So how do you measure trust and transparency in a business? One way is through team member and 360 degree feedback loops. These allow individuals to share their thoughts (sometimes in an anonymous fashion) with business leaders, peers and subordinates. *The Personal Social Responsibility 360 Barometer* is great to use as it specifically measures the degree of trust that other team members have with you and also how you create and add to the Flow in the company.

> **You can find out more about *The Personal Social Responsibility 360 Barometer* and how it can enable team members to increase their personal awareness and responsibility of how they are showing up in the team, whilst also providing insights to the entire team on the importance of collective accountability to improve the levels of Trust and Flow within the team at *www.businesshorsepower.com/psr***

Trust is measured in five areas, namely:

1. Innovation: The degree to which your team trusts that you can be consistently relied on to come up with creative solutions and plans.
2. Communication: The degree to which your team trusts that you can be consistently relied on to share information and listen effectively.
3. Service: The degree to which your team trusts that you can be consistently relied on to look after customers and team members.
4. Measurement: The degree to which your team trusts that you can be consistently relied on to measure and refine your own performance.
5. Spirit: The degree to which your team trusts that you can be consistently relied on to remain resilient and positive.

Whilst Flow is measured in terms of:

1. Initiative: The degree to which your team experience that you consistently contribute your ideas and plans for improvement effectively, such that they add to the success of the company.
2. Respect: The degree to which your team experience that you consistently collect and share suggestions and feedback from customers and partners with the team for effective action, resolution and improvement.
3. Presence: The degree to which your team experience that you consistently invest the time to be present for the team, and to be proactive in seeking and finding solutions to improve the well-being and harmony of the team.

4. Discipline: The degree to which your team experience that you consistently maintain a high level of caring and sharing in how you manage time, performance measures and financial responsibility.
5. Perseverance: The degree to which your team experience that you consistently work with the end in mind and find paths to success for the team and company without giving up.

Furthermore, the success of any business is also measured in its financial results – revenue, profits, earnings per share – as well as in terms of its contribution to society. In *Firms of Endearment: How World Class Companies Profit From Passion and Purpose*, Raj Sisodia and his co-authors discovered that companies with great corporate cultures, and which focused on all the stakeholders benefiting from the companies existence, over a 15-year period outperformed the S&P 500 index by a factor of 10.5. Whilst the authors had anticipated that well-managed businesses with loyal team members and customers would perform well for investors, as they have a holistic, well-balanced approach to business and focus on delivering value, what surprised them was the extent to which these businesses outperformed the market.

The fact that purpose-driven companies with a high-performance culture outperform the market has also been reported by Gallup, which has found that in high-performance businesses the ratio of "engaged" to "non-engaged" team members is a ratio of 10:1, compared to a ratio of 1.8:1 for average companies. Clearly, therefore, the benefits of mastering the three foundational cornerstones of the *Joined Up Business Blueprint™* are fundamental to evolving a high-performance culture.

CASE STUDY:

SOUTHWEST AIRLINES

Whenever a business wants to shift direction, implement a new strategy, change their structure or execute a new system, culture comes into play. In the airline industry, Southwest Airlines in particular provides a great example of that.

Southwest's culture is one that clearly supports its strategy. This has led to Southwest consistently being a winning business. That is understandable, because firms with long-term success usually have cultures aligned to support their strategy and structure.

Southwest is a low-cost airline that executes rapid turnaround in preparing planes for their next flight and offsets some of the inconvenience of travel with humour. They have an efficient route structure as well as a job structure that allows people to share jobs and be very responsive to whatever it takes to get the plane back in the air quickly.

People at Southwest are highly collaborative and flexible. Everybody, from the gate agents to the flight attendants and even the pilots, pitches in to prepare the plane for turnaround. Southwest is able to turn planes around in roughly half the time of many other airlines.

Additionally, Southwest is the only airline that has made money every year for the past five years "in the turbulent airline industry. Its strategy has always been to provide low-cost, point-to-point travel in a way that is appealing to customers. The key to doing that is embedded in the culture."

The low-cost message is further communicated in the culture through practices such as flight attendants wearing shorts and polo shirts in the warmer months, and through the fun they have with the fact that people "fly for peanuts". Their values focus on accountability through ownership and commitment, healthy state of mind through their positive attitudes, collaboration through teamwork, and flexibility and agility in dealing with change.

In many ways, you could say that culture is Southwest's main strategy. As former CEO Herb Kelleher has said, "We market ourselves based on the personality and spirit of Southwest."

To systematically create and sustain their culture, people are carefully selected and oriented to fit their brand and constant reinforcement takes place. The flight attendants, customer service reps and baggage handlers are encouraged to take whatever action they feel is appropriate to meet customer needs or help fellow workers, even if that means breaking company policies. When team members make mistakes in judgement, they are rarely punished, but instead are given feedback and coaching on how to improve next time. There is even a tradition of celebrating errors with the intent of turning those lessons into personal growth opportunities. All of these cultural practices reinforce the self-worth of employees.

There is a strong emphasis on what we would call "organisational health" or people's state of mind.

A portion of Southwest Airlines' mission statement states that customer service will be "delivered with a sense of warmth, friendliness, individual pride and company spirit."

> *Southwest's culture is a reflection of its leader, former CEO Kelleher. He is famous for his humorous and eccentric behaviour. He has rolled up on his Harley at 2:00 a.m. to host parties for mechanics working the night shift. He has worn costumes and sung rap songs at company events. He has served beverages and handed out snacks to passengers alongside flight attendants. At the same time, he's been a hard-working, results-focused leader.*
>
> *As a result, the culture is an interesting blend, in which people take their jobs very seriously, but don't take themselves too seriously. This leads to a light-hearted spirit and comfortable informality that is directly translated into the customer experience.*

CULTURAL MISMATCH

In Chapter Ten, we examined the implications of hiring the wrong people, people who were not a cultural fit into the team. Just as team members can be a mismatch, so can other companies. As business becomes more global, the need for collaboration between companies across the globe will increase. Mergers and acquisitions are more common than ever in today's business climate. The chances are, if you haven't yet worked at a company going through some sort of integration, you will.

Yet studies show that many – if not most – mergers are doomed to fail. The failures result in poor shareholder returns, lay-offs and, in some cases, a complete dissolution of the merger.

Why? Sometimes, as with MCI WorldCom and Sprint, they fall apart due to regulatory pressure before they ever take place. Sometimes, as with Quaker and Snapple, it is because one company overestimated the worth of the other – and overpaid. Sometimes, as with Kmart and Sears, it is simply poor product, market or resource synergy.

When mergers come up, these are the causes often discussed. But **culture**, in part because it is so difficult to measure or manage, is all-too-often overlooked. Yet according to The Society for Human Resource Management (SHRM), over 30% of mergers fail because of simple culture incompatibility. [51]

An example of a successful corporate merger was that of Andersen UK and Deloitte UK. From an insider's perspective working in the firm at the time, there were definite challenges but overall, to me as a team member, the integration appeared pretty seamless. It is not surprising, therefore, that the then Andersen UK Managing Partner, John Ormerod, is quoted as saying: *"We see a strong cultural fit between the firms' partner groups, and are confident that our partners and staff will prosper under the Deloitte banner".*

Contrast this with the failed $350 billion merger of Time Warner with AOL, where a culture clash was widely blamed for the failure of the joint venture. Richard Parsons, president of Time Warner, is quoted as saying: *"I remember saying at a vital board meeting where we approved this, that life was going to be different going forward because they're very different cultures, but I have to tell you, I underestimated how different… It was beyond certainly my abilities to figure out how to blend the old media and the new media culture".* The result was that in 2008, you could buy Time Warner stock for less than $15, down from a high in January 2000 of $71.88.

This example clearly reveals the importance of culture to the success of any business, and if there is a mismatch, the consequences can be dire. The outcome of a *Joined Up* business which *Energises The Culture* in effect forms the heart of the business. It is what

319

can create and sustain business success, and it is what can cause businesses to fail. The health of a business is a direct reflection of the health of its heart (aka its culture).

Chapter Sixteen:

Creating a High-Performance Culture

Takeaways:
- The culture of a business describes the character of a group of people and how they think and act as collective.
- Trust and transparency are the two main characteristics of business culture that directly impact results.
- Business success is inextricably linked to corporate culture.
- Culture fit is a key consideration, not just when hiring team members, but also when considering potential joint venture and business partners.
- The best deals on paper will never succeed unless the business cultures of the two businesses can be aligned.
- The health of a business is a direct reflection of the health of its heart (aka its culture).

History has shown that one cannot legislate a culture of integrity. And yet, one of the paramount responsibilities and challenges of corporate leadership is to ensure such a culture.

Preet Bharara

CHAPTER SEVENTEEN: ALL JOINED UP

"A STRONG CULTURE CAN HELP OR HURT PERFORMANCE. CULTURE CAN ACCOUNT FOR UP TO HALF THE DIFFERENCE IN OPERATING PROFIT BETWEEN TWO ORGANISATIONS IN THE SAME BUSINESS. SHAPING A CULTURE IS ONE OF A LEADER'S MOST IMPORTANT JOBS: IT CAN BE IGNORED, BUT ONLY FOR SO LONG AND AT ONE'S PERIL."

JAMES HESKETT, HARVARD BUSINESS SCHOOL

In a sense, you don't change culture but rather you shift the behaviours of individuals within the culture by creating a business that is *Joined Up*. Behaviour change needs to be led in the first instance by the *Joined Up Leader* being aligned within themselves and acting in a consistent, congruent manner. This is why Edgar Schein says, *"Culture is not a surface phenomenon, it is our very core."*

If change is taking place, it is observable and therefore it is measurable. The key thing to remember is that business transformation will not take place without personal transformation. Just like a body cannot change without the individual cells that comprise the body changing, business cannot change unless all the stakeholders within the business change and a business structure that accommodates the change is created.

When a team and a business can learn to operate in a healthier state by being *Joined Up*, they can dramatically increase their performance. They can:

- Reach good decisions more easily and quickly
- Be more supportive internally and more competitive externally
- Align and positively energise the business
- Handle whatever comes along, with greater grace and ease

This is the type of environment that team members would want to work in, one where they feel valued and know they are making a contribution; here they know they can bring the hidden 90% of their potential to work, it is a place where work is fun and engaging.

Creating a business-wide collaborative culture supports high performance on a sustained basis. It unlocks this hidden 90% of human potential and unleashes the productive energy of team members. Productive energy means team members choosing to give of themselves because they are in Flow; it distinguishes high-performance cultures from others. Businesses that succeed in unleashing this hidden aspect of human potential win every time. As Tony Hsieh, CEO of Zappos, said, *"If you get the culture right, most of the other stuff will just take care of itself."*

However, collaboration will look more like chaos if there is no overall framework. There needs to be clarity about how team members should work together to support critical performance priorities. As Jim Collins noted, *"A culture of discipline is not a principle of business; it is a principle of greatness".* Discipline is required to create a framework where the habits and routines are implemented to facilitate change in thinking and behaviour, and in turn enable leveraging and aligning the culture. And why would you do this? Because, as Jim Collins observed, strong, well-aligned cultures are six times more effective than their competitors.

COMMON BARRIERS TO SUCCESS

As we have moved through the three foundational cornerstones, we have identified a number of factors that impede team members accessing the hidden 90% of their potential and so create a high-performing business. Use this checklist to examine which ones, if any, exist in your business:

1. There are no clarity of purpose and shared values that the team members can align with. It is this purpose that is the magnetic force that unleashes the drive, energy, creativity and courage needed to reach an objective. In many ways, a clear vision represents "magnetic north" for employees within a high-performance business. It also represents the idealised picture of what the company and its employees can become. A vision

is much more than just a goal or picture of a future; it evokes a strong feeling. It is the feeling, not the goal, which inspires high energy and commitment.
2. Leaders do not model the way and walk the talk regarding the company values. Leaders fail to exhibit the traits of having courageous impact.
3. Hierarchical top-down tendencies and a boss-driven leadership style mean that team members are not empowered to be creative and deliver real value to the business. Leaders have an entitlement mindset and poor empowerment skills.
4. Team members are not given roles and accountabilities that make best use of and nurture their talents and, as a consequence, the team is unbalanced. This creates internal competition between business units and functions – turf issues and "we-they" attitudes.
5. To escape conflict, honest conversations are avoided and polite but passive-aggressive behaviours result.
6. Decision-making is not delegated down the business for fear of getting it wrong. As a result, bureaucratic tendencies and the need to control stifle creativity and innovation.
7. Lack of agility or ability to quickly adapt. Inability to foster and support diversity of ideas and people. This makes team members feel suffocated and so they don't deliver their best.
8. The business environment fails to recognise change and respond appropriately; there is a lack of knowing when a winning strategy becomes a losing strategy.
9. Lack of accountability, excessive blaming and excuses – "not my fault". There is a win-lose culture.
10. Trust issues and hidden agendas hinder the creation of a high-performance culture.

As *Joined Up Leaders* seek to influence change in their businesses, it is useful to remember that the behaviours required for creating a healthy, high-performance culture are the same ones individuals need to create a fulfilling life. A winning culture in business means collaboration, personal responsibility, learning and growing, respect and trust, to name just a few. These are behaviours we don't have to learn, we are innately born with them, and they show up automatically when we are at our best, in Flow, accessing the hidden 90% of our potential.

How different business and life would be if we all operated from a place of collaboration rather than a place of isolation and 'me-ness'! This is the quest that all *Joined Up Leaders* and business owners are on – to find a way to get more commitment from themselves and others and in doing so create a sustainable workplace that meets the needs of all its stakeholders and adds value to the community within which it operates. For business to succeed in the future, it can no longer be based on exploitation and coercion. Co-operation and voluntary exchange must prevail. Trust must be fostered, both individually and collectively, so that a win-win situation exists for everyone and harmony results.

Apple is one company that has embraced the concept of collaboration and created an innovative *Joined Up* business. Here is what the late Steve Jobs had to share at the D8 Conference in June 2010.

Steve Jobs On The Collaborative Culture At Apple

- *"Apple is an incredibly collaborative company."*
- *"We have no committees at Apple. We are organised like a start-up. One person in charge of each product or area of focus."*

- *"There is tremendous teamwork at the top of the company which filters down to tremendous teamwork throughout the company."*
- *"Teamwork is dependent on trusting the other folks to come through on their part without watching them all the time."*
- *"We're great at figuring out how to divide things up into these great teams that we have and all work on the same thing, touch bases frequently, and bring it together into a product."*
- *"What I do all day is meet with teams of people and work on ideas and solve problems."*
- *"If you want to hire great people and have them stay working for you, you have to let them make a lot of decisions, you have to be run by ideas and not hierarchy."*
- *"The best ideas have to win, otherwise good people don't stay."*

Steve Jobs Interview at D8 Conference, June 2010

Zappos, too, is a company that has fully embraced the concept of collaboration and having a *Joined Up* business; they have taken it a stage further, implementing a structure called a Holacracy. The new system replaces the conventional command-and-control workplace with a series of self-governed teams known as "circles." The framework streamlines and optimises decision-making by honouring multiple perspectives – without getting lost in a swamp of indecision. It respects personal expertise, fuels innovation and invites engagement; sparks creativity and leverages process for purpose-driven results. Recognising that this is currently an unconventional approach to running business, the CEO Tony Hsieh has offered an exit strategy to those team members not sold on this new approach and who feel that they cannot adapt to the organisational changes. This is a great way to ensure that all remaining team members are on board and fully supportive of this new initiative and are working in collaboration to ensure its success because any discord or silo mentality will impact its success and could adversely impact the new business culture.

In conclusion, culture is a measure of the health of a business. It is what sustains business success or brings it crashing down. It is made up of a complex, interrelated and interdependent set of variables – an **Energised Culture** is only possible when the three foundational cornerstones of **Expand The Leader, Empower Others To Act** and **Engage The Environment** are all aligned and operating in harmony to evolve a business that is *Joined Up*.

The business culture is therefore a barometer for the success of the business and if it is in any way out of balance, this is sure sign that something else is misaligned, either within the leadership, with the stakeholders or in the environment. The health of a business's culture is a symptom, not the cause of the problem; the cause will be found at a more foundational level of the business, typically with the business leaders.

It was day seven of my time in Wyoming and at last the sun was shining. In fact, there was a double rainbow over the Dimmock Ranch where I had been staying. As I stood next to my little wild mustang, Cody, I mused on the journey we had taken over the last seven days. To see his transformation had been incredible. Now I was standing next to a proud, courageous little horse, as opposed to the trembling wreck he had been on day one.

He had learnt to trust me. I had to shown up as a leader for him and, by my consistent actions, shown that I was a competent individual with integrity, whom he could trust. I had helped him engage with me and shown him the value of making great decisions. By my learning to communicate with him in his language, we had been able to start a dialogue that had built trust and respect between us.

Furthermore, I had created an environment for him where he could safely explore who he was. I had done this by providing him with a routine and rewarding positive behaviour. Sure, he was out of his comfort zone, being in a pen rather than out on the open range, but I had carefully managed the situation to help him expand his comfort zone, rather than remaining in his fear zone.

It took me three days to even be able to get close enough to touch Cody. Building trust takes time; but once we had this solid foundation in place, his pace of learning rapidly increased. By day four, he was wearing a halter, and on day five I had started to be able to lead him. Now as I stood with him, his new owner, Sue, was cutting off his BLM tag, with his number 0786. He was now officially adopted and had a new home. He was no longer number 0786 but Cody, a proud mustang with a good future. He had excelled and had accessed that 90% of his hidden potential.

Sure, it is early days and Cody has a whole lifetime ahead of time to develop his skills and learn more and more; but like everything, great things start with tiny steps and Cody had taken the first of these. His courageous spirit had pulled him through to heights that seven days prior I had seriously wondered if we could accomplish.

And just as it happened for Cody, creating and responding to change in business takes time. It is a step-by-step process. It won't happen overnight, but if you set up the system and recognise the interrelatedness and interdependence of everything, then change is possible.

Together, all the business stakeholders can co-create a collaborative and co-operative way of working together in a *Joined Up* manner, inspired by the power of the herd and nature's natural laws, where wastage is minimised, and performance and connection are optimised.

A LEADER IS BEST WHEN PEOPLE

BARELY KNOW HE EXISTS,

WHEN HIS WORK IS DONE,

HIS AIM FULFILLED,

THEY WILL SAY:

WE DID IT OURSELVES.

LAO TZU

CHAPTER EIGHTEEN: FINAL THOUGHTS

Having read and understood the concepts of creating a business that is *Joined Up*, many of my clients ask me where do they start. Since developing a *Joined Up* business starts with the developing of *Joined Up Leaders*, I always suggest this is the best starting point. After all, the leader sets the purpose and tone of the business.

So, how do I suggest they do this? Quite frankly, I encourage them to learn straight from the horse's mouth! Yes, really I do suggest that all my clients engage in learning leadership from horses.

Now some of you might think that this sounds strange, but as we have seen, you can't learn leadership in the classroom. It is an embodied process that can only be experienced through being. Partnering with horses allows people to experience first hand many of the qualities of how to lead with courageous impact. Horses teach us how to be authentic, trustworthy, present, pay attention, and be respectful and responsible. Horses model for us how to collaborate and share leadership. They show us how to build relationships and live in harmony with a shared common purpose.

How specifically you be a leader and how you act is as unique and personal to you as your DNA. How I lead is not how you might lead. Our differing perspectives, experiences and frame of reference make learning how to lead a very personal experience. There is no manual to follow, no one formula to follow. The one thing I do know, however, is that horses will provide you with real honest feedback on how effective your leadership has been. If you are not compelling and inspiring, they simple won't want to be with you, and unlike team members, they will vote with their hooves and not engage. This is the power of learning leadership with horses as it allows you to explore what approaches work and which don't and then to calibrate and try something new based on the feedback. Just like your team members, horses are individuals and each one needs to be led differently. If you don't believe me, just try it and experience this for yourself.

Working with horses certainly helps leaders develop agility and learn how to lead On-The-Hoof. You never know what the horse will do. There is no rulebook. Sometimes the horse may decide to stand still, while at other times it might decide to walk. Some days he might run away and others he might connect. Horses teach us how to master our emotions and make informed decisions from a place of vulnerability and uncertainty. They show us how to build trust and respect. After all, you can't simply control 600 kg of horse and if you believe you can, then you are deluding yourself. Like team members, you can only influence, inspire, encourage and motivate, and trust they deliver the outcome you desire. Not because they feel they have to, but because they really want to collaborate and contribute and be part of a partnership focused on something bigger.

Working with horses will test your leadership skills beyond measure revealing to you how persistence, perseverance, adaptability and determination are required to navigate the uncertain conditions that business operates in today. They help you experience the fine balance of combining focus with energy in order to get into flow and the need for clarity in all your communications. Quite simply, the horses are masters at helping you develop authentic communication skills as they read your non-verbal communication cues and if these are misaligned in any way, they will feed that back to you.

When you experience true connection walking with a horse beside you at liberty, with no ropes to keep him in place, then you are both truly *Joined Up* and aligned and connected. By taking this experience back into business leaders report they can now fully engage and access the real power of being *Joined Up* with everything aligned and where true potential is unleashed for the organisations success.

If you are curious to explore more on how horses can help you and your team become *Joined Up Leaders*, then please connect with me for a complimentary consultation to see what is possible for you and your organisation when you take the lessons from the barn and nature and apply them to creating boardroom success.

Do more than is required. What is the distance between someone who achieves their goals consistently and those who spend their lives and careers merely following? The extra mile.

Gary Ryan Blair

ACKNOWLEDGEMENTS

There are so many people that have touched me during my life and that have in some small way contributed to the ideas in this book. The sense of accomplishment and relief at finishing this book has been extraordinary, mainly because the book was not really planned. However, the ideas and concepts that have emerged along the way so define who I am and the legacy I want to leave in the world.

I am indebted to my book coach Ruth Klein for helping to draw this content out of me with her laser questions and for seeing what was possible before I had the slightest inkling of what was happening. She challenged and motivated me in ways that I have never experienced before and kept me on track. She believed in me when sometimes I just thought I was never going to get this completed.

Grateful thanks also go to my good friend Helena Holrick who diligently read the early drafts and provided insightful feedback on the structure and content on the book. Her patience with me did not go unnoticed. She was so inspiring and fun to work with that it made the early edits so much less painful. I am also appreciative of the great work that Jennifer Manson did of providing a thorough edit of this manuscript.

To the team at AuthorCraft, and in particular Chris Day, who guided me on the book publishing journey, dealing with all my unreasonable requests with such great humour. To Richard Duszczak of Cartoon Studio Ltd, who created the inspiring cartoons that really helped bring the book to life.

I am also indebted to the business leaders who so feely shared their valuable time with me to help provide some real insights for the book. Special thanks go to John Connolly, former CEO of Deloitte UK; Karen Boswell, Managing Director of Hitachi Rail Europe; Tony Troy, CEO Principal of Hayley Hotels and Conference Venues; and Hollie Delaney, Head of People Happiness at Zappos.

Thank you, Roger Hamilton and Michelle Clarke, for opening my eyes to Talent Dynamics and first planting the seed that there were lessons that business could learn from nature, if we just opened our eyes. It makes so much sense to me that business is just another ecosystem, but one that typically operates out of balance. What massive potential could be unlocked if we just acknowledged the laws of nature and how they apply to business.

My equine mentor, Carolyn Resnick, needs special recognition for sharing with me her wisdom on herd dynamics and psychology. It is her incredible depth of knowledge and invaluable insights that enabled me to take the lessons of the herd and translate these into how they apply to business, thus bridging the gap between these two worlds and, in doing so, helping me define my true identity.

Finally, thanks go to my amazing herd of horses – Toby, Charlie, Bracken and Thistle – and Bunny and Red, and, of course, little Cody. You have taught me the best business lessons that anyone could ever learn and I am grateful that you now allow me to help others experience the same. You always help keep me *Joined Up*, aligned and authentic.

APPENDIX
JOINED UP BUSINESS ASSESSMENT

JOINED UP BUSINESS BLUEPRINT™ ASSESSMENT

Please answer these questions scoring them on a scale of 1-5 where

1 = No: Activity is not in place or major improvement is needed
2 = Rarely: Activity is sometimes implemented but only when requested
3 = Occasionally: Activity is partially in place but improvement is needed
4 = Mostly: Activity is implemented most of the time
5 = Yes: Activity is consistently and effectively implemented

then total each of the three different sub-sections within the cornerstone to see how you have faired.

	Question:	Rating: 1-5
	EXPAND SELF	
	PURPOSE AND VALUES	
1	Does the business have a clear purpose for why it is in existence?	
2	Is there a clear compelling vision that is consistently communicated and shared with the team?	
3	Are the conditions of success are known and there are team members assigned responsibilities to achieve these?	
	TOTAL	
	LEADING WITH COURAGEOUS IMPACT	
1	Do the leaders walk the talk and do what they say they will do?	
2	Do the leaders share the power as a means for increasing power?	
3	Do the leaders exercise emotional agility and resilience and notice what triggers them?	
	TOTAL	
	EMPOWER RATHER THAN DELEGATE	
1	Do the leaders rely significantly on peer problem solving?	
2	Do the leaders understand the difference between delegation, empowerment and shared leadership and know when to use them?	
3	Do the leaders acknowledge there is more than one way to be right and just because someone doesn't do it their way doesn't make it wrong?	
	TOTAL	
	TOTAL EXPAND SELF	

339

Question:	Rating: 1-5
ENABLE OTHERS TO ACT	
KNOW YOUR PLACE IN THE HERD	
1 Are team members are assigned to roles that maximize their strengths?	
2 Are team members are hired based on character rather than competency?	
3 Is there is a diverse mix of individuals with the team reflecting all the different energies?	
TOTAL	
THE POWER OF COURAGEOUS CONVERSATIONS	
1 Is the environment safe for team members to say what is on their mind without fear of retribution?	
2 Do team members quickly and constructively confront behavioural issues with others?	
3 Do team members understand and engage in active listening?	
TOTAL	
PURPOSE DRIVEN DECISION MAKING	
1 Is decision making responsibility devolved to the people closet to the information?	
2 Are team members given an active role in decision making that impacts them?	
3 Do processes exist so that all stakeholders have an equal say in decision making?	
TOTAL	
TOTAL ENABLE OTHERS TO ACT	

Question:	Rating: 1-5
ENGAGE THE ENVIRONMENT	
IS THE BUSINESS ENVIRONMENT KILLING YOU?	
1 Does the environment encourage openness and transparency to mitigate stress and fear?	
2 Does the environment encourage collaboration: the "we" rather than the "me" approach?	
3 Do team members feel values and cared for?	
TOTAL	
HARNESSING NATURE'S NATURAL RHYTHM	
1 Is it clearly understood which season the business is in and leadership matched to this?	
2 Are clearly delineated spaces allocated for the different types of business activities?	
3 Are team members personal rhythms recognized and work hours assigned appropriately?	
TOTAL	
CREATING A WIN-WIN SITUATION	
1 Do team members understand that business is a win-win situation rather than a win-lose?	
2 Are systems in place so that team members know how they are progressing towards goals?	
3 Is an entrepreneurial spirit encouraged within a framework of governing rules?	
TOTAL	
TOTAL ENGAGE THE ENVIRONMENT	

BEING TRUSTED	
1 Do you know where you are most trusted in business?	
2 Do you know how to build and sustain trust?	
3 Do team members share trust in order to get trust?	
TOTAL	

341

SUMMARY:	
PURPOSE AND VALUES	
LEADING WITH COURAGEOUS IMPACT	
EMPOWER RATHER THAN DELEGATE	
EXPAND SELF	
KNOW YOUR PLACE IN THE HERD	
THE POWER OF COURAGEOUS CONVERSATIONS	
PURPOSE DRIVEN DECISION MAKING	
ENABLE OTHERS TO ACT	
IS THE BUSINESS ENVIRONMENT KILLING YOU?	
HARNESSING NATURE'S NATURAL RHYTHM	
CREATING A WIN-WIN SITUATION	
ENGAGE THE ENVIRONMENT	
BEING TRUSTED	

Now that you have completed the assessment and tallied the results you can clearly see which of the three cornerstones you should tackle first. Rank them in accordance of priority and then within that cornerstone identify which of the three attributes you should work on first.

If you want any help interpreting the results please connect with me to arrange a complimentary strategy session so that I can help you get clarity on how to move forward.

ENDNOTES

CHAPTER ONE: THE QUEST

[1] Radicati Group, Inc. (March 2015) http://www.radicati.com/wp/wp-content/uploads/2015/02/Email-Statistics-Report-2015-2019-Executive-Summary.pdf

[2] Gunelius, Susan. *The Data Explosion in 2014 Minute By Minute.* http://aci.info/2014/07/12/the-data-explosion-in-2014-minute-by-minute-infographic/

[3] The Hay Group: *Building The New Leader: Leadership Challenges of the Future Revealed*, 2014 www.haygroup.com/leadership2030

[4] The Hay Group: *Building The New Leader: Leadership Challenges of the Future Revealed*, 2014 www.haygroup.com/leadership2030

[5] Deloitte University Press. *Global Human Capital Trends 2015. Leading In the New World Of Work.* Deloitte University Press, 2015

[6] Cooper, Robert K. *The Other 90%: How To Unlock Your Vast Untapped Potential For Leadership And Life.* New York: Three Rivers Press, 2001 p12

[7] Deloitte University Press. *Global Human Capital Trends 2015. Leading In the New World Of Work.* Deloitte University Press, 2015

[8] Baldoni, J. *Employee Engagement Does More Than Boost Productivity.* Harvard Business Review. July 2013 www.HBR.org

[9] Mackey, John & Sisodia, Raj. *Conscious Capitalism: Liberating The Heroic Spirit of Business.* Boston: Harvard Business School Publishing Corporation, 2014, P 29

CHAPTER THREE: THE JOINED UP BUSINESS BLUEPRINT™

[10] NLP Perceptual Perspectives

CHAPTER FOUR: SETTING THE GPS FOR YOUR BUSINESS

[11] Aberdeen Research. *Executive Dashboards: The Key to Unlocking Double Digit Profit Growth.*

[12] EMA/9sight Big Data. *Operationalizing the Buzz: Big Data 2013.* http://www.pentaho.com/resource/operationalizing-buzz-big-data-2013

CHAPTER SIX: APPLYING TRUST IN A JOINED UP BUSINESS

[13] Covey, Stephen M. R. *The Speed Of Trust: The One Thing That Changes Everything.* New York: Simon & Schuster, Inc, 2006

[14] Branson, Richard. *Richard Branson On Customer Service.* Entrepreneur.com/article/217846

CHAPTER SEVEN: PURPOSE AND VALUES

[15] Deloitte, *Mind The Gaps: The 2015 Millennial Survey.* (2015) p3 http://www2.deloitte.com/global/en/pages/about-deloitte/articles/millennialsurvey.html

[16] Deloitte Survey 3rd annual Deloitte Core Beliefs & Culture Survey. *Strong Sense Of Purpose key Driver Of Business Investment.* April 2014. www.deloitte.com

[17] A Miller, F & Brown, D & Garber, A *As One: Better Collaboration Where It Counts Most.* Deloitte Review, Issue 12, 2013. www.deloittereview.com

[18] Confino, J Paul Polman: *The power is in the hands of the consumers.* The Guardian November 2011, http://www.theguardian.com/sustainable-business/unilever-ceo-paul-polman-interview

[19] Trotman, Andrew *I will take Tesco back to core values, says new chief Dave Lewis.* Sept 2014. The Telegraph http://www.telegraph.co.uk/finance/newsbysector/retailandconsumer/11076599/I-will-take-Tesco-back-to-core-values-says-new-chief-Dave-Lewis.html

[20] Edeleman Trust Barometer 2012. http://www.edelman.com/insights/intellectual-property/2012-edelman-trust-barometer/

[21] Deloitte Survey 3rd annual Deloitte Core Beliefs & Culture Survey. *Strong Sense Of Purpose key Driver Of Business Investment.* April 2014. www.deloitte.com

[22] *A Strong and Well Communicated Corporate Purpose Can Significantly Impact Financial Performance,* According to IMD/Burson-Marsteller Corporate Purpose Impact Study - See more at: http://www.burson-marsteller.com/press-release/a-strong-and-well-communicated-corporate-purpose-can-significantly-impact-financial-performance-according-to-imdburson-marsteller-corporate-purpose-impact-study/#sthash.r0QBmwcf.dpuf

CHAPTER EIGHT: LEADING WITH COURAGEOUS IMPACT

[23] Greenleaf, Dr. Robert, 1997 and Patterson, Dr. Kathleen, 2003. Servant Leadership: *A Journey into the Nature of Legitimate Power and Greatness*

CHAPTER NINE: EMPOWER RATHER THAN DELEGATE

[24] Lorinkova, N *Examining the Differential Longitudinal Performance of Directive versus Empowering Leadership in Teams.* Academy of Management. 2012

[25] Gallup. *State of the Global Workplace.* 2013. http://www.gallup.com/poll/165269/worldwide-employees-engaged-work.aspx

[26] The Conference Board. *CEO Challenge 2014.* People and Performance – Reconnecting with Customers and Reshaping The Culture of Work. www.conferenceboard.org

CHAPTER TEN: KNOW YOUR ROLE IN THE HERD

[27] Krotoski, A. *Robin Dunbar: We Can Only Ever Have 150 Friends At Most.* The Guardian. March 2010. http://www.theguardian.com/technology/2010/mar/14/my-bright-idea-robin-dunbar

CHAPTER ELEVEN: THE POWER OF COURAGEOUS CONVERSATIONS

[28] The McKinsey Quarterly: *The War For Talent.* 2007. http://www.executivesondemand.net/managementsourcing/images/stories/artigos_pdf/gestao/The_war_for_talent.pdf

[29] CPP Global Human Capital Report. *Workplace Conflict and How Business Can Harness It To Thrive.* 2008. https://www.cpp.com/pdfs/CPP_Global_Human_Capital_Report_Workplace_Conflict.pdf

[30] Gallup. *State of the Global Workplace.* 2013. http://www.gallup.com/poll/165269/worldwide-employees-engaged-work.aspx

[31] Quantum Workplace. *2015 Employee Engagement Trends* http://www.quantumworkplace.com/resources/whitepapers/research-and-trends/2015-employee-engagement-trends-report/

CHAPTER TWELVE: PURPOSE-DRIVEN DECISION-MAKING

[32] Douglas, K (2011) *Decision Time: How Subtle Forces Shape Your Choices.* New Scientist, 14 November 2011, 38-41

[33] Robinson, L & Baawden, D (2009). *The dark side of information overload, anxiety and other paradoxes and pathologies.* Journal of Information Science 35, 5.

[34] Knoblauch, Max. *Internet Users Send 204 Million Emails Per Minute* (2014) http://mashable.com/2014/04/23/data-online-every-minute

[35] Hemp, P (Sept 2009). *Death By Information Overload.* Harvard Business Review, 87, 9 83-89

[36] Mack, A and Rock, I (1998). *Inattentional Blindness.* MIT Press, Cambridge

[37] Commonly attributed to Einstein but is now thought to be a misattribution

[38] Associated Press (2008). *Nokia Sales Increased 4 per cent in Quarter.* New York Times. 18 July 2008

[39] The Associated Press (2008). *Obama on Vacationing and Time To Think.* New York Times. http://www.nytimes.com/2008/07/27/us/politics/27CHAT.html

347

[40] Hayek, FA (1945) *The Use of Knowledge In Society.* American Economic Review, 35, 4, 519-530

[41] CVS Health *This Is The Right Thing To Do.* 2014 http://www.cvshealth.com/research-insights/health-topics/this-is-the-right-thing-to-do

CHAPTER THIRTEEN: IS THE BUSINESS ENVIRONMENT KILLING YOU?

[42] Sinek, Simon. *Leaders Eat Last: Why Some Teams Pull Together And Others Don't.* New York: Penguin Group, 2014, p20

[43] Deloitte Centre For The Edge. *Deloitte Shift Index 2010. Measuring The Forces Of Long Term Change.* 2010. http://www2.deloitte.com/us/en/pages/center-for-the-edge/topics/deloitte-shift-index-series.html

CHAPTER FIFTEEN: CREATING A WIN-WIN SITUATION

[44] Glassdoor Employment Confidence Survey (Q1 2014) *Average US Employee Only Takes Half of Earned Vacation Time.* 2014 http://www.glassdoor.com/blog/average-employee-takes-earned-vacation-time-glassdoor-employment-confidence-survey-q1-2014/

[45] BBC News: *Virgin's Richard Branson offers staff unlimited holiday* http://www.bbc.co.uk/news/business-29356627

[46] Mochari, I *The Wishful Thinking of Unlimited Vacation Policies.* Oct 2014. Inc Magazine   http://www.inc.com/ilan-mochari/unlimited-vacations.html

[47] Shellenbarger, S *Companies Deal With Employees Who Refuse to Take Time Off by Requiring Vacations, Paying Them to Go.* August 2014. Wall Street Journal http://www.wsj.com/articles/companies-deal-with-employees-who-refuse-to-take-time-off-by-requiring-vacations-paying-them-to-go-1407884213

CHAPTER SIXTEEN: ENERGISING A HIGH-PERFORMANCE CULTURE

[48] Kotter, John &. Heskett, J *Corporate Culture and Performance.* Free Press. 2011.

[49] Smith, Greg. *Why I Am Leaving Goldman Sachs.* New York Times. March 2012. http://www.nytimes.com/2012/03/14/opinion/why-i-am-leaving-goldman-sachs.html?_r=0

[50] Sam, K. *How Tatas Responded After Mumbai Terrorist Attacks.* March 2012. http://karmarkars.net

[51] SHRM Case Study. *Culture Management and Merger Acquisitions.* March 2005. https://www.shrm.org/publications/hrmagazine/editorialcontent/documents/cms_011564.pdf

BIBLIOGRAPHY

Ambler, George: *11 Practices of Collaborative Leaders*. www.georgeambler.com. September 2013.

Baghai, Mehrdad & Quigley, James. *As One: Individual Action Collective Power.* Portfolio Penguin, 2011

Branson, Richard. *Richard Branson On Customer Service.* Entrepreneur.com/article/217846

Childre, Doc, Cryer, Bruce. *From Chaos To Confusion: The Power To Change Performance.* Boulder, Heart Math LLC, 2008

Cooper, Robert K. *The Other 90%: How To Unlock Your Vast Untapped Potential For Leadership And Life.* New York: Three Rivers Press, 2001

Cooper, Robert and Sawaf, Ayman, Executive EQ: Emotional Intelligence in Leadership and Organisations (New York: Grosset/Putnam 1997) p68

Covey, Stephen M. R. *The Speed Of Trust: The One Thing That Changes Everything.* New York: Simon & Schuster, Inc, 2006

Csikszentmihalyi, Mihaly. *Flow: The Psychology Of Optimal Experience.* HarperCollins. 2009

Deloitte Business: *Confidence Report 2014: The Gap Between Confidence and Action.* www.deloitte.com

Deloitte Consulting LLP & Bersin by Deloitte. *Global Human Capital Trends 2014. Engaging the 21st Century Workforce.* Deloitte University Press, 2014

Deloitte LLP. *3rd annual Deloitte Core Beliefs & Culture Survey.* www.deloitte.com

Deloitte LLP. Strong Sense of Purpose Key Driver of Business Investment.

Deloitte University Press. *Global Human Capital Trends 2015: Leading In The New World Of Work.* January 2015

Duhigg, Charles. *The Power of Habit: Why We Do What We Do And How To Change.* London: Random House. 2012

EY. *The Power Of Many: How Companies Use Teams To Drive Superior Corporate Performance.* EYGM Limited. 2013

Haines, Nicholas. *The Vitality Test.* www.fiveinstitute.com

Hamilton, Roger. *Your Life, Your Legacy.* Achievers International, 2006

Hamilton, Roger James. *The Millionaire Master Plan: Your Personalized Path To Financial Success.* New York: Hachette Book Group, 2014

Hamilton, Roger & Clark, Michelle. *Team Dynamics.*

Hay Group. *Building The New Leader: Leadership Challenges Of The Future Revealed.* Hay Group. 2014

Kotler, Stephen. *The Rise of Superman: Decoding the Science of Ultimate Human Performance*. New Harvest. 2014

Kotter, John &. Heskett, J *Corporate Culture and Performance*. Free Press. 2011.

Kruse, Kevin. *Leadership Secrets From Yum!. Brands CEO David Novak*. Forbes.com. June 2014

Kuppler, Tim & Garnett, Ted & Morehead, Tom. *Build The Cultural Advantage: Delivering Sustainable Performance With Clarity And Speed*. Michigan, The Cultural Advantage. 2014

Larcker, David F, & Saslow, Scott *2014 Report On Senior Executive Succession Planning and Talent Development*. IED and Rock Center for Corporate Governance. 2014

Lencioni. Patrick. *The Five Dysfunctions of a Team*. John Wiley & Sons. 2002.

Mackay, John & Sisodia, Raj. *Conscious Capitalism: Liberating The Heroic Spirit of Business*. Boston: Harvard Business School Publishing Corporation, 2014

Mauboussin, Michael J. *The True Measure Of Success*. Harvard Business Review, October 2012

McFee, Andrew & Brynjolfsson. *Big Data: The Management Revolution*. Harvard Business Review, October 2012

Maxwell, John C. *The 21 Irrefutable Laws of Leadership – follow them and people will follow you*. Nashville, Thomas Nelson, 2007

Maxwell, John C. *Developing the Leader Within You*. Nashville, Thomas Nelson, 1993

Maxwell, John C. *The 17 Indisputable Laws of Teamwork*. Nashville, Thomas Nelson, 2001

Kouzes, James M. and Posner, Barry Z. *The Leadership Challenge– Five Practices of Exemplary Leaders*. San Francisco, Josey-Bass, A Wiley Imprint, 2002

Page, S.E *The Difference: How The Power of Diversity Creates Better Groups, Firms, Schools and Societies*. Princeton University Press, Princeton. NJ. 2007

Ricci, Ron and Wiese, Carl. *The Collaboration Imperative: Executive Strategies For Unlocking Your Organization's True Potential*. 2011

Rohn, Jim. *The Seasons Of Life*. Texas: John Rohn International, 2002

Rodenburg, Patsy. Presence: *How To Use Positive Energy For Success*. Penguin. 2007

Scharmer, Otto & Kaufer, Karin. *Leading From An Emerging Future – From Ego-System To Eco-System Economics*. San Francisco, Berrett-Koehler Publishers, Inc. 2013

Senge, Peter M. *The Fifth Discipline: the Art & Practice of the Learning Organisation*. Random House Business. 2006.

Senn, Larry & Hart, Jim. *Winning Teams: Winning Cultures*. California: Senn-Delaney Leadership Consulting Group. LLC. 2010

Shapiro, Mary. *The Team Equation: Managing Teams That Deliver.* Harvard Business Review, 2014

Sinek, Simon. *Leaders Eat Last: Why Some Teams Pull Together And Others Don't.* New York: Penguin Group, 2014

Sinek, Simon. *Start With Why: How Great Leaders Inspire Everyone To Take Action.* New York: Penguin Group, 2011

Smith, David & Silverstone, Yaarit & Breecher, Deborah & Upadhyaya, Punya. *Leadership Imperatives For An Agile Business.* Accenture Strategy. 2015

Squires, Susan, Smith, Cynthia, McDougall, Lorna, Yeack, William. *Inside Arthur Andersen: Shifting Values, Unexpected Consequences.* New Jersey: Pearson Education Inc. 2003

Strozzi, Ariana. *Horse Sense for the Leader Within.* Bloomington. Author House. 2004

Tardanico, Susan. *10 Traits of Courageous Leaders.* Forbes.com. 15th Jan 2013

Wolfe, Alexander. *Big Data At Work: Decline Of The HiPPO.* Forbes Blog, 2013

Business HorsePower
—— Unleashing Hidden Potential ——

Julia Felton is the Herd Leader of Business HorsePower, a firm dedicated to helping service-based businesses, just like you, operate more effectively and efficiently through developing better leadership and teamwork skills and creating a high-performance Joined Up business culture

Visit www.businesshorsepower.com and explore:

Consulting, Coaching and Mentoring:
Improve your strategy and organisational alignment to create a Joined Up purpose-driven, sustainable business where no resources are wasted.

Leadership:
Become a Joined Up Leader through innovative, experiential leadership development workshops with horses to develop agile *On-The-Hoof* leadership skills.

Teamwork:
Get the best out of your team by aligning their skill set and helping them find their flow thereby increasing engagement and delivering improved productivity and profitability.

Books:
The Alchemy of Change: Ancient Wisdom To Unleash The Potential In Leaders and Teams
Unbridled Success: How The Secret Lives Of Horses Impact Leadership, Teamwork and Communication